I0651221

Thornley Smith

The History of Joshua

Viewed in Connection with the Topography of Canaan, and the Customs of the

Times in which he Lived. Second Edition

Thornley Smith

The History of Joshua
Viewed in Connection with the Topography of Canaan, and the Customs of the Times in which he Lived. Second Edition

ISBN/EAN: 9783337202835

Printed in Europe, USA, Canada, Australia, Japan

Cover: Foto ©Lupo / pixelio.de

More available books at **www.hansebooks.com**

THE

HISTORY OF JOSHUA:

VIEWED IN

CONNECTION WITH THE TOPOGRAPHY OF CANAAN, AND THE

CUSTOMS OF THE TIMES IN WHICH

HE LIVED.

BY THE

REV. THORNLEY SMITH,

AUTHOR OF 'THE HISTORY OF JOSEPH,' 'THE HISTORY OF MOSES,' ETC

SECOND EDITION.

EDINBURGH: WILLIAM OLIPHANT AND CO.
LONDON: HAMILTON, ADAMS, AND CO.

—

MDCCCLXX.

MURRAY AND GIBB, PRINTERS, EDINBURGH.

PREFACE TO THE SECOND EDITION.

Since the publication of the First Edition of this work, several attacks have been made on some of the Historical Books of the Old Testament, and especially on the Pentateuch and the Books of Joshua. But these books have stood the test, and it may be safely affirmed that they rest upon as firm a basis as ever, and one from which future criticism will not remove them. In the Keil and Delitzsch series of translations, published by the Messrs. Clark, another Commentary on Joshua has appeared, similar in character to the larger work to which frequent reference is made in these pages. The writer says: " Even if the Book of Joshua was not composed till some time after the events recorded (and the authorship cannot be determined with certainty), this does not affect its *historico-prophetic character*, for both the contents and form of the book show it to be an independent and simple work, composed with historical fidelity, and a work which is as thoroughly pervaded with the spirit of the Old Testament revelation as the Pentateuch itself."

On the standing still of the sun, the writer makes no reference to Keil's interpretation in the larger work, but speaks of it as an optical stoppage of the sun, or rather a continuance of the visibility of the sun above the horizon, by celestial phenomena which are altogether unknown to us, or to naturalists in general. I confess, however, that I still lean to the view given in this volume ; nor do I see any reason for alteration in other particulars of importance. The work is re-issued with the hope that it will still commend itself to the judgment of careful readers of the word of God, and be found a help in the study of this portion of inspired Scripture.

T. S.

October 28, 1869.

PREFACE.

A HISTORY of JOSHUA must necessarily differ in many respects from a Commentary on the Book of Joshua. It will be seen, however, that this volume comprises such explanations of each chapter of that book as to render it almost as valuable as a commentary, and to the general reader it will perhaps be more attractive in this form than it would have been in another. The utmost care has been bestowed on its preparation, and all available helps have been made use of; yet it has not been written amidst learned leisure, but amidst numerous ministerial duties, often in hours stolen from recreation and rest.

Our language contains but few works on the subject. The Commentaries of Calvin and of Keil, which have been translated into it, and the Notes of Bush, an American writer, are the principal. It cannot, then, be said that such a work as this is uncalled for; the only question will be, whether it supplies the desideratum felt.

Among the old folios of the seventeenth century, is a work by Thomas Fuller, entitled 'A Pisgah Sight of Palestine and the Confines thereof.' This work, which is now somewhat scarce, professes to give a geographical account of the Holy Land, and is illustrated by a number of curiously-executed maps. Considering its date, it is a remarkable book, and it is full of the quaint observations for which its author was so celebrated. But it furnishes a striking contrast with modern works on the subject; and the comparison shows how great an advancement has been made in recent times in the knowledge of the geography of the land of Canaan. Fuller's work has suggested to the author some valuable thoughts.

It has very recently been observed, that the close, microscopic examination of the Book of Life is daily bringing its secret beauties into clearer light. There are some readers of that book, however, who care very little for its secret beauties; and as for its topography and antiquities, they never trouble them. For anything they know of the physical character of Palestine, the events of which it was the theatre might have taken place in America or in Japan; and, as a necessary consequence of their ignorance, they have no vivid picture before them of the scenes depicted in the Bible, and are quite unable to understand many of its allusions. For such readers a work like the present will have no attractions, and the probability is, that, if they open it at all, it will soon weary them. But there is another class of Bible readers—and it is believed that the number is constantly increasing—who deem nothing that the Holy Spirit has thought proper to place on the pages of inspiration unimportant, even though it be only a genealogical table, or a list of towns and cities. For Bible readers of this class, the author has written, with the hope of affording them a little help to the better understanding of this portion of the Word of God. He has not written for the learned, but for inquirers, he being but an inquirer himself, and glad to avail himself of all such aids as are furnished by others, of whatever name. Critical remarks he has introduced but seldom; historical and topographical inquiries he has entered into with some minuteness. It will be found that, for the sake of clearness, and to prevent the necessity of referring the reader back to a previous page, a topographical statement has occasionally been repeated. It has been thought best to quote, in most instances in which they are referred to, the words of Robinson and other travellers, rather than to give the substance of what they say, that so the reader who has not access to their works may have the benefit of their own remarks.

As no special reference is made in the body of this work to the Authorship of the Book of Joshua, it is desirable that the question should be considered here. Neology has done its utmost to prove that the work is fragmentary, and that it was written by different persons, and at different times. But the shafts of its criticisms have been turned aside; for it is abundantly evident, as Keil and others have shown, that the book consists of three portions only: the first, chap. i. to xii., containing an account of the conquest of Canaan; the second, chap. xiii. to xxi., an account of its partition among the tribes of Israel; and the third, chap. xxii. to xxiv., a narrative of the return of the Reubenites to their possessions, and of the last days and death of Joshua. Nor can any unprejudiced mind, especially after reading Keil's introduction, entertain a doubt either as to the unity of the work, or as to its early date. Havernick is of opinion that the first half of it was written by Joshua himself; and, though Keil doubts this, there is very much to be said in its favour. It is highly probable that Joshua, following the example of Moses, his illustrious predecessor, would write a history of the conquest in some form or other; and that he did write something, is expressly stated in chap. xxiv. 26. It is true that, in the first part of the book, the expression, 'unto this day,' several times occurs—chap. iv. 9, v. 9, vi. 25, vii. 26, etc.,— as it also does in the second part of the book; a fact which seems to intimate, that the first part of the book must have been written after Joshua's death. It is remarkable, however, that Joshua makes use of this phrase when addressing the Reubenites, chap. xxii. 3, 17, xxiii. 8, 9; and though in these passages it bears a somewhat different sense, yet, as he lived several years after the conquest, he may very well have used it in the sense in which it occurs in chap. iv. 9, where it is said of the stones set up in the Jordan, that 'they are there unto this day;' and in chap. vi. 25, where of Rahab it is said, 'she dwelleth in Israel unto this day.' Both these passages, and especially the latter, are surely decisive against the opinion that the book was written even as late as the times of Saul; and hence, if Joshua himself was not the author of it, or of any portion of it, *in its present form*, he must have left materials for it; for who but himself could have furnished the accounts he gives of his interviews with the Lord Jehovah, chap. i. 1–9, v. 13–15, etc.? And it must have been compiled from such materials, and others possessed by the writer, *within a few years after Joshua's death.* Calvin ascribed it to Eleazar, Lightfoot to Phinehas, and Keil to one of the elders who outlived Joshua. The latter view meets all the necessities of the case, and is, on the whole, the most satisfactory. What more probable than that one of these elders, spared for some years after the death of Joshua, and well acquainted with the events which appear to have taken place subsequent to Joshua's death—as the capture of Hebron, of Debir, and of Leshem—would be led by the Holy Spirit to place the entire history of Joshua on permanent record, for the instruction of succeeding generations? It would have been strange if this had not been done; and we can no more conceive that the events of these times were left for several generations to the uncertainty of tradition, than that those of the times of Moses were so left.

But there is a class of critics in this country who, following in the wake of Ewald and others, of the German school of Rationalists, are determined, if possible, to get rid of the historical books of the Old Testament, and who hold that both the Pentateuch and the Book of Joshua were compiled from ancient documents, and especially from two, called respectively the Elohistic documents, and the Jehovistic; and, moreover, that these books did not assume their present form until a short time before the captivity of the Jews in Babylon! Any one must see that, if this theory is correct, but very little dependence can be placed on the historical accuracy of these works; and, indeed, it is the object of the writers referred to, to prove this. What success have they met with? In Germany their theory has been long since exploded; and, though it is still thrust forward before the eyes of the British public, its fate is sealed, as may be seen from the able and unanswerable work of the Rev. D. Macdonald —' Introduction to the Pentateuch'—recently issued from the press of Messrs Clark of Edinburgh. A more thorough work on the subject has not appeared either in this country or in any other; it is one of the most valuable contributions to our Theological Literature of recent date, and will, no doubt, operate as an antidote to much of the poison which has lately come forth from higher quarters.

The usual objections to the authenticity of the Book of Joshua are referred to in the following pages. Its place in the Jewish Canon has never been disputed, and there are several references to it, as to a well-known work, in the Scriptures of the New Testament: Acts vii. 45; Heb. xi. 30, 31; James ii. 25. Some editions of the Septuagint contain the following passage at the close of the book :—' In that day the children of Israel took the ark of God, and carried it about among them: and Phineas became priest instead of Eleazar his father, until he died, and he was buried in Gabaar, his own place. But the children of Israel departed every one to their own place, and to their own city. And the children of Israel worshipped Astarte, and Astaroth, and the gods of the nations round about them; and the Lord gave them into the hands of Eglon, king of Moab, and he reigned over them eighteen years.' But this passage has no authority, and is evidently made up from Judges ii. 12–14, iii. 7–12.

The present volume completes the series of three Scripture

Biographies—Joseph, Moses, Joshua—which the Author con
templated. He acknowledges with gratitude the kind reception
given to the two former, especially beyond his own section of
the Church; and should the third be deemed worthy of an
equal measure of attention, he will venture to hope that he has
done something, though but little, towards the elucidation of these
eventful histories. There are other Old Testament Biographies
which require similar treatment, especially those of Daniel,
Queen Esther, Ezra, and Nehemiah; but whether providential
circumstances will permit the Author of this series to deal with
them, the future must decide.

BOLTON, *Feb.* 10, 1862.

CONTENTS.

LIST OF ILLUSTRATIONS.

MOSES AND JOSHUA IN THE TABERNACLE.

CHAPTER I.

JOSHUA THE MINISTER OF MOSES.

IN writing the life of any man of eminence, the biographer seldom fails, if he possesses the requisite materials, to commence with some account of the parentage, the birth, and the childhood of his hero; while upon the events of his boyhood, and the circumstances under which his mental powers began to be developed, he usually dwells with very special interest. And if, as a poet of our own has said, 'the child is

father of the man,' this is but natural, for every one is gratified
in being able to trace the story of a life to its source; and to
study the connection between the boyhood and the manhood of
an illustrious individual, is often both a pleasant and an instruc-
tive task.

But of the early lives of some great men we know next to
nothing.   Like the sources of some of the grandest rivers, they
are wrapped in obscurity and mist.   How little, for instance,
do we know of the boyhood of our great dramatist, William
Shakespeare!   Beyond the fact that he was born at Stratford-
upon-Avon, April 23, 1564, the notices which have come down
to us of his early life—that he received his education at the
Free Grammar School of Stratford, that he was bound appren-
tice by his father to a butcher, and that whilst comparatively a
young man he became a schoolmaster in the country—are but
traditional and uncertain; and hence the great secret of the
spring and origin of his power remains to this day unexplained.

Such is the case with respect to Joshua, the faithful minister
and the valiant successor of Moses, the deliverer and lawgiver
of the Israelites.   We were able to begin the History of Moses
with an account of his birth, of his infancy, and of his early perils
and deliverances; but the very first notice in the Bible of Joshua
is as the victorious commander of the Israelites in the battle
fought with Amalek.[1]   Thus suddenly does he step forth on the
great theatre of life, fully armed, like Minerva from the head of
Jupiter; and respecting his early days we can gather but a few
incidental facts.

He was a descendant of Joseph through his younger son
Ephraim; and it is somewhat remarkable that his pedigree is
preserved in the First Book of Chronicles in a more perfect form
than that of any of his contemporaries.[2]   If the genealogical
tables of that book are genuine—and there is no reason to sup-

[1] Ex. xvii. 8–16.   [2] 1 Chron. vii. 20–27.

pose them otherwise—between Ephraim and Joshua there were eighteen generations,—a fact to which we referred in a former work as one proof, among others, of the lengthened sojourn of the Israelites in Egypt.[1] Bertheau and Kurtz, however, read the passage thus:—'The sons of Ephraim are Shuthelah, and his son Bered, and his son Tahath, and his son Eladah, and his son Shuthelah, and Ezer and Elead. And the men of Gath that were born in that land slew them (Ezer and Elead), for they had gone down to take their cattle : and their father Ephraim mourned many days, and his brethren came to comfort him. And he went in to his wife, and she conceived and bare a son, and called his name Beriah, for it went evil with his house.' Supposing the correctness of this explanation, Ephraim was the father of Beriah, and between Ephraim and Joshua there were ten generations, namely, Ephraim, Beriah, Rephah, Resheph, Telah, Tahan, Laadan, Ammihud, Elishama, and Nun. But on a very moderate calculation these ten generations are amply sufficient to fill up the 430 years of the sojourn in Egypt, and our former conclusion on that point remains, therefore, undisturbed.[2]

There is every reason to suppose that Joshua was born in the land of Goshen ; and it is not improbable that his father was one of Pharaoh's slaves, and was subject to the lash of the Egyptian taskmasters. The year of Joshua's birth is uncertain ; but if we suppose, with Jewish chronologers, that he lived in Canaan twenty-seven years after its conquest, we must infer that at the time of the Exodus he was forty-three ; for he lived forty years in the wilderness, and at his death he was a hundred and ten years old. Now, according to the Hebrew chronology, the year of the Exodus was 1491 B.C., and 43 added to 1491 is 1534, whence it follows that this was the year of Joshua's nativity. At the time

[1] 'The History of Joseph,' p. 173.
[2] See Kurtz on 'the Old Covenant,' vol. ii., p. 178. Clark.

of the Exodus Moses was eighty years of age, so that Joshua was
thirty-seven years younger than he ; and as Moses was upwards
of forty years of age[1] when he fled into the land of Midian,
Joshua was at that time an infant three years old.

It was, then, during the period of the residence of Moses in a
strange land that Joshua grew up to youth and manhood,—a
period this of great sorrow and affliction to the Israelites, for
then it was that they were greatly oppressed, and ' sighed by
reason of their bondage, and cried.'   As Joshua, or, as he was
then called, Hoshea,[2] became old enough to understand the
nature of things, his father Nun, and perhaps his mother too,
though she is nowhere mentioned, would relate to him the history
and fortunes of their people, and would tell him, especially,
of Joseph, their own illustrious ancestor.   In their custody,
probably, was Joseph's mummy, standing upright in its case in
some corner of their dwelling ; and pointing to it, they would
say to the boy,—' We are now an enslaved and afflicted people,
but ere Joseph, our great progenitor, died, he said, " God will
surely visit you, and bring you out of this land unto the land
which He sware to Abraham, to Isaac, and to Jacob, and ye
shall carry up my bones from hence."[3]   And see! his bones are in
that coffin, waiting for the day when our bonds shall be broken
asunder, and our liberty proclaimed.'   And oh ! how the youth
would exult in the prospect, and how ready he would be to take
the oath of fidelity to Joseph, which had probably been taken by
all Joseph's descendants![4]   On Joshua, if his father had died in
Egypt, would have devolved the task of taking charge of Joseph's
mummy ; but as his grandfather Elishama was alive at the time
of the Exodus,[5] it is probable that his father Nun was alive
also.   Yet a high honour would Joshua deem it to take any part
in the preservation of that treasure, and the constant sight of it

[1] Acts vii. 30.   [2] Num. xiii. 16.   [3] Gen l. 24.
[4] Gen. l. 25.   [5] See Num. i. 10.

would inspire his mind with hope. He would hear, too, from the lips of his parents and his friends the remarkable story of Jochebed and her son; of Moses' refusal to become the son of Pharaoh's daughter; and of his flight from Egypt, they knew not whither. And what would be his joy when, having arrived at man's estate, he heard one day that this same Moses had returned, bearing a commission from the God of Israel to demand of Pharaoh the liberation of the tribes! His father Nun (or his grandfather Elishama) was probably one of the elders to whom Moses and Aaron announced the fact of their commission, and Joshua would doubtless receive the intelligence with the highest satisfaction. Nor would the long delay shake his confidence in the promises of God. He would hear of the interviews of Moses with Pharaoh, and he would witness the plagues which desolated the land; and when, at length, the night of the deliverance came, he would partake, with the family of which he was a member, of the paschal lamb; and, in a dwelling, the door-posts of which were sprinkled with its blood, would wait the signal which proclaimed them free. That signal was soon given. A great cry was heard in Egypt; for there was not a house in which there was not one dead. The pride of Pharaoh was humbled; the might of the oppressor was destroyed; all was ready, and presently the tribes were on their march to Rameses, where probably they were organized for their future journeys.

The tribe of Ephraim, to which Joshua belonged, occupied, at a subsequent period of the march, the seventh place in the order of the tribes, and was immediately preceded by the Kohathites bearing the sanctuary.[1] This was probably its position from the first; and from the first, Elishama, the grandfather of Joshua, was at its head.[2] Where, then, was Joshua himself but with his honoured grandsire, commanding, under him, a division of the tribe, which numbered no less than forty thousand

---

[1] See Num. x. 21, 22.   [2] Num. x. 22.

and five hundred?[1] Strong, vigorous, and heroic, he was prepared to contend with the difficulties of the journey, and was perhaps often seen encouraging the faint-hearted, and cheering the more feeble of the tribe. A wise commander never places an untried soldier in a position of extraordinary difficulty ; and we may be sure, therefore, that ere Moses summoned Joshua to choose out men and to fight with Amalek, he had had ample proof of his bravery and skill. Does a young man aspire to some post of honour in the great battle-field of life ? He must show himself worthy of it by faithfully discharging the duties of the station he already occupies. Mere drones can never be entrusted with the leadership of an enterprise. Joshua was already a man of mark, or he would not have been chosen to the command of the army which was to conquer the Amalekites. The Jew Philo calls Joshua ' the friend and pupil' of Moses ; and says that he ' lived with him under the same roof, and shared the same table with him ;' and that he ' performed other services for him in which he was distinguished from the multitude, being almost his lieutenant, and regulating, with him, the matters relating to his supreme authority.'[2] Whether this was the case or not, one thing is certain, that Moses had the most perfect confidence in Joshua, and knew him to be a valiant soldier, worthy to be entrusted with this most important enterprise.

Nor did Joshua disappoint the expectations of his friend. As Moses made choice of him to take the command of the army, so did he himself make choice of others to compose that army ; and, with a number of picked men in whom he could confide, he rushed forward, sword in hand, to meet the first enemies of the Israelites in the wilderness. On a lofty hill in Horeb sat Moses, with uplifted hands, from morning until sunset, watching the fierce onset of the wild Arab horde ; ' and it came to pass, when Moses held up his hand, that Israel prevailed ; and when

[1] Num. i. 33.   [2] Philo ' On Humanity,' ii.

he let down his hand, Amalek prevailed.' We have elsewhere represented the uplifted hands of Moses as the sign of prayer; but Kurtz entertains another view, which is perhaps worthy of attention. 'The attitude of Moses was rather that of a commander, superintending and directing the battle. This is evident from the simple fact, that the elevation of the hand was only a means; the raising of the *staff*, which was held up before the warriors of Israel as the signal of victory, was really the end. It was not to implore the assistance of Jehovah that the hand and the staff were raised, but to assure the Israelites of the help of Jehovah, and serve as the medium of communication. It was not a sign for Jehovah, but for Israel: it was rather a sign *from* Jehovah, of whom Moses was the representative. So long, therefore, as the warriors could see the staff of God lifted up, by which so many miracles had already been wrought, their faith was replenished with divine power, inspiring confidence and ensuring victory; and they became strong to smite Amalek in the name of the Lord.'[1]

We must suppose, then, that the hill on which Moses sat was behind the Amalekites, and right in front of Joshua and his band. But the hands of Moses were heavy, and now and then the rod dropped, in spite of his utmost efforts to hold it up. Aaron and Hur, therefore, 'stayed up his hands, the one on the one side, and the other on the other;'[2] and then Joshua's forces were encouraged, and, though the battle was severe, and lasted until the going down of the sun, the victory was at length won, and the enemy was put to flight.

That was an eventful day in the history of Joshua. According to the above representation of the case, Moses was, in one sense, the commander of the army, but Joshua was in fact its leader, and to Joshua belonged, in great part, the honour of the victory. Had he been timid, faint-hearted, and fearful, the

<hr/>

[1] 'History of the Old Covenant,' vol. iii. 51, 52. [2] Ex. xvii. 8–13.

Amalekites would have smitten his forces to the ground ; but he led on his followers with the bravery of a true hero, inspired them with confidence, and thus won the day.

When David won *his* first victory—the victory over Goliath, the champion of the Philistines—the women of Israel came out with instruments of music, and sang in praise of the youthful hero, with exulting joy ; and when, in later times, our own illustrious commander, Wellington, as Colonel Wellesley, gained *his* first victory—the battle of Assaye—he returned to England as a Knight of the Bath, and was everywhere received with the highest honours. Was no honour done to Joshua by the hosts of Israel ? were no songs chanted in his praise by the females of the tribe of Ephraim ? The sacred narrative is silent on these points, but we may be sure that some demonstrations of gladness would be witnessed in the camp ; and, that the event might not be forgotten, Moses was commanded to write it for a memorial in a book, and to rehearse it in the ears of Joshua, inasmuch as, on account of Amalek's unprovoked attack upon His people, God had determined to put out his remembrance from under heaven.[1] JEHOVAH-nissi, said Moses, as he built an altar on the spot,— ' The Lord is my banner ;' and to Amalek's ultimate destruction he looked forward with confidence and hope.

From that day Joshua would become dearer to him than ever. He had proved himself worthy of the confidence reposed in him, and Moses felt assured that in him he had a friend on whom he would ever be able to rely. We are not surprised, therefore, to find, that when Moses went up into the mount of God, Joshua accompanied him, and that he went farther than even Aaron, Nadab, and Abihu ; for they were evidently left behind, whilst Moses and Joshua proceeded towards the summit.[2] Yet into the midst of the cloud—into the presence-chamber of Jehovah—Moses went alone, leaving Joshua, as it were, to watch

---

[1] Ex. xvii. 14; Num. xxiv. 20; Deut. xxv. 19.   [2] Ex. xxiv. 13, 14.

and wait until he returned. And watch and wait he did during the whole period of Moses' absence, sustained miraculously, as was Moses himself; for no intimation is given that he returned to the camp, but, on the contrary, when Moses was descending with the tables of stone in his hand, there was Joshua still in the mount; and, hearing the noise of the people as they shouted on the plain below, he said unto Moses, 'There is a noise of war in the camp.' Alas! no; it was worse than that. Moses had already learnt from God, what Joshua had not, that the people had made the molten calf, and were worshipping it; and he replied, 'It is not the voice of them that shout for mastery, neither is it the voice of them that cry for being overcome; but the noise of them that sing do I hear.'[1] How would the noble-minded Joshua grieve at this intelligence! To him, as well as to Moses, that scene of revelry and mirth would, as they approached it, appear most revolting, and he would almost wish that he had been in the camp to remonstrate against an act so foolish. But there were probably other remonstrants there, for the Levites had not yielded to the tempter's power; and they, led perhaps by Joshua, were now called to execute summary justice on the people.

Joshua is designated the *minister* of Moses,—a word which signifies servant or attendant, and which, in military language, would be expressed by aid-de-camp. Never, perhaps, did any one fulfil the duties of such an office more honourably; never, perhaps, was any one more truly a helper to the general under whom he served. Upon the fidelity and heroism of an aid-de-camp has the result of many a momentous conflict been suspended; and in how many instances Moses found Joshua of essential service to him in the numerous difficulties he met with in the wilderness, who can tell? Joshua never betrayed his trust; and, as in modern times a faithful aid-de-camp has sometimes, after the death of his commander, succeeded to the generalship of the

[1] Ex. xxxii. 17, 18.

army, so Joshua was ultimately called to fill the place of his illustrious guide and friend.

When the tabernacle had been set up in the wilderness, the princes of Israel, heads of the house of their fathers, brought their offerings to the Lord ; and among them came Elishama the son of Ammihud, prince of the children of Ephraim ; and his offering was 'one silver charger, the weight whereof was an hundred and thirty shekels, one silver bowl of seventy shekels, after the shekel of the sanctuary, both of them full of fine flour mingled with oil, for a meat-offering : one golden spoon of ten shekels, full of incense : one young bullock, one ram, one lamb of the first year, for a burnt-offering : one kid of the goats for a sin-offering : and for a sacrifice of peace-offerings, two oxen, five rams, five he-goats, five lambs of the first year. This was the offering of Elishama the son of Ammihud.'[1] Was Joshua standing by, as his worthy grandsire brought these gifts to the door of the tabernacle ? or did he himself assist in their presentation ? That he took some part in the ceremony we cannot doubt ; and happy would he be to witness the imposing scene, and to help his aged relative in the task. The offerings of all the princes were alike, and very valuable they must have been ; but God had first given unto them, ere they left the land of Egypt, and of His own only did they render to Him again. But very beautiful must have been the sight, as, for twelve successive days, the twelve princes of the people came to Moses, accompanied, no doubt, by many of the elders of their respective tribes, bringing those gifts for the service of the sanctuary ; and very gratifying would it be to all concerned—and to Joshua no less than to others—to see their offerings accepted, and to know that Jehovah deigned to confer on His people the honour of contributing to the worship of the tabernacle.

One incident is mentioned in the Book of Numbers which

[1] Num. vii. 48–53.

shows that Joshua was not a little jealous for the honour of Moses. The seventy elders were prophesying near the tabernacle, when the Spirit came down upon two others also, Eldad and Medad, and they likewise prophesied. What said Joshua? Thinking that they had no right to prophesy, he said, 'My lord Moses, forbid them.'[1] No doubt Joshua's motive was pure enough; but in this instance he was mistaken, as many perhaps are who would prevent others from doing good because, as they happen to think, they have not been ordained or set apart to the work. Or perhaps Joshua thought that they had no right to prophesy because they remained in the camp, and did not come unto the tabernacle; just as, in the days of our Lord, John said to Him on one occasion, 'Master, we saw one casting out devils in Thy name, and we forbade him, because he followed not us.'[2] But to Joshua's request Moses said, 'Enviest thou for my sake? Would God that all the LORD's people were prophets, and that the LORD would put His Spirit upon them!' A noble answer, and one which only a generous mind could have conceived. And why, indeed, should one servant of God grieve because honour is conferred upon another? St Paul rejoiced though Christ was preached even of envy and strife.[3] And thankful should we ever be if good be done, though it be done by those who are not of our party; for there is ample room in the world for every one to work who will, and ample need, too, that every one should work who can. Joshua was silent, for he perhaps saw his error; and though himself one of the elders, as some at least have supposed, he was willing that Eldad and Medad should continue to prophesy as the Spirit gave them power.

Four days after this event the children of Israel pitched in the wilderness of Paran, on the borders of the land of promise; and thence, Moses, by the commandment of the Lord, sent spies to visit the country, of whom Oshea, or Joshua, was one. The

---

[1] Num. xi. 27–29.   [2] Luke ix. 49, comp. John iii. 26.   [3] Phil. i. 18.

number of the spies was twelve, one being selected from each tribe;[1] and Joshua and Caleb seem to have been the leaders of the party. It was on this occasion that Moses called Oshea Jehoshua or Joshua—the one name signifying 'salvation,' the other 'the Lord of salvation.' The latter name occurs previously, not because, as Hengstenberg thinks,[2] that it was given before, and now only renewed, but by a prolepsis, of which other examples occur in the Pentateuch. 'The alteration in Joshua's name,' says Kurtz, 'was a *God speed*. There was something apparently significant in the fact that they had an Oshea among them. Moses not only brought this to mind, but strengthened it, by connecting the name of Jehovah, which brings salvation, with that of Oshea, which promised salvation; whilst his previous life was a pledge that Jehovah is salvation.'[3] Philo represents this change of Joshua's name as displaying the distinctive qualities of his character; 'for,' he observes, 'the name Oshea is interpreted "What sort of a person is this?" but Joshua means "the salvation of the Lord," being the name of the most excellent possible character; for the habits are better with respect to those persons who are of such and such qualities being influenced by them: as, for instance, music is better in a musician, physic in a physician, and each art of a distinctive quality in each artist, regarded both in its perpetuity, and in its power, and in its unerring perfection with regard to the objects of its speculation.'[4] This, after Philo's manner, is somewhat too recondite; yet Joshua was doubtless worthy of this distinguished title, and, as we shall hereafter see, the name then given to him was prophetic of the great work he was to accomplish for God's people.[5]

[1] That of Levi excepted, Num. xiii. 5–16.

[2] 'Authenticity of the Pentateuch,' vol. ii., p. 323.

[3] 'History of the Old Covenant,' iii., p. 284.

[4] 'On the Change of Scripture Names,' xxi.

[5] The Septuagint calls him 'Ιησοῦς, which is also the name given him in Heb. iv. 8.

With this ' *God speed*,' the party set out upon their important errand. We have elsewhere followed them on their journey to Rehob in Mount Hermon, and thence back to Hebron and the Valley of Eshcol, where they obtained grapes, and pomegranates, and figs ; and we have also referred to the report they brought of the land, and to the timidity of ten out of the twelve spies, who greatly exaggerated the difficulties of its conquest, and thereby discouraged the congregation of the people.[1] Caleb was the first to still them, and said, ' Let us go up at once, and possess it, for we are well able ;'[2] and subsequently Joshua also assured the murmurers that they had nought to fear.[3] But he and Caleb had well nigh lost their lives for their fidelity ; for, had not God interfered on their behalf, the people would have stoned them. That was a sad and calamitous day ; for the ten unfaithful spies died by the plague before the Lord, and from that hour the tribes were driven back into the wilderness, there to wander for forty years, until that generation perished, Caleb and Joshua alone excepted. ' Your carcases,' said the Lord, ' shall fall in this wilderness ; and all that were numbered of you, according to your whole number, from twenty years old and upward, which have murmured against Me, doubtless ye shall not come into the land concerning which I sware to make you dwell therein, save Caleb the son of Jephunneh, and Joshua the son of Nun.'[4]

It is seldom that God grants to any one a certain lease of life, even for a year ; but here were two men who were assured that they should live for at least forty years, and that they should see, during that period, a whole generation gathered to their fathers. What must have been the emotions of Caleb and Joshua at this intelligence ! Let the reader imagine that he himself is informed that he will certainly live for nearly half a century, and

---

[1] See the ' History of Moses,' p. 258, etc. [2] Num. xiii. 30.
[3] Num. xiv. 6-9. [4] Num. xiv. 29, 30.

that he will see, meanwhile, all his coadjutors and friends drop, one after another, from the stage of time, and an entirely new race spring up before his eyes. Would not feelings of sadness predominate in his breast? and would he not be disposed to shrink from the ideas that would naturally enter his mind? It is well, then, that as a rule men are kept in ignorance of the future; and foolish beyond measure is the man who attempts to draw aside the curtain that hides it from his view. But Joshua and Caleb received the promise of lengthened days as a reward for their fidelity; and though they would probably start back at the thought of seeing all who had come up with them out of Egypt die in the wilderness, the more youthful part of the community excepted, yet, trusting in the all-sufficiency of God, they would at the same time look forward, through the long vista of forty years, to the day of their entrance on the land of promise, and exult in the thought that that land would, after all, become the inheritance of the tribes of Israel.

Of Joshua's fortunes during the years the people wandered in the wilderness we know nothing. Those years are a blank in his history, as they are in the history of the Israelites generally. We must, therefore, pass them over, and must now look at the events which occurred, in relation to our hero, on the plains of Moab, just prior to the death of Moses. Philo represents Moses as lifting his virgin hands towards heaven, and saying, 'Let the Lord God of the spirits and of all flesh look out for Himself a man to be over this multitude, to undertake the care and superintendence of a shepherd, who shall lead them in a blameless manner, in order that this nation may not become corrupt like a flock which is scattered abroad as having no shepherd.'[1] But the very words of his prayer, as given in the sacred narrative, were, 'Let the LORD, the God of the spirits of all flesh, set a man over the congregation, which may go out before them, and which

---

[1] 'On Humanity,' ii.

may go in before them, and which may lead them out, and which
may bring them in; that the congregation of the Lord be not as
sheep which have no shepherd.'[1] Moses had sons or *grandsons*
living. The *descendants* of Gershom and Eliezer were alive,
though they—Gershom and Eliezer—in all probability, were
not. But he was not so anxious for the honour of his own family
as for the general welfare of the people; and he would not, therefore, appoint either Shebuel the son of Gershom, or Rehabiah
the son of Eliezer,[2] to the important office; but besought God
Himself to choose a successor, knowing that human wisdom was
inadequate to the task, and that no one but the man whom the
Lord appointed would be equal to the enterprise of leading the
people into Canaan.

The prayer of Moses was heard, and he was commanded to
lay his hand upon Joshua, a man in whom was the Spirit, and
to set him before Eleazar the priest, and before the congregation.
Moses was by no means grieved or disappointed because one of
his own kindred was not chosen to succeed him, for he himself
probably thought that there was no man so worthy of the honour
as his long-tried friend and minister; and he proceeded, therefore, to fulfil the important task of presenting him to the people
as their future guide. It was a deeply solemn and interesting
occasion. Aaron was now dead, and Eleazar, his son, was the
high-priest in his stead. And now, clad in his pontifical robes,
he is standing at the door of the tabernacle, before which a vast
concourse of people is assembled, as if waiting for some great
event. Presently the venerable form of Moses is seen approaching, and with him the manly and noble-minded Joshua. A
solemn silence pervades the assembly, and Moses addresses them,
and says, 'I am an hundred and twenty years old this day; I
can no more go out and come in: also the Lord hath said unto
me, Thou shalt not go over this Jordan. The Lord thy God,

[1] Num. xxvii. 16, 17.   [2] 1 Chron. xxiii. 16, 17.

He will go over before thee, and He will destroy these nations before thee, and thou shalt possess them : and Joshua, he shall go over before thee, as the Lord hath said.' And, having further encouraged the people, he calls Joshua forward, sets him before Eleazar the priest, and laying his hands upon him, says, 'Be strong, and of a good courage : for thou must go with this people unto the land which the Lord hath sworn unto their fathers to give them ; and thou shalt cause them to inherit it. And the Lord, He it is that doth go before thee ; He will not fail thee, neither forsake thee : fear not, neither be dismayed.'[1]

History presents no parallel to this scene. That of Samuel anointing David king over Israel in the place of Saul is, perhaps, the nearest approach to it ; and that of Hamilcar, the Carthaginian general, causing his son Hannibal to take a solemn oath at the altar of eternal hostility to Rome, can only be mentioned as a striking contrast. True, Joshua was to look upon the Canaanites as his enemies and not to spare them ; but it was because they were the enemies of the Lord Jehovah, and had now filled up the cup of their iniquities. Did he accept the task assigned him? He had no alternative, for it was God's requirement ; and to have shrunk from it would have been an act of rebellion against Heaven. However arduous an enterprise may be, the man who is called to undertake it by the Lord Jehovah and refuses, does so at his peril, even though he may plead as the ground of his refusal, his unfitness for the work. But Joshua grasped the banner which was put into his hands, confiding in the strength of the Lord God of his fathers ; and Moses, well satisfied to leave the future guidance of the people in his hands, went to the top of Pisgah, beheld the land, and died.

It is a great satisfaction to the monarch of an empire, or to the commander of an army, to know that when he dies the sceptre or the sword will be wielded by skilful hands ; and many an il-

---

[1] See Deut. xxxi. 2–8; and comp. Num. xxvii. 18–23.

lustrious general has resigned his charge to his successor with the utmost pleasure, knowing him to be a man of the highest courage, integrity, and skill. But perhaps there never was an instance in which an eminent functionary gave the baton of office to another with greater confidence, than did Moses to his minister Joshua; and doubtless this was one of the circumstances which rendered the death of Moses, solemn and mysterious as it was, so calm and peaceful to himself. How Joshua fulfilled his trust, it will be our object in the following chapters to show.

BASHAN

CHAPTER II.

JOSHUA THE SUCCESSOR OF MOSES.

THE greatest men have no successors, taking that word in its widest acceptation. Every representative man occupies a niche in the great temple of society which, when vacated by his death, is never occupied by an individual man again,—the great purpose for which he was raised up and placed in it having been accomplished by his personal labours. The Prophet Samuel had no successor, nor the Psalmist David, nor John the Baptist, nor Paul the Apostle. Nor had Cyrus any successor, nor Alexander the Great, nor Julius Cæsar, nor the Emperor Constantine. Neither, in later times, can any one be named as the successor of Wickliffe, or of Luther, or of Knox, or of Cromwell. All these men, and others who might be named, stood related to the age in which they lived as no other men did; and when they passed away, it was found that, though they had left behind them large gaps in society, yet that none were ready to step forth and fill them, and that each gap must be filled, if filled at all, not by one man, but by several men.

If, then, we speak of Joshua as the successor of Moses, we use the term in a limited sense only. As a legislator, Moses had no successor. 'There arose not a prophet since in Israel like unto Moses, whom the Lord knew face to face.'[1] His work was done, his mission was accomplished. No one could fill the place he filled, nor was it requisite that any one should. He had left nothing unaccomplished but the conquest of Canaan; and only as the captain of the hosts of Israel was one now needed, —only as the captain of the hosts of Israel was Joshua appointed as his successor.

Joshua's induction into office probably took place immediately after that great man's death. God said unto him, perhaps in a dream or vision of the night, 'Moses My servant is dead: now therefore arise, go over this Jordan, thou, and all this people, unto the land which I do give to them, even to the children of Israel.'[2] 'Moses My servant is dead!' Was this the first certain intimation of the fact which Joshua received? It may have been; for no one was on Mount Nebo when Moses died, and no one, therefore, could be sure of his demise unless informed of it by God. Yet Joshua, no doubt, knew that Moses had gone up to the mount to die; and, as Moses did not return, he would naturally conclude that his death had taken place, and that now their illustrious leader was no more. He was not in haste, however, to assume the responsibilities of office, and hence God had to summon him to the work before him. How would he receive

[1] Deut. xxxiv. 10. [2] Josh. i. 2.

the announcement? what would be his feelings when at length the solemn fact rushed upon his mind, that the reins of government were actually in his hands? We have heard of princes and of rulers who, at the moment of their accession to the throne, have wept under an almost overwhelming sense of the magnitude of the task they saw before them; and that Joshua would thus feel, on taking the command of that vast multitude, is more than probable. Hence the promise, which he doubtless needed: ' There shall not a man be able to stand before thee all the days of thy life: as I was with Moses, so will I be with thee: I will not fail thee, nor forsake thee.' Encouraging words! Well did Joshua know that God had been with Moses,—with him when an infant, exposed to the waters of the Nile; with him when a youth, amidst the fascinations of Pharaoh's court; with him when a man, an exile in a foreign land; and with him when the leader of the hosts of Israel through all the toils and perils of the wilderness. And now Joshua was assured that God would be with *him* in like manner; and that, whatever difficulties might arise, he should bring the people into the land which God sware unto their fathers to give them. Yet the promise was conditional. He must be strong, courageous, and obedient to all the injunctions of the law. His prosperity and success were to depend upon his fidelity. Day and night he was to meditate in that book which Moses had left for the instruction of the people, and, with unwavering confidence in the power of God, he was to prosecute the enterprise which was now before him. Then, not a man would be able to resist him; then, not an enemy would have courage to withstand him; then, not a weapon formed against him would prosper. Resistless as the lightning, he would be able to scatter all his foes as the leaves are scattered by the autumnal blast; and, ere he terminated his career, victory would crown his arms, and he would see the Israelites in peaceful possession of the land.

The true secret of prosperity in any enterprise, great or small, lies in obedience to the divine commands. This lesson we may learn not only from the history of Joshua, but from that of Joseph,[1] from that of Moses,[2] from that of Saul,[3] from that of Uzziah,[4] and from that of Hezekiah.[5] Nay, it is the great lesson which runs through the pages of inspiration, and which is enforced by universal observation and experience. Wicked men may appear to prosper for a while, and God's people are sometimes staggered, as David was, because they seem to flourish like a green bay tree. But their triumphing is only for a season. Often, very often, are their schemes thwarted and their plans frustrated, and often is the cup of pleasure dashed from their lips just when they imagine that they have reached the object of their ambition, and are about to grasp the wreath of honour and of fame. Or, if godless men prosper even to the end of life,— if every plan they undertake succeeds,—if every purpose they devise is realized,—if they amass riches, and dwell in palaces, and ride in chariots, and are clothed in purple,—if their persons are had in honour, and men bow down at their approach,—and if, when they die, they are buried with funereal pomp, and a marble cenotaph is erected over their dust, and poets and historians hand down their names to future generations, and tell posterity of their riches and their glory,—to what does it amount, and what does it all avail? Will such prosperity secure the happiness of the deathless spirit? We know that it will not; and hence, when the Psalmist understood their end, he ceased to fret at their success; for he said, 'How are they brought into desolation, as in a moment! they are utterly consumed with terrors. As a dream when one awaketh; so, O Lord, when Thou awakest, Thou shalt despise their image.'[6]

To Abram God said, 'Unto thy seed have I given this land,

[1] Gen. xxxix. 23. [2] Exod. iii. 12. [3] 1 Sam. xv. 23.
[4] 2 Chron. xxvi. 5. [5] 2 Chron. xxxi. 21. [6] Ps. lxxiii. 19, 20.

from the river of Egypt unto the great river, the river Euphrates.'[1] And now, in allusion to this original promise, God
says to Joshua, 'Every place that the sole of your foot shall tread
upon, that have I given unto you, as I said unto Moses. From
the wilderness and this Lebanon, even unto the great river, the
river Euphrates, all the land of the Hittites, and unto the great
sea, to the going down of the sun, shall be your coast.' These,
then, were the utmost boundaries of the land to be possessed.
Far in the north were the mountain ranges of Lebanon and Anti-
Lebanon, their summits capped with perpetual snow, and their
sides adorned with the cedar and the fir. On the west was the
Mediterranean Sea, into which the evening sun seemed to drop
as into a bed, amidst a flood of golden light. Eastward was
the Euphrates, on the banks of which Babylon was already rising
in her pride, the destined scourge of Judah, when Judah should
forget her God. And on the south was the wilderness, stretching far away to Egypt's famous Nile, the river of whose luscious
waters the Israelites had so often drunk. It was a wide and
ample territory, and it lay in the very centre of the then civilized
world. But the limits here given do not correspond with the
actual limits attained;[2] for no one advanced as far as the Euphrates ere David did, nor did the Israelites ever extend their
boundaries to the Nile, or ever think of doing it. Yet the words
נהר מצרים in Gen. xv. 18, rendered in our version 'the river of
Egypt,' undoubtedly refer to the Nile, and not, as some have
supposed, to the brook of Egypt—נחל מצרים—mentioned in Num.
xxxiv. 5; Josh. xv. 4, 47, etc., etc., which was unquestionably
the Wady-el-Arish, near the village of that name, anciently called
Rhinocura. How, then, are the discrepancies to be met? We
reply, with Hengstenberg,[3] Keil,[4] and others, that these promises

---

[1] Gen. xv. 18.   [2] See Num. xxxiv.; Josh. xiii. xix.
[3] 'Genuineness of the Pentateuch,' vol. ii. p. 216.
[4] 'Commentary on Joshua,' p. 67   Clark.

partake of a rhetorical character, and merely indicate in a general way certain well-known points that were to constitute the limits within which the land to be given to the Israelites would lie; as is evident from this fact, among others, that between the Nile and the Euphrates nations such as the Ammonites and the Moabites dwelt, whose extinction or expulsion was expressly and strictly forbidden to the Israelites.

Animated by the divine promises which were thus addressed to him, Joshua proceeded at once to make the necessary preparations for taking possession of the land. There were certain officers amongst the people, called shoterim or scribes (γραμματεῖς), whose duty it was to take charge of the genealogies of the tribes, and who assisted in levying troops for military service. These were commanded by Joshua to pass through the host, and to say to the people, 'Prepare you victuals; for within three days ye shall pass over Jordan, to go in to possess the land, which the Lord God giveth you to possess it.' A skilful general is always attentive to the commissariat of his army, well knowing that if the temporal necessities of the forces under his command be not supplied, they will be unfitted to sustain the difficulties of the campaign. This, then, was a wise and prudent measure; and the officers, seeing its importance, would hasten to fulfil the task assigned to them. Their numbers were probably considerable; and they were soon in the midst of the host, passing from tribe to tribe, and from tent to tent, and animating the people to prepare for the conquest of the land. In three days from that time they were *to be ready to cross the Jordan*, though, as we shall hereafter see, they did not actually cross it until at least seven days after. How busy, then, they presently became! They were to prepare victuals; by which we are not to understand manna, as, although that had not yet ceased, it would not have kept longer than a day; besides which, they were in an inhabited country, and had already conquered several of the nations on

that side the river.   What the victuals were, then, it is not difficult to conceive.   They consisted of corn, sheep, oxen, and
other produce of the neighbourhood, which, though not scanty,
would nevertheless require considerable effort to collect.   Now,
therefore, the young men would sally forth into the country round
about, and would gather in whatever provisions they could find
in the conquered territory; and now each family would be employed in the preparation of these victuals, that, when the command to advance was issued, there might be no lack of food and
no unnecessary waste of strength.   In some respects the scene
now witnessed would be similar to that of the solemn night when
they prepared and ate the paschal lamb, just prior to their departure from Egypt.   And yet how different were the two events!
Not the present generation, but a former one, ate of that lamb;
and there were few who would remember the events of that
night.   Would they not, however, be reminded of those events?
and would they not converse about them on this occasion?   It
is not improbable; and, as they contrasted their condition with
that of their fathers, and thought of God's goodness to them
during their wanderings in the wilderness, their hearts would
glow with holy gratitude, and they would be encouraged to
place confidence in the promise they had received.

Another proof of Joshua's foresight presents itself before
us.   The tribes of Reuben and Gad, having a great multitude of
cattle, had, at their own request, been permitted by Moses to
choose their inheritance on the east of the Jordan; for ' when
they saw the land of Jazer, and the land of Gilead, that, behold,
the place was a place for cattle; they spake unto Moses, and to
Eleazar the priest, and unto the princes of the congregation,
saying, Ataroth, and Dibon, and Jazer, and Nimrah, and Heshbon, and Elealeh, and Shebam, and Nebo, and Beon, even the
country which the Lord smote before the congregation of Israel,
is a land for cattle, and thy servants have cattle: wherefore, said

they, if we have found grace in thy sight, let this land be given unto thy servants for a possession, and bring us not over Jordan.' It appeared to Moses a selfish request, and, moreover, calculated to discourage the hearts of the people; so that at first he opposed it, and remonstrated with them. But they assured him that their object was not to shrink from taking their share in the conquest of the country beyond the Jordan; for that, leaving their cattle and their little ones behind, they themselves would go armed before their brethren and assist them in their arduous enterprise. The proposal was an honourable one, and the conditions were accepted. 'If ye will do this,' said Moses, 'if ye will go armed before the Lord to war, and will go all of you armed over Jordan before the Lord, until He hath driven out His enemies from before Him, and the land be subdued before the Lord; then afterward ye shall return, and be guiltless before the Lord, and before Israel; and this land shall be your possession before the Lord,' etc.[1] And, lest they should forget their obligation, Moses, at a somewhat later period, reminded them of their promise;[2] and now Joshua calls upon them to fulfil it. 'Remember,' said he, 'the word which Moses, the servant of the Lord, commanded you, saying, The LORD your God hath given you rest, and hath given you this land. Your wives, your little ones, and your cattle, shall remain on this side Jordan; but ye shall pass before your brethren armed, all the mighty men of valour, and help them; until the LORD your God have given your brethren rest, as He hath given you, and they also have possessed the land which the LORD hath given them; then ye shall return unto the land of your possession, and enjoy it, which Moses, the LORD's servant, gave you on this side Jordan, toward the sun-rising.'[3]

Vows and promises should never be forgotten. It often happens that men make them without intending to keep them;

[1] Num. xxxii. 1–24.   [2] Deut. iii. 18–20.   [3] Josh. i. 13–15.

and in that case, when they are reminded of them, and are called
upon to perform them, they profess to have forgotten them, or
treat them lightly. Happily for the Reubenites, they were of
another spirit. God held them to their word, and they were
ready to go whithersoever Joshua would send them. They felt
themselves under a solemn obligation to assist their brethren,
and they were quite prepared to take their share in the difficulties
connected with the conquest of the country.

And under a solemn obligation they were; for had not their
brethren assisted *them* in the conquest of the territory which *they*
had received for an inheritance? Would the Reubenites, and
the Gadites, and the half-tribe of Manasseh, have been able *of
themselves* to gain possession of the fertile territories of Jazer
and of Gilead? No. In the war with the Midianites a thousand
of each tribe of the Israelites were engaged; and thus the two
tribes and a half were greatly indebted to their brethren, and
were in justice bound to stand by them to the end.

Let us survey for a moment the country of which they had
become the possessors. The territory of Reuben was bounded
on the south by the river Arnon and the land of Moab, on the
west by the Dead Sea and a small portion of the Jordan, on the
north by the territory of Gad, and on the east by the land of
Ammon. In the days of Abraham it was occupied by a numerous race of giants called the Emim, whose name is said to signify
terror,[1] but the Moabites had dispossessed them of it;[2] and they,
in their turn, were driven out of it by the Amorites, in whose
possession it was when the Israelites conquered it.[3] Its capital
was Heshbon, which afterwards became one of the Levitical
cities,[4] and the site of which was visited by Seetzen, Burckhardt,
Irby and Mangles, and other travellers, who found, on the side
of an insulated hill, considerable ruins bearing the name of Heshbon, and who saw from the summit of the hill the ruins of many

[1] Gen. xiv. 5   [2] Deut. ii. 10.   [3] Num. xxi. 26.   [4] Josh. xxi. 39.

other cities. Here too, on the north bank of the river Arnon, was Aroer,[1] the name of which is still attached to a heap of ruins discovered by Burckhardt, on the summit of a lofty wall of rock which bounds the Modjib or Arnon. Three miles north of Aroer stood Dibon, called also Dibon-Gad, because it was fortified by the Gadites after the conquest.[2] Bamoth-baal, or the heights of Baal, from which Balaam saw the outskirts of Israel, was also situated in the vicinity of the Arnon; and under the name of Myun, Burckhardt discovered Beth-baal-meon, about two miles south-east of Heshbon. The positions of Jahaza, where Sihon was defeated,[3] of Kedemoth, Mephaath, Kirjathaim, and other towns mentioned in Joshua xiii. 18–20, have not been satisfactorily identified with any existing ruins; but Beth-peor is said to have stood opposite Jericho, and not far from it were the cliffs of Pisgah, whence Moses was permitted to survey the land.

The Reubenites were not mistaken when they said that this country was a place for cattle. It is 'a land of which travellers say, that in beauty and fertility it as far surpasses western Palestine as Devonshire surpasses Cornwall,'[4]—a remark which also applies to the territories which fell to the tribe of Gad and the half-tribe of Manasseh. Buckingham observes, that east of Jordan there are two ranges of hills, the first of which consists in general of white limestone, and the second of a mixture of many other kinds of rock. Both these ranges are comparatively barren; but no sooner has the traveller passed the western one, than he finds himself on plains eight hundred feet above the stream of the Jordan, and different from anything to be seen in Palestine. 'We were now,' says our authority, 'in a land of extraordinary richness, abounding with the most beautiful prospects, clothed with thick forests, varied with verdant slopes,

---

[1] Deut. ii. 36.   [2] Num. xxxii. 34.   [3] Num. xxi. 23; Deut. ii. 32.
[4] Stanley's 'Sinai and Palestine,' p. 332.

and possessing extensive plains of a fine red soil, now covered with
thistles as the best proof of its fertility, and yielding in nothing
to the celebrated plains of Zabulon and Esdraelon in Galilee and
Samaria.'[1]

'Let Reuben live, and not die,' said Moses; 'and let his men
be few.' It was even so. Unstable as water, he did not excel.
The tribe had to strive hard for existence, and never attained to
any particular eminence—never took part in the great struggles
of the nation. Instead of going up with Deborah against Sisera
and Jabin, the Reubenites abode by their rivers and their sheep-
folds, where, as Deborah afterwards complained in her beautiful
ode, there were great thoughts of heart—great deliberations and
debates—but no resolution to engage in the struggle. Far more
agreeable to them was the bleating of the sheep[2] than the sound
of the trumpet; and, for anything they cared, Sisera and Jabin
might drive Deborah and Barak from the field. At a later
period, however,—in the days of Saul,—there were among the
Reubenites some valiant men, who, together with some of the
Gadites and of the half-tribe of Manasseh, made war upon the
Hagarites, and took from them fifty thousand camels, two hundred
and fifty thousand sheep, two thousand asses, and a hundred
thousand men.[3] But this was the only great exploit recorded
of the tribe; and, the first of the Israelites to gain their inheritance, they were the first to lose it; for they transgressed against
the Lord God of their fathers, and were carried away captives
into Assyria by Tiglath-Pileser, in the days of Pekah king of
Israel.[4]

To the tribe of GAD was assigned the principal portions of
the mountains of Gilead; respecting which Buckingham observes,
'We continued our way over this elevated tract, continuing to
behold with surprise and admiration a beautiful country on all

[1] 'Travels in Palestine,' vol. ii., p. 104, 2d edit. 1822.
[2] Judg. v. 15, 16.   [3] 1 Chron. v. 18–21.   [4] 2 Kings xv. 29.

sides of us; its plains covered with a fertile soil, its hills clothed with forests, at every new turn presenting the most magnificent landscapes that could be imagined.' The eastern boundary of this tribe is not defined; but to the south it extended to Jazer, supposed by Seetzen to be represented by the ruins of Szîr, fifteen miles north-west of Heshbon, and to Aroer that is before Rabbah,—the latter town being the capital of the Ammonites, which probably remained in their possession. Northward, the territory of Gad seems to have diminished in breadth to a narrow tract along the Jordan, so that the domain of the half-tribe of Manasseh extended on its north-eastern border. The principal towns of Gad were, Ramoth-Gilead or Ramoth-Mizpeh, which was probably identical with the present es-Salt, and which was given to the Levites and became one of the cities of refuge, and Mahanaim on the north of the Jabbok, where Ishbosheth was proclaimed king, and whither David fled from Absalom.

'Gad, a troop shall overcome him: but he shall overcome at last,' was Jacob's prophecy. Whilst Moses said of him, 'Blessed be he that enlargeth Gad: he dwelleth as a lion, and teareth the arm with the crown of the head. And he provided the first part for himself, because there, in a portion of the lawgiver, was he seated; and he came with the heads of the people, he executed the justice of the LORD, and His judgments with Israel.'[1] His name signified 'a troop of plunderers;' and the prophecy of Moses was fulfilled, and the character of the tribe illustrated, when (in the days of David) Ezer, Obadiah, Eliab, and several others, whose 'faces were like the faces of lions, and who were swift as the roes upon the mountains,' crossed the Jordan when it had overflowed all its banks, and joined the outlawed David, and helped him against the band of the rovers.[2] In the days of Solomon twelve officers were appointed to provide victuals for the king and his household, each man for one month in a year;[3]

[1] Deut. xxxiii. 20, 21.   [2] 1 Chron. xii. 8–21.   [3] 1 Kings iv. 7–14.

and of these, Geber the son of Uri is said to have been the only
officer in the country of Gilead, whilst his son was prefect in
Ramoth-Gilead and several other towns, and Ahinadab the son
of Iddo had charge of Mahanaim and the territory round about
it.   We may infer from this fact, that the fruits and products of
this land were plentiful; and rich, no doubt, would be the supply
of provisions which Solomon would receive from these purveyors.
And, indeed, it was to this trans-Jordanic territory that Moses
specially referred when he said, ' The Lord hath made him to
ride upon the high places of the earth, that he might eat the increase of the fields; and He made him to suck honey out of the
rock, and oil out of the flinty rock; butter of kine, and milk of
sheep, with fat of lambs, and rams of the breed of Bashan, and
goats, with the fat of the kidneys of wheat; and thou didst drink
the pure blood of the grape.'[1]

The half-tribe of Manasseh had not joined in the request of
the tribes of Reuben and Gad; but the children of Machir, the
first-born of Manasseh, were animated with a martial spirit, and
took the land of Gilead from the Amorites who dwelt there.   Jair
took sixty cities or villages, and called them Havoth-Jair, that is,
hut-villages of Jair; and Nobah took Kenath and its villages,
and called it after his own name.[2]   Moses, therefore, gave them
this territory; and a rich and ample one it was.   It extended
from Mahanaim on the south, and included not only the province
of Bashan, but the whole kingdom of Bashan, which embraced
the northern portion of Gilead with its two principal cities,
Ashtaroth and Edrei.[3]   Ashtaroth was the residence of Og king
of Bashan, and became one of the Levitical cities.   Edrei is supposed by Porter and others to be identical with Edhra or Adralia,
a village on the south banks of the Wady ed-Dan.   Of this
country as a whole Buckingham says, ' The general face of the

_____

[1] Deut. xxxii. 13, 14.   [2] Num. xxxii. 39–42; Josh. xiii. 29–31.
[3] 1 Chron. v. 23, 24.

region improved as we advanced farther in it, and every new direction of our path opened upon us views which surprised and charmed us by their grandeur and beauty.   Lofty mountains gave an outline of the most magnificent character; flowing beds of secondary hills softened the romantic wildness of the picture; gentle slopes, clothed with wood, gave a rich variety of tints, hardly to be imitated by the pencil; deep valleys, filled with murmuring streams and verdant meadows, offered all the luxuriance of cultivation; and herds and flocks gave life and animation to scenes, as grand, as beautiful, and as highly picturesque, as the genius or taste of a Claude could either invent or desire.' Nor is this description of it at all exaggerated, for it is almost surpassed by that of Lord Lindsay; and every traveller who has visited the region speaks of it with like enthusiasm.

This territory included one half of Gilead, the other half of which lay in the country assigned to Gad.   The mountains of Gilead commence at a little distance from Mount Hermon, and extend southwards to the sources of the Jabbok and the Arnon. 'As it was thus first occupied by the Israelites, so it subsequently became the border-land between Palestine and the nations of eastern Asia.   From its midway position it necessarily bore the brunt of all the incursions of the Syrians of Damascus, when Ramoth-Gilead became the scene of so many sieges and battles, as the fortress for which both kingdoms contended; and for the same reason it was the first to resist and the first to fall before the arms of the Assyrian Tiglath-Pileser.   In this respect the range of Gilead remained faithful to the description given by the two patriarchs who of old parted on its summit, as the boundary-line between the tribes of Canaan and those of Mesopotamia.   "This heap is a witness between me and thee this day. . . .   The God of Abraham and the God of Nahor judge betwixt us."'[1]

---

[1] Stanley's 'Sinai and Palestine,' pp. 320, 321.

Such is but a hasty view of the trans-Jordanic territories assigned to Reuben, Gad, and the half-tribe of Manasseh. Having received such an inheritance, it was but just and right that they should not sit down and rest until the country west of the Jordan was also conquered; and, as we shall hereafter see, a considerable portion of them went with Joshua to the war, and subsequently returned to the lands assigned to them. Joshua, like Moses, was a lover of justice; and though he could doubtless have conquered Canaan without the aid of the two tribes and a half, yet he chose to act on the principles of his predecessor, and demanded as a right what was not perhaps a matter of necessity.

HOUSE ON THE WALL

CHAPTER III.

THE SPIES SENT TO JERICHO.

THE Israelites still abode in Shittim, where they had encamped prior to the death of Moses. It was in the
desert plains of Moab; and was so called from the
acacia groves which line both the eastern and the western banks
of the Jordan. 'Their tents were pitched,' observes Mr Stanley, 'from Abel-Shittim on the north, to Beth-Jeshimoth on the
south (Num. xxxiii. 49),—from the "*meadow*" which marked

c

the limit of those "*groves,*" to the "*hamlet*" or "*house*" which
stood in the "*waste,*" or the shores of the Dead Sea.' Very
beautiful must have been the view of them which Balaam saw
from 'the top of the rocks' on which he stood, and thus he
described the scene before him :—

> 'How goodly are thy tents, O Jacob!
> Thy tabernacles, O Israel!
>> As the valleys are they spread forth,
>> As gardens by the river's side,
>> As the trees of lign-aloes which the Lord hath planted,
>> As cedar-trees beside the waters.'

Just opposite their encampment, and sixty stadia east of the
Jordan, was Jericho, the city of palm-trees; and here, the frontier
town of the land of promise. It was one of the walled cities of
which ten of the spies who went to search out the land were so
much afraid, and of which they brought so alarming an account.
Yet it was absolutely essential that Joshua should take it, for it
was the key of Palestine, and would form the basis of all future
operations. And take it he would, for God had promised it to
him. But he was cautious, and neglected no means likely to
facilitate its conquest. For his own satisfaction, as it would
appear, he sent two spies, saying unto them secretly or apart,
'Go view the land, and especially Jericho.' 'He sent them away
privately,' says Keil, 'partly in order that the inhabitants of the
land might not receive any intimation of it, and partly also that
the Israelites themselves might not be disheartened by the report, if it should prove unfavourable, as they had formerly been
in the time of Moses.'[1]

If the Jordan was now overflowing its banks, the two spies
must have crossed it by swimming; and no sooner were they on
the opposite bank, than they proceeded towards Jericho and
entered one of its gates. Against the wall of the town they

[1] 'Commentary on Joshua,' p. 79. Clark.

found the house of a harlot named Rahab, and, to avoid suspicion, they entered it and there lodged. Some have supposed that Rahab was not a harlot, but an innkeeper; but there is no evidence that inns were kept in those days, and the word rendered harlot, זוֹנָה, is certainly from the root זָנָה, to commit whoredom, and not, as Schleusner and others have represented, from זוּן, to feed.

They, of course, told the woman their errand, and probably informed her—what, indeed, she must have heard already—that their people were encamped in vast numbers on the eastern bank of the river, that they intended to invade the land, and that Jericho was doomed to fall into their hands. She believed their words, and resolved to aid them to the utmost of her power. Fearing that the entrance of the spies into her house had been observed, and that the king of Jericho would hear of it and send messengers to seize them, she took them to the top of the building, which was flat, and there hid them under the stalks of flax which she had laid in order on the roof. In Egypt flax grows to the height of three feet and upwards; and, as the climate of Jericho was similar to that of Egypt, the plant would attain the same height in that neighbourhood. Now these long stalks of flax had been piled up on the top of Rahab's house to dry in the sun, and were very suitable for the purpose to which they were now put.[1]

The king of Jericho speedily received intelligence of the arrival of the spies; for there were, no doubt, guards appointed to watch the city gates, and to give notice to the king of the entrance of any strangers. And, as Rahab had apprehended, the king's messengers soon appeared at her door, and demanded that she should give up the men who had lately entered her dwelling.

---

[1] From Exod. ix. 31, it appears that flax and barley ripened together. But this was the time of the barley harvest in Canaan, and, we may infer, of the flax harvest too. Hence the flax on Rahab's house had just been gathered in. See Blunt's 'Undesigned Coincidences,' p. 105, 6th edit.

It may appear surprising that they did not forcibly enter the house and search it, as would be done under such circumstances in our day; but in the East, as Dr Kitto observes, the privacy of a woman was respected, even to a degree that might be called superstitious; and no one will enter the house in which she lives, or the part of the house she occupies, until her consent has been obtained, if, indeed, such consent be ever demanded.'[1] The king's messengers, then, only appeared at the door of Rahab's house, and there made their demand. But the spies had been *already* hid—for it is not likely that the messengers were kept waiting at the door whilst she was concealing the two men—and she was resolved not to comply with the king's request. Rahab said therefore, 'There came men unto me, but I wist not whence they were: and it came to pass, about the time of shutting of the gate, when it was dark, that the men went out; whither the men went, I wot not: pursue after them quickly: for ye shall overtake them.'[2] She was a sharp-witted woman; and very artful was this reply. But what shall we say of the falsehoods it contained? Was it a lawful deception which Rahab thus practised on the messengers? or may we conclude, with Grotius, that 'before the Gospel, a lie which contributed to the safety of good men was not regarded as a sin?'[3] No; a lie is a lie, and was such in all ages; and of the sin of lying, Rahab was unquestionably guilty. But she was a heathen, and her notions of morality were doubtless of the lowest kind. Had she been better taught, she would have known that to resort to any such sinful expedient as this was quite unnecessary, inasmuch as God would have taken care both of her and of His servants. But, though Rahab had a little faith—faith to believe that God was about to give the victory to the Israelites, her faith did not go so far as this, and hence she deemed it necessary to tell a false-

---

[1] 'Daily Readings,' vol. ii., p. 243.   [2] Josh. ii. 4, 5.
[3] Quoted by Keil, Comm. in loco.

hood in order to screen the spies from harm. Yet 'her faith was counted unto her for righteousness, and her sins, which were many, were forgiven.'[1] And according to St James, she was justified by works also;[2] 'because her works were a necessary part of that inherent righteousness which must be in every one that lives by faith.'—'Had she said unto these messengers only thus—I believe the God of heaven and earth hath given you this whole land for a possession, yet I dare not show you any kindness in this city—her belief would have been as dead as a body without breath or motion.'[3] But her faith was a living, operative faith; and by her works it was made manifest, and became acceptable to God.

It has always been customary in the East to close the gates of walled cities in the evening, and not to permit any person to pass through them without special authority. The messengers of the king had such authority, and they immediately sallied forth in quest of the supposed fugitives. It was getting dusk, for the sun had already set; but it is probable that the men spent three days in pursuit of the spies, perhaps, as is often done in some countries to this day, following upon what they fancied were their foot-prints with the utmost care. There were several fords over the Jordan, which, if the river was not yet full, they might have crossed. But it is scarcely probable that they would venture to the opposite bank; for there the Israelites were encamped, and they would be in danger of being taken prisoners.

But now Rahab returned to the two spies. There they were on the top of the house, trembling with apprehension lest they should be betrayed, or lest the messengers, whose approach they had heard, should force their way to their hiding-place, when Rahab came to them and quieted their fears. She told them that she knew something of their history,—how the Lord

---

[1] Heb. xi. 31. [2] James ii. 25.
[3] Dr Thomas Jackson's Works, vol. iii., p. 182. Oxford edit.

had dried up the waters of the Red Sea before them,—how they had smitten Sihon and Og, the two kings of the Amorites,—and how, when these tidings reached the ears of her countrymen, their hearts melted and their courage failed them ; and she now entreated them to swear that, when they entered the city as conquerors, they would show kindness to her and to her family, and save her father, and her mother, and her brethren, and her sisters from death. It was a touching appeal. Harlot as she was, she had not lost her affections for her kindred. In some other part of the city her parents were living, and her brethren, and her sisters ; and for these, as well as for herself, she interceded with the spies, believing that they would be able to preserve them from the general destruction which awaited the inhabitants. How could the spies resist her appeal? They knew the doom that hung over the city, for they knew that God had commanded Joshua to slay utterly old and young ; but they doubted not that, having experienced such kindness from Rahab, they might give her the assurance of protection. She urged her request on the ground of the favour she had conferred on them. 'I have showed kindness to you,' she said : 'swear therefore that ye will also show kindness unto me.' They promised that they would. 'Our life for yours,' they replied, 'if ye utter not this our business. And it shall be, when the Lord hath given us the land, that we will deal kindly and truly with thee.'

It is observable that in this address of Rahab the name Jehovah occurs ; but was she—a heathen woman—acquainted with this mysterious name, or was it merely put into her lips by the historian? That she knew its full import, or that she had already become a worshipper of Jehovah, we cannot suppose ; but that she might have heard that this was the name·of the God of the Israelites, is just as probable as that she had received the intelligence of their passage through the Red Sea. It may be difficult to some minds to conceive how she could receive intelligence respecting them at all; but surely such stirring events as had occurred on the east of the Jordan would be reported on the west of it. Would there not be many stragglers from the armies of Sihon and of Og who would seek refuge beyond the river, and carry with them the alarming tidings of the people who had come out of Egypt, and who were sweeping away everything before them? If Balak king of Moab heard of Israel's conquests and took the alarm ere yet the territory east of the Jordan was entirely in their hands, well might the king of Jericho hear of them and tremble when the Midianites also had been subdued.

Rahab would be satisfied with nothing but an oath from the spies. 'Swear unto me by Jehovah,' said she; or, literally, 'give me a token of truth.' 'The material man is not contented with a word alone; for greater security he requires a material token, a visible pledge of the word, which may serve either to remind the other of his oath, or, if he break it, to convict him of perjury. It has therefore been a custom with all nations to give such tokens in connection with oaths and treaties. They have only been driven out by the written signature of oaths, contracts, and other things of the same description, the document in writing taking the place of a token chosen at pleasure.'[1] And with the words, 'Our life for yours,' or 'our souls shall die for you,' the spies took the required oath; for they meant by this, 'We place our life and soul in the hand of God, as a pledge for thee, in order that He may destroy us if any one injures thee or thine.'

But how were they to know Rahab's house again? or how were Joshua and his people to distinguish the habitation in which she and her family would remain? In the storming of a city it is no easy thing for the conquerors to show favour to a single family within it; for there is generally so much confusion, and the inhabitants crowd together in such wild consternation, that

[1] Keil on 'Joshua,' p. 88. Clark.

families are lost one among another, and the nearest relatives
are often unable to recognise each other. The spies therefore
required Rahab, as the conditions on which their oath should be
binding, that she should bring all the members of her family into
that house, and that from its window she should bind a scarlet
cord, which, it is probable, they themselves gave her for the
purpose. It was a cord spun of crimson threads, a colour
obtained from the insect *Coccus illicis*, the dead bodies of the
females of which, together with their eggs, furnish a splendid
deep red dye. This insect 'is found abundantly upon a small
species of evergreen oak (*Quercus coccifera*), common in the south
of France and many other parts of the world, and has been employed to impart a blood-red or crimson dye to cloth from
the earliest ages, and was known to the Phœnicians before the
time of Moses under the name of Tola or Tolath (תּוֹלַע), to the
Greeks under that of *Coccus* (Κόκκος), and to the Arabians and
Persians under that of *Kermes* or *Alkermes;* whence, as Beckman
has shown, and from the epithet *vermiculatum*, given to it in the
Middle Ages, when it was ascertained to be the produce of a
worm, have sprung the Latin *coccineus*, the French *cramoisi* and
vermeil, and our crimson and vermilion.'[1] In the passage before us—Josh. ii. 18—the word used is simply shani, שָׁנִי, which,
according to some authorities, signifies double-dyed, or, according to others, deep red, bright dye.[2] As the curtains of the
tabernacle contained threads of this colour (Exod. xxvi. 1), it is
probable that the spies had had the scarlet cord with them ; and
its brilliant colour rendered it the most suitable for the purpose
to which it was now to be applied, as it could be easily observed
at a considerable distance. 'Behold,' says Bishop Hall, 'this
is the saving colour: the destroying angel sees the door-cheeks
of the Israelites sprinkled with red, and passes over them ; the

---

[1] Kirby and Spence's 'Entomology,' one vol., edit. 1858, pp. 181, 182.
[2] See Beckman's 'History of Inventions,' vol. i., pp. 392, 393. Bohn's edit.

warriors of Israel see the window of Rahab dyed red, and save her family from the common destruction. If our souls have this tincture of the precious blood of our Saviour upon our doors and windows, we are safe.'[1]

When the king's messengers left the city in pursuit of the spies, 'they shut the gate.' It was therefore impossible for the two men to depart in the ordinary way that night; and had they remained until the next day, the vigilance of the king's servants would have prevented their escape. Under these circumstances, there was but one expedient to which they could resort. Happily for them, Rahab's house was on the town-wall—the back of it, in which there was a window, probably jutting out beyond the wall over the path beneath. What then does this friendly woman? With a strong cord she lets them down, one after the other, out of this window, and in a few moments they are both safe outside the city. That a woman could let down two men in such a way, may seem incredible; but she would have the assistance of one of them whilst the other was let down, and the first would no doubt assist his companion in *his* descent. Besides which, we need not suppose that the window was very high; so that, with care, the task would easily be accomplished.[2]

We have already mentioned the conversation relative to the scarlet thread; but it should be observed that it actually took place under the window of the dwelling,—for they said, 'Behold, when we come into the land, thou shalt bind this line of scarlet thread in the window which *thou didst let us down by;*' so that both the order in which the circumstances are narrated, and the form of the words here employed, lead to the conclusion that this arrangement was made with Rahab *after* she had let them down out of the window. The scarlet thread, however, was not,

[1] 'Contemplations,' Book viii.

[2] In a similar manner did Saul of Tarsus escape from the city of Damascus. Acts ix. 25.

as some have supposed, the cord she used, for that is called by another name, *chevel* (חֶבֶל); so that they no doubt fastened the scarlet thread to the rope, which she drew up and took care of until the time when it would prove of such essential value.

Rahab had probably provided them with food, and advised them to go into the mountain and hide themselves three days, lest the pursuers should meet them. They acted on her advice, and fled to the mountain. There were mountains on the west of the town, on the north, and on the south. It is not probable that they would go to the west, as they should then have been at a considerable distance from the camp; they would most probably choose the north, where the mountains are situated, to which the name Quarantana was afterwards given, and by the Arabs *Kŭrŭntal*. Following the tradition that this was the scene of our Lord's temptation, Milton happily describes it thus:—

> ‘ It was a mountain at whose verdant feet
> A spacious plain, outstretched in circuit wide,
> Lay pleasant; from his side two rivers flowed,
> Th’ one winding, th’ other straight, and left between
> Fair champaign with less rivers interveign’d,
> Then meeting, joined their tribute to the sea;
> Fertile of corn the glebe, of oil, and wine;
> With herds the pastures throng’d, with flocks the hills;
> Huge cities, and high tower’d, that well might seem
> The seats of mightiest monarchs; and so large
> The prospect was, that here and there was room
> For barren desert, fountainless, and dry.
> To this high mountain, too, the tempter brought
> Our Saviour, and new train of words began.’[1]

Josephus places the ancient Jericho near a fountain, called the fountain of Elisha, which ‘runs very plentifully, and is very fit for watering the ground.’[2] Most modern travellers admit that he is correct; and if so, the spies would have but a quarter of a

---

[1] ‘ Paradise Regained,’ Book iii. 256.

[2] ‘ Wars of the Jews,’ Book iv. chap. viii. 3.

mile to walk ere they found themselves on the mountain-side. It rises precipitously twelve or fifteen hundred feet above the plain, and its eastern front is full of natural caverns and artificial grottoes, once the abodes of superstitious hermits.[1] In one of these caverns the spies might easily hide themselves from their pursuers; and here it was, no doubt, that they remained three days, patiently waiting until they could, without much danger, venture back to the camp. They were worthy men, and performed their task well. But as they were absent so long, Joshua would perhaps be somewhat anxious respecting them; and when at length they stood before him, he would give them a most cordial greeting.

Very different was their report to that of the ten men who had accompanied Joshua and Caleb nearly forty years before, and glad would Joshua be that their fears on this point were not realized. 'They told him all things that befell them: and they said unto Joshua, Truly the Lord hath delivered into our hands all the land: for even all the country do faint because of us.' It was principally to gain information relative to the feelings of the Canaanites that Joshua sent the men, and now this is their report: The people are afraid of us; they have heard of our conquests, and are faint-hearted and discouraged; they are filled with consternation on account of what Jehovah has done for us, and they are utterly unprepared to resist our arms. Quickly the tidings would spread throughout the camp; and instead of the murmurings which were heard aforetime, there would now be rejoicings and congratulations, and with brave hearts and fearless spirits the people would prepare to march forward to the conquest.

And would not the name of Rahab be in honour? She had protected and shown kindness to the spies. But for her, they might have been taken prisoners and put to death. To her,

---

[1] Robinson's 'Researches,' vol. i., p. 567. 2d edit. Murray.

therefore, the whole multitude were not a little indebted, and
every one would approve of the promise given her of protection,
and be willing to pledge himself that the promise should be
kept.   How it was kept, and how Rahab was preserved, we
shall see hereafter; but we must here glance for a moment at
her subsequent history.   She doubtless abandoned heathenism,
and with it the sins to which she had been addicted; and such is
the divine mercy, that she obtained the righteousness which is of
faith, was received as a proselyte into the Jewish Church, and
became a partaker of the privileges of God's people.   Hebrew
tradition affirms that she became the wife of Joshua himself,
and the ancestress of Jeremiah, Maaseiah, Hanameel, Shallum,
Baruch, Ezekiel, Neriah, Seriah, and Huldah the prophetess.[1]
But from Matthew i. 5 it appears that she was married to Salmon the son of Naason, or Nahshon, and became the mother of
Boaz, and through his line an ancestress of our Lord and Saviour.   It is true that doubts have been entertained, on chronological grounds, whether the Rachab of this passage was the
Rahab of the Book of Joshua; but, as Olshausen observes, the
expression ἡ ʹΡαχάβ (with the article) clearly points to the known
Rahab, and the chronological difficulties are by no means insurmountable.   'Nahshon, the father of Salmon, the prince of
Judah (1 Chron. ii. 10), offered his offering at the setting up of
the tabernacle (Num. vii. 12), thirty-nine years before the taking
of Jericho.   So that Salmon would be of mature age at or soon
after that event, at which time Rahab was probably young, as
her father and mother were living.'[2]   The difficulty, however,
lies in the fact, that according to the received chronology, a
period elapsed between Rahab and David of upwards of four
hundred years, which would give for the four generations men-

---

[1] See Lightfoot's 'Hor. Heb.' in loco.

[2] Alford's 'Greek Test.,' vol. i., Matt. i. 5; and Lange's Com. on St Matt.,
p. 64. Clark.

tioned—Salmon, Boaz, Obed, and Jesse—an average of more than one hundred years. Either, then, the chronology is incorrect, and must be considerably reduced, as several authorities affirm, or Matthew has not included all the generations, as Olshausen, Keil,[1] and others suppose. And this is the more probable solution of the difficulty, as it is certain that the Jews did not insert all names into their genealogical lists.

What an honour, then, was conferred on Rahab, that she, a poor Gentile, should become, however remotely, an ancestress of the Messiah! The same honour was conferred on another Gentile woman—Ruth the Moabitess;[2] and thus the genealogy of our Lord is not purely Jewish, but contains these Gentile elements, as if to intimate that He was to become, as we know He has become, the Saviour of the Gentiles as well as of the Jews. And that Rahab had her full share in the blessings of redemption, who can doubt? Whether her faith apprehended the promise of the Messiah, received by tradition through Abraham, we know not; but when she became the wife of Salmon, if not before, she would doubtless hear of the expected Deliverer, and would believe in Him. Dante, therefore, places her in Paradise, and says:—

> ' Know, then, the soul of Rahab
> Is in that gladsome harbour, to our tribe
> United, and the foremost rank assign'd.
> She to this heaven, at which the shadow ends
> Of your sublunar world, was taken up,
> First in Christ's triumph, of all souls redeem'd:
> For well behoved, that, in some part of heaven,
> She should remain a trophy, to declare
> The mighty conquest won with either palm;
> For that she favour'd first the high exploit
> Of Joshua on the Holy Land.'[2]

This is not mere poetry. Rahab was indeed a trophy of redeeming love; and her history, like that of many others, affords

---

[1] ' Comm. on Joshua,' p. 172, note. [2] Ruth iv. 17, comp. Matt. i. 5.
[2] Carey's Dante, ' Paradise,' Canto ix.

ground of hope for sinners of more than ordinary guilt. If this poor Gentile harlot obtained mercy, while yet the Gentiles as a race were strangers to the covenant of promise, who need now despair, since the door of faith has been opened to the Gentile and the Jew alike? But her history presents to us another lesson also. It reminds us of the saying of St Paul, 'Be not forgetful to entertain strangers: for thereby some have entertained angels unawares.'[1] To her the spies were as angels, sent to warn her of coming judgments. She received them, she lodged them, she sent them away in peace; 'therefore her reward was sure, so that she was not only preserved in life, but received more grace unto salvation, for the sake of her vigorous first faith. And with her we may compare those who are disposed to come out of the world, and enter among the people of God, who receive the disciples of Christ and give them food in His name, because they are His disciples.'[2] None such shall lose their reward; for an act of kindness done to one of His servants is considered by our Lord as done to Himself, and He will remember it in the day when He shall call the nations to His bar. To such as Rahab it will be said in that day, 'I was a stranger, and ye took Me in.'

Returning to the narrative, we find the vast camp of the Israelites once more in motion; for 'Joshua rose early in the morning; and they removed from Shittim, and came to Jordan, he and all the children of Israel' (chap. iii. 1). The words are brief, but they present to us a picture of the most lively interest. Several months had elapsed since the people pitched their tents in that locality, during which many events of thrilling importance in their history had occurred, such as the stratagem of Balak, the defeat of Sihon, the battle at Edrei, and the death of Moses; but now their tents were once more struck, and, with the exception of the families of Reuben, Gad, and the half-tribe of

---

[1] Heb. xiii. 2.   [2] Stier on 'St James,' p. 359. Clark.

Manasseh, the whole assembly of the children of Israel left the desert plains of Moab, and moved towards the valley of the Jordan, preparatory to the transit of the river and their entrance on the promised land. This valley, which is called by the Arabs El Ghor, is here fifteen miles in breadth, two-thirds of which lie on the western side of the river; so that the people must have spread themselves up and down its banks for a distance of several leagues. Forty years before, their fathers had stood in like manner on the banks of the Red Sea, soon after their departure from Egypt; and, as children, many of the present generation too were there. But the greater number of them would have but a faint recollection of that event; and though they had heard from their parents of the wondrous miracle which God then wrought on their behalf, they would possess but a very inadequate conception of the scene which then occurred. Now, however, they were about to witness another display of Jehovah's power; and their enemies would hear that He who had divided the waters of the Red Sea before them, was still their Deliverer and their God.

Three days were spent in this locality, during which all possible attention would, of course, be paid to the preparations necessary for conducting the host, the women, the children, and the cattle, over the river with as little confusion as possible. At the end of the three days the Shoterim went through the host, giving instructions to the people that when they saw the ark of the covenant of the Lord their God, borne by the Priests and Levites, they should follow it; leaving, however, a space between it and them of two thousand cubits, that they might know the way by which they should go, for they had not passed that way before. It has been supposed that this injunction was given because of the sacredness of the ark; but this space was to intervene that the people might see their way, for, as Keil observes, had they 'followed *en masse* close upon the heels of the priests who were carrying the ark, from the pressure of the crowd, those who were nearest it would have completely hidden it from the rest, and thus have prevented the more distant from seeing the way which it opened before them.' And now the voice of Joshua was heard, and his words were conveyed to the utmost extremity of the camp—'Sanctify yourselves; for to-morrow the Lord will do wonders among you.' It was a similar command to that given by the Lord to Moses just prior to the promulgation of the law: 'Go unto the people, and sanctify them to-day and to-morrow, and let them wash their clothes, and be ready against the third day.'[1] God was about to reveal His presence in an extraordinary manner on the following day, and to perform a miracle before the eyes of the people, equalled only by the dividing of the Red Sea; and now, therefore, they were to prepare themselves for His coming, by washing their clothes, by abstinence from all sensual enjoyments, and by a renewed consecration of themselves to His service. The solemn injunction was obeyed; and that night the camp would present an extraordinary scene of humiliation, fasting, and prayer; whilst many thousands would perhaps wash themselves in the waters of that river, on the opposite shores of which they were soon to stand.

When an entire people is on the eve of some great national event, the excitement increases as the anticipated hour draws nigh. How intense must have been the emotions of the Israelites as the hours of that evening sped away, and as the dawn of the following morning broke upon the camp! Early would their slumbers cease, and soon the entire multitude would be in readiness for the expected sign. And what congratulations would be heard among the different tribes! 'We are to pass over the river this day. This day we are to take possession of the land which God promised unto our fathers. We are now about to begin the conquest of the country which is to be our resting-place

[1] Exod. xix. 10, 11, and 14, 15.

and home.' Thus would parents address their children, and thus would friend converse with friend; and every countenance would beam with joy, and every heart be animated with hope. No anxiety would be felt as to the result, for the people's confidence in God, and in His servant Joshua, was now firm and fixed. For murmuring there was no room. They saw that the Lord Jehovah was in their midst; they were satisfied that their commander was acting under His directions and control; and, whatever difficulties they might have to encounter, they believed that before the advancing hosts all such difficulties would give way.

MEMORIAL STONES

CHAPTER IV.

THE PASSAGE OF THE JORDAN.

ALL was ready, and early that morning Joshua said unto
the priests, 'Take up the ark of the covenant, and pass
over before the people' (chap. iii. 6).

But 'the Jordan overfloweth all his banks all the time of
harvest' (iii. 15); a statement which is confirmed by other passages in the writings of the Hebrews. In 1 Chron. xii. 15 it is
said, 'These are they that went over Jordan in the first month
(about the latter end of March), when it had overflown all its
banks.' From Jer. xlix. 19, l. 44, we learn that these swellings

drove the lion from his lair; and the writer of the apocryphal book of Ecclesiasticus says, 'He maketh the understanding to abound like Euphrates, and as Jordan in the time of harvest' (chap. xxiv. 26). To understand the position of the Israelites at this moment, it will be necessary to inquire into the nature of these 'swellings,' and to ascertain, if possible, their extent; the more so, as several objections have been raised to the accuracy and truthfulness of the Biblical representation. 'It is,' however 'a plain and honest statement of a simple fact, as literally true now as when Joshua led the ransomed tribes into Canaan. All we need in order to clear the passage from obscurity and doubt, is an adequate acquaintance with the phenomena of the country and the river.'[1]

The Jordan—or, as the word signifies, 'the Descender'— takes its rise in the far north, at the base of the snowy Hermon. Here there are innumerable springs and fountains, which find their way southwards, and probably unite with what are supposed by most authorities to be the two principal sources of the river,—the cave of Banias, and the hill of Dan. Of the former, Josephus, who calls it Panim, says, 'This is a very fine cave in a mountain, under which there is a great cavity in the earth; and the cavern is abrupt and prodigiously deep, and full of still water. Over it hangs a vast mountain, and under the cavern arise the springs of the river Jordan.' The latter is called by the same writer the source of the Lesser Jordan; but it is here that the largest fountain in Syria takes its rise; and as Dr Thomson witnessed it, he thus wrote:—'The young Jordan! type of this strange life of ours! Bright and beautiful in its cradle, laughing in its merry morning away through the flowery fields of the Hûleh; plunging, with the recklessness of youth, into the tangled brakes and muddy marshes of Merom; hurrying

---

[1] 'The Land and the Book,' by W. M. Thomson, D.D., p. 619. English edit. Nelson.

thence, full-grown, like earnest manhood with its noisy and bus-
tling activities, it subsides at length into life's sober midday in
the placid Lake of Gennesaret.   When it goes forth again, it is
down the inevitable proclivity of old age, sinking deeper and
deeper, in spite of doublings and windings innumerable, until
finally lost in the bitter sea of Death, that melancholy bourne
from which there is neither escape nor return.'[1]

There is reason to believe that there are at least four principal
sources of the Jordan, with several smaller ones, all which meet
before the river enters the Lake Hûleh, and all which are more
or less affected by the melting of the snows of Hermon.   'The
Jordan is made up from the joint contributions of great permanent springs; and in this fact we find the explanation of the
overflow of the river so late in the season as March.   These
immense fountains do not feel the effects of the early winter
rains at all.   It requires the heavy and long-continued storms of
mid-winter before they are moved in the least; and it is not until
toward the close of winter, when the melting snows of Hermon
and Lebanon, with the heavy rains of the season, have penetrated
through the mighty masses of these mountains, and filled to
overflowing their hidden chambers and vast reservoirs, that the
streams gush forth in their full volume.   The Hûleh—marsh
and lake—is filled, and then Gennesaret rises, and pours its ac-
cumulated waters into the swelling Jordan about the 1st of
March.   Thus it comes to pass that it does actually "overflow
all its banks during all the time of harvest;" nor does it soon
subside, as other short rivers do, when the rains cease.   These
fountains continue to pour forth their contributions for months
with undiminished volume, and the river keeps full and strong
all through March into April, and the proper banks of the river
are still full to overflowing in the time of harvest.'

Such is the explanation of the swelling of the Jordan given

[1] 'The Land and the Book,' p. 214.

by Dr Thomson, who also observes, that he visited the scene of
the miracle on the 1st of April, and 'found the river full to the
brim, and saw abundant evidence that it had overflowed its banks
very recently.'[1]   Dr Robinson, however, says that the Hebrew
expressions signify nothing more than that the Jordan 'was full,
or filled up to all its banks,' meaning 'the banks of its channel.'[2]
Yet he himself observes, that when he saw it on the 12th of May
1838, the low banks of the channel, in the vicinity opposite
Jericho, were *covered* with water, and that there was a still,
though very rapid, current.   That the Jordan does not, like the
Nile, cover a vast tract of country by its overflow, is acknowledged; but the river may be said to have 'three sets of banks;
viz., the upper or outer ones, forming the first descent from the
level of the great valley; the lower or middle ones, enclosing
the tract of canes and other vegetation; and the actual banks of
the channel.'   Now the water sometimes rises to the very tops
of these inner banks, and even reaches to the roots of the bushes
in the middle ones; the breadth of the stream is then from eighty
to a hundred feet, its depth ten or twelve feet, and its current
so strong that an experienced swimmer will be carried down
several yards in crossing.[3]

The course of the Jordan is not more, in a straight line,
than 70 miles; but such is its tortuosity, that its actual length
was found by the American expedition, under Captain Lynch,
to be at least 200 miles.   The Sea of Tiberias is 328 feet below
the level of the Mediterranean, and the Dead Sea 1311 feet,—a
difference in the level of the two seas of 983 feet, giving room
for three cataracts, each equal to the Niagara.   And cataracts
there are, with many rapids.   Captain Lynch passed down 27 of
the latter which were very threatening, together with several

---

[1] 'The Land and the Book,' p. 619.   [2] 'Researches,' vol. i., p. 536.
[3] Robinson, vol. i., p. 536, etc.; comp. 'Lord Lindsay's Letters,' and Van
de Velde's 'Syria and Palestine,' vol. ii., p. 322, etc.

others of a less fearful character.[1]   Well, then, may the river be called the Descender, and well may its current, when it overflows its banks, be formidable to encounter, even by those accustomed to such tasks.

We may now form a conception of the position of the Israelites at this moment.   They had encamped in the Ghor, on the upper banks of the river ; but they were now commanded to strike their tents and to proceed towards the lower banks, which were covered with bushes of luxuriant green.   There, however, the waters were before them, rolling down, if not impetuously, yet with considerable rapidity, and reaching to the roots of the trees that ran along the river's side.   What was that vast multitude of men, women, and little children, together with all their droves of cattle and of sheep, to do?   How were they to pass the flood, and to reach in safety the farther side of the stream?   When, in the fourth century of the Christian era, the Goths, amounting to nearly a million of persons of both sexes and of all ages, crossed the Danube, which had been swelled by incessant rains, a large fleet of vessels, of boats and of canoes, was provided ; yet many days and nights they passed and repassed with indefatigable toil, and, notwithstanding the most strenuous efforts of the officers, many were swept away and drowned by the rapid violence of the current.[2]   But here were two millions of people, who, in some way or other, must be transported to the opposite banks of the river which was before them.   It is evident, then, that God must interfere on their behalf.   And interfere He did. ' This day,' said He to Joshua, ' will I begin to magnify thee in the sight of all Israel, that they may know that, as I was with Moses, so I will be with thee.   And thou shalt command the priests that bear the ark of the covenant, saying, When ye are

---

[1] Lynch's ' Narrative of the United States Expedition.'

[2] See the account in Gibbon's ' Decline and Fall,' etc., Milman's edit., vol. iii., p. 321.

come to the brink of Jordan, ye shall stand still in Jordan' (chap. iii. 7, 8). Joshua then addressed the people, and said, 'Come hither, and hear the words of the Lord your God;' and, repeating, as it were, God's message, he told them that, as a pledge of future victories over the Canaanites and other inhabitants of the land, the ark of the covenant of the Lord would pass over before them into the river, and that as soon as the soles of the priests' feet rested on the river's brink, it would be cut off, and the waters above would stand upon a heap. The people doubted not his word. All were ready to obey the signal. All were prepared to follow their guides.

And now the ark of the covenant, which, from the dedication of the tabernacle, had been the appointed symbol of God's gracious presence, is lifted up on the shoulders of the priests, and borne towards the brink of the descending river. When the Red Sea was divided before the Israelites, Moses lifted up his rod, for then the ark had not been made; but 'where the ordinary means of grace exist, the goodness and power of God operate through them, and not directly;'[1] and, therefore, now the miracle is wrought through the medium of this symbol of Jehovah's power. Slowly and solemnly the priests advance with their precious treasure, when no sooner do their feet touch the Jordan, than instantly its progress is arrested, and the waters stand up in a heap, 'far from the city Adam, which is beside Zaretan,' leaving the channel of the river dry for a distance of several miles.

Zaretan is no doubt identical with the Zarthan of 1 Kings vii. 46, where all the brazen vessels of the temple were cast, 'in the plain of the Jordan, in the clay ground between Succoth and Zarthan.' Succoth lay on the eastern bank of the Jordan, not far from Beisan or Bethshean; and accordingly Van de Velde identifies Zaretan with Surtabeh, on the western bank, a pe-

[1] Keil's Comm. *in loco.* Clark.

culiar mountain group in the Ghor, south of Wady-el-Feirah, on the highest peak of which, called Kurn el-Surtabeyh, he found 'the ruins of an ancient castle, probably the citadel of the proper town of Zarthan, which must have been at its base.' The city Adam he supposes to have stood between the mountain and the Jordan, where large hewn stones are found scattered about; but the name of the city has not been preserved.[1]

Here, then, ten miles above Jericho, and upwards of twenty above the Dead Sea, did the waters of the Jordan stop, as if a bar of ice had suddenly been formed across the river to prevent their progress; and this entire space, of between twenty and thirty miles, formed a passage for the mighty host. For the waters below would, of course, rapidly run off into the sea, and, though the bed of the river would not become perfectly dry, it would be sufficiently so to render the passage easy even for children; nor would there be, even on the right hand of the people, any sign of danger, for 'the heap,' into which the river 'rose up,' would be far away out of their sight.

Having entered the bed of the river, there the priests remain; and so long as the ark of the covenant is there, the waters are obedient to their Creator's word. 'How observant are all the creatures to the God that made them! How glorious a God do we serve, whom all the powers of the heavens and elements are willingly subject unto, and gladly take that nature which He pleases to give them! He could have made Jordan like some solid pavement of crystal for the Israelites' feet to have trod upon, but this work had not been so magnificent. Every strong frost congeals the water in a natural course; but for a river to stand still, and run on heaps, and to be made a liquid wall for

---

[1] 'Syria and Palestine,' vol. ii., p. 323, and Memoir accompanying the Map, p. 354. Comp. Stanley's 'Sinai and Palestine,' p. 302, and Keil's 'Commentary on 1 Kings,' vol. i., p. 135. Clark.

the passage of God's people, is for nature to run out of itself, to do homage to her Creator.'[1]

At the distance of a mile from the ark of the covenant the people commenced their march, and thus the vast host see clearly the way which it has gradually opened up before them. The foremost ranks soon reach the bed of the river, where they find the ark resting on their right; and rank after rank of soldiers clad in armour, of women and of children, and of herdsmen with their droves of cattle, pass through the Jordan, some of them but just able, if at all, to see the symbol of the divine presence by which they are preserved, but all of them exulting in the mighty work which the Lord Jehovah is performing before their eyes. And none of that great multitude, save those who have already received their inheritance, are left behind. 'The priests, that bare the ark of the covenant of the Lord, stood firm on dry ground in the midst of Jordan, and all the Israelites passed over on dry ground, until all the people were passed clean over Jordan.'[2] And now they wend their way up the western banks to the vast plain—which, according to Robinson, is from ten to twelve miles in breadth,[3]—that lies on the western side of the river; the foremost ranks reaching it, ere the hindermost have entered the river's bed. We hear of no song of praise as they set foot in the land promised to their fathers, like that with which they rent the air after their passage through the waters of the Red Sea; but could they refrain from giving expression to their emotions? Would there be no burst of joy and thankfulness for this signal proof of God's goodness and power? Doubtless there would: for the Lord magnified Himself that day before their eyes, and gave them a pledge of glorious conquests hereafter to be won.

It was fitting that some memorial should be raised to cele-

[1] Bishop Hall's 'Contemplations,' Book viii. [2] Josh. iii. 17.
[3] 'Researches,' vol. i., p. 559.

brate the event, and to perpetuate the knowledge of it to future generations. Already twelve men had been chosen, one from each tribe, who were now commanded to go into the midst of the Jordan, and take thence each man a stone, such as he could bear upon his shoulder; and these stones were brought together, and placed in the midst of the camp. Whether they were set up side by side, or one upon another, we are not informed; but Josephus says that an altar was constructed of them, and Dr Kitto observes, that 'as the stones were not, singly, larger than one man could carry, this seems not unlikely.'[1]

But ere these stones were actually set up, 'Joshua set up' other 'twelve stones in the midst of the Jordan, in the place where the feet of the priests who bare the ark of the covenant stood.'[2] Commentators and critics have stumbled at this verse, and have supposed it to be spurious; whilst others have contended that it is a short and somewhat different account of the same event. Both these views are manifestly incorrect. It is true that we do not read of any command given to Joshua to set up these twelve stones, but the divine commands are not all expressly reported in this book; and if it be objected that such a memorial, erected in the bed of the river, would have been of no use, we may reply, with Calvin, that 'the top of the heap may have been sometimes seen when the river fell.' Keil supposes that the priests did not stand in the bed of the river, but upon the eastern banks, and that these stones were set up there; so that when the waters returned to their proper channel, the stones would be left dry. And what if this memorial did not remain long! It was designed for the existing generation, and especially, perhaps, for the two tribes and a half whose inheritance was on the eastern side of the river. We have no doubt, then, that the historian is perfectly correct; and that, as the LXX. and the Vulgate read the passage, 'other

---

[1] 'Pictorial Bible' *in loco*.   [2] Josh. iv. 9.

twelve stones'—αλλους δωδεκα λιθους—were set up here, to mark the very spot where the feet of the priests had stood. Perhaps they were larger stones than the others; and it may be, that if they were ever thrown down by the violence of the current, the people would re-erect them, and thus preserve the memorial for years.

Let us now picture to ourselves the scene at this moment. The day is far spent; the twelve stones have been set up in the Jordan—the priests bearing the ark still waiting there, until this work also is accomplished; the twelve men with the other twelve stones are proceeding towards the place where the people are to encamp; and the whole of the nine tribes and a half, together with forty thousand armed men of the other two tribes and a half, have reached in safety the western plain; when Joshua, at God's command, says to the priests, ' Come ye up out of Jordan.' Solemnly, and not in haste, they also cross the river, and, per-haps passing through the midst of the vast assembly, proceed again to the front; and no sooner are the soles of their feet planted on the dry land, than the waters return unto their place, and flow over all their banks as they did before. Thus does the Lord magnify Joshua in the sight of all Israel. Yet ' this was not,' as Calvin observes, ' the chief design of the miracle, to exalt the power and authority of Joshua. But as it was of the greatest importance to the people generally that the government of Joshua should be firmly established, it is very properly mentioned as the crowning advantage resulting from it, that he was, as it were, invested with sacred insignia, which produced such veneration among the people that no one dared to despise him.'

To the spot whither the people journeyed that day, was subsequently given the name Gilgal, which occurs in chap. iv. 19, 20, by anticipation. According to Josephus, it was about six miles from the river, and ten from Jericho;[1] and in the time

---

[1] 'Antiq.' v. 1, 4.

of Jerome the site of the encampment was still distinguishable. But the exact position of Gilgal has not been ascertained. Dr Thomson observes, that if Joshua crossed due east of Jericho, and if Josephus is correct in his numbers, then Gilgal must have been very near the present Riha; an opinion also entertained by Dr Robinson. There are, however, no traces of antiquity here, except a fragment of sienite granite, and some foundations of unhewn stones; so that if Gilgal became an inhabited place, it was probably abandoned at an early period.[1]

Here, then, the 'sons of Israel,' בְּנֵי יִשְׂרָאֵל, as they are called, because each one represented the tribe to which he belonged, set up the twelve stones which they had taken out of the river; and then Joshua addressed the people, and said, ' When your children shall ask their fathers in time to come, saying, What mean these stones? then ye shall let your children know, saying, Israel came over this Jordan on dry land. For the Lord your God dried up the waters of Jordan from before you, until ye were passed over, as the Lord your God did to the Red Sea, which He dried up before us, until we were gone over; that all the people of the earth might know the hand of the Lord, that it is mighty; that ye might fear the Lord your God for ever.'[2] It was a solemn and interesting scene; and the address of Joshua intimates that the design of the two miracles was to prove to the heathen the omnipotence of Jehovah, and to induce the Israelites to continue in the practice of the worship of their father's God. National favours call for national acknowledgments and praise; and the erection of these stones was a significant mode of giving expression to the feelings of the people, as well as of raising a memorial which should perpetuate the remembrance of the event in future years. Similarly did Jacob, centuries

---

[1] 'The Land and the Book,' p. 612; Robinson's 'Researches,' vol. i., p. 557.

[2] Josh. iv. 21-24.

before this, set up the stone which had served for his pillow at
Bethel, and pour oil upon the top of it;[1] and similarly did
Samuel, two hundred years after, set up a stone between Mizpeh
and Shen, and call it Ebenezer, or the stone of help, saying,
'Hitherto hath the LORD helped us.'[2] These twelve stones, like
Samuel's one, might have been called, and were called in effect,
Ebenezer also, for God had hitherto helped His people in an
extraordinary way; and well might they have sung—as perhaps,
indeed, they did—'Thou hast with Thine arm redeemed Thy
people, the sons of Jacob and Joseph. The waters saw Thee,
O God, the waters saw Thee: they were afraid; the depths also
were troubled.'—'Thy way is in the sea, and Thy path in the
great waters, and Thy footsteps are not known.'[3]

It is to be regretted that in modern times memorial stones
are not more frequently set up. We rear, in these days, monuments to great men: why should we not more frequently rear
alms-houses or sanctuaries in remembrance of great national
events? We have heard of memorial trees planted in comme-
moration of royal visits, and a memorial church is to be erected at
Cawnpore in remembrance of the sad events and gracious deliverances which occurred there during the Indian Mutiny; but
why should not this Christian land be studded with memorial
buildings commemorative of plentiful harvests, of the cessation
of war, of religious progress, and of other national events which
often call for our gratitude as a people? The memory of the
nation is not more retentive of its mercies than is that of the
individual; and hence we need such public monuments to remind
us of our obligations to the Great Supreme—monuments to
which we could point our children, and say, 'In such a year God
delivered us from the pestilence;' or, 'In such a year He gave us
abundant harvests;' or, 'In such a year He visited us with a
great revival of religion.' Such memorial buildings would be

[1] Gen. xxviii. 18. [2] 1 Sam. vii. 12. [3] Ps. lxxvii.

ornaments to our country, and would do honour to our country's piety and zeal.

At Gilgal Joshua was commanded to renew the rite of circumcision, which, during the thirty-eight years' wanderings in the wilderness, had not been observed. All the males who came out of Egypt forty years before were circumcised, but they fell in the wilderness; and their sons, who were born in the wilderness, had not been circumcised. Now, therefore, must this rite, which had been instituted in the days of Abraham, and which was the outward sign of the covenant into which God had entered with Abraham's posterity, be solemnly regarded, and performed on all the males. The instruments used are called 'sharp knives,' but literally 'knives of flint,'—such instruments being frequently employed both in earlier and in later times.[1]

In answer to the question, Why was this sign of the covenant not observed during the sojourn in the wilderness? Kurtz replies,—' The circumcision of the new-born was omitted from the time of the departure from Egypt,—at first, no doubt, on account of the difficulty of the journey; for, when the camp was broken up, and the orders were given to advance, it was impossible to make allowance for any of the families which might require longer rest, on account of the new-born infants being ill at the time with the fever which followed circumcision. On the other hand, they could not be left behind; and therefore nothing remained but to suspend the circumcision altogether. The whole period of the journey through the desert was one of affliction, which fully warranted the omission. It was undoubtedly their intention at the time to repair the omission on reaching the Holy Land. And this continued to be the case even after the sentence of rejection, by which the entrance into the promised land was postponed for thirty-eight years.'

We cannot but think, however, though Dr Kurtz repudiates

[1] Josh. v. 2–8.

the notion, that this was not the only, nor the principal reason; but that the covenant itself was for a time suspended, and that, therefore, the sign of it during that period was omitted. The rising generation, it is true, were not the parties on account of whose guilt the entrance into the promised land was postponed; but that generation necessarily shared in the consequences of their fathers' sins, and during the whole of the thirty-eight years the entire nation suffered a partial withdrawal of the divine favour, and bore the punishment of their iniquities.[1] For His own sake, and for the sake of their progenitors, God did not utterly cast them off; but for a while they were under a dark and mysterious cloud, lost to history, and exposed to the perils of the wilderness; and only when the new generation emerged from behind that cloud did the covenant into which God had entered with them again come into force, and therefore not until then was the sign of the covenant observed.

And that this view of the case is the correct one, appears from the fact, that the Lord said unto Joshua, 'This day have I rolled away the reproach of Egypt from off you.' Now, as Keil observes, by the reproach of Egypt, is necessarily meant 'the reproach which is cast upon you by the Egyptians.' And what was that reproach? That they were an uncircumcised people? No; for there is no evidence whatever that the Egyptians themselves were all circumcised, and hence they could not reproach the Israelites on this ground. The reproach was nothing less than that God had brought them into the wilderness to destroy them. The Egyptians had often said—just what Moses often feared they would say—'For mischief did He bring them out, to slay them in the mountains, and to consume them from off the face of the earth;'[2] for during the thirty-eight years' wanderings they would doubtless hear of their condition, and this was the conclusion to which they would naturally come.

[1] See Num. xiv. 34.   [2] Exod. xxxii. 12; Num. xiv. 13–16 · Deut. ix. 28.

The subject of reproach was their rejection, which was made manifest by the cessation of the outward sign of the covenant. But now God had re-admitted them into His favour; now He had brought them into the land of promise; now the sign of the covenant was restored; and now, therefore, the reproach of the Egyptians was for ever rolled away. Hence to the place of their encampment where the rite was renewed, the name Gilgal was given; i.e., a rolling away.[1]

And now that the covenant was renewed, and the reproach was rolled away, the plains of Jericho witnessed also the celebration of the Passover. The first Passover the Israelites observed after leaving Egypt was at Sinai, in the second year of their journey in the desert. That same year they were driven back into the wilderness from Kadesh-Barnea, and from that time the feast of the covenant had never once been kept for eight and thirty years. But the period of its celebration had now arrived. On the tenth day of the first month, they had crossed the Jordan;[2] during the three days following, the rite of circumcision was performed; and now the fourteenth day of the month Nisan[3] (on the evening of which day, just forty years before, the Passover was instituted in the land of Egypt) dawned upon them, and found them once more in close covenant-relationship with God. Now, therefore, the paschal lamb was slain, and its blood sprinkled upon the mercy-seat, in the tabernacle, which had been pitched for the first time in the land of promise. What joy and rejoicing would there be on the occasion! With what grateful feelings would that vast assembly join in the celebration of the feast! To the greater portion of them it would have the charm of novelty; and, as they sat down in their tents and par-

---

[1] The name Gilgal occurs in Deut. xi. 30; whence it follows that the name was not now given to the locality for the first time. It was now, however, called Gilgal again, in reference to the event which had just occurred.

[2] Josh. iv. 19.   [3] Exod. xii. 18; Lev. xxiii. 5; Num. xxviii. 16.

took of the repast, they would contrast their position with that of their fathers on the night when first the festival was observed, and they would eat it with a glad and thankful heart.

But by 'the Passover,' in chap. v. ver. 10, is included, at least in part, the feast of unleavened bread; for in the succeeding verse it is said that on the morrow after the Passover they ate of the produce of the land; and, according to the law, this could not be done until the sixteenth day of the month, after the presentation of the first fruits to the Lord. Our translators say, 'They did eat of *the old corn* of the land on the morrow after the Passover;' but the Hebrew word does not bear this meaning, but signifies merely the *fruit* or *produce* of the land.[1] The plains of Jericho are exceedingly fertile; and, according to Dr Robinson, the wheat-harvest is not completed until about the 13th of May. Doubtless, then, abundance of corn was still standing in the neighbourhood of Gilgal, and thus were the necessities of the people met. But the law said, 'Ye shall neither eat bread, nor parched corn, nor green ears, until the self-same day that ye have brought an offering unto your God;'[2] and this offering was to consist of a sheaf of barley, and was to be presented on the 16th day of the month Nisan, or on 'the morrow after the Sabbath.' There is no difficulty in conceiving how all this was done, if we suppose that the historian uses the term 'Passover' not in its limited sense, but as including, in part, the feast of unleavened bread which followed. The law was in every point strictly observed. On the fourteenth and fifteenth days the paschal lamb was eaten, and the feast of unleavened bread commenced. On the sixteenth day a sheaf of barley was presented to the Lord, the produce of the land in which the people had encamped; they then were at liberty to eat of the corn now ready for the

---

[1] The word is עָבוּר, and is rendered by the LXX. σῖτος, and in the Vulgate *frux*, in the plural.

[2] Lev. xxiii. 14, 15.

sickle; and the self-same day they made of it unleavened cakes, or baked it at the fire.[1]

The manna now ceased to fall: 'Neither did the children of Israel eat manna any more.' In Exod. xvi. 35 it is said, 'And the children of Israel did eat manna forty years, until they came to a land inhabited, until they came unto the borders of the land of Canaan.' We are not to understand from these passages that manna was the only food of the Israelites during their sojourn in the wilderness; quails were sometimes sent; and there can be little doubt that they were able to procure many other kinds of food. Manna, then, was the extra supply; and, miraculous in its nature, it continued to fall, in greater or in less quantities, as it was required; until, now that the people had come into a land inhabited, it definitely ceased. In its failure, they must have seen 'an additional attestation of the kindness of God, inasmuch as it was thence apparent that the manna was a temporary resource, which had descended, not so much from the clouds, as from a paternal Providence.'[2]

For all these ceremonial observances the season of the year was highly favourable, as, in Palestine, no rain falls during the time of harvest.[3] In the open air, under a bright and beautiful sun, could the vast thousands of Israel enjoy their solemn feasts. Nor were they under any fear of being molested by the inhabitants of the land; for the inhabitants of the land were smitten with terror and had no heart to venture out of their cities to attack them. How easy a prey would the Israelites have been, just after they had received the rite of circumcision! But their enemies were held back by an invisible hand, and neither the Amorites nor the Canaanites had any power to injure them.

---

[1] Parched corn is much used in the East, and, mixed with honey, butter, or spices, is greatly relished. See Harmer's 'Observations,' vol. i., p. 475, etc.

[2] Calvin *in loco*.   [3] See 1 Sam. xii. 17.

JERICHO.

CHAPTER V.

THE SIEGE OF JERICHO.

'ART thou for us, or for our adversaries?' said Joshua, with some degree of trembling and anxiety. He had left the camp at Gilgal, and had come near to Jericho, probably to reconnoitre, when suddenly 'there stood a man over against him, with a drawn sword in his hand.' There was doubtless something in the aspect of the warrior of unusual majesty, and, not knowing who or what he might be, Joshua unhesitatingly inquired whether he was on their side or on that of their enemies. The reply was, 'Nay; but as prince of the army of Jehovah am I now come.' The 'nay' implied that he was neither a Canaanite

nor an Israelite; the words which followed it were an assurance
to Joshua that the stranger was on their side, and that they had
nought to fear.

Who was this august personage? Does He now appear on
the stage of history for the first time, or have we any records of
Him previously? To Moses God said, just after the giving of
the law in Mount Sinai, 'Behold, I send an Angel before thee,
to keep thee in thy way, and to bring thee into the place which
I have prepared,' etc. Can there be a doubt in any unprejudiced
mind that this was any other than that same Angel? Invisibly
He had been with the Israelites in all their wanderings; but now
that a decisive blow was to be struck, He appeared to Joshua
in the form of a man, to reassure him of His presence, and to
encourage him in the prosecution of his task.

But was he merely a created angel? Such was the opinion
of the Jewish Rabbins, who went so far as to affirm that he was
the archangel Michael, whom they supposed to be a created
angel only. And this view of the case has been advocated in
recent times by many able commentators, among whom may be
mentioned Dr Tholuck[1] and Dr Kurtz.[2] But, on the other
hand, Hengstenberg and Keil have, we think, proved most con-
vincingly, that this Angel was none other than the second person
of the Trinity, the Son of God,—the great Revealer of the
Father from the earliest times. For what says this Angel to
Joshua? He claims divine honour, and says, as He did to Moses
in the bush, 'Loose thy shoe from off thy foot; for the place
whereon thou standest is holy. And Joshua,' who had already
fallen on his face and worshipped Him, 'did so.' Besides, in
chap. vi. 2 the Angel is expressly called Jehovah; 'for,' as Hengstenberg observes, 'it is evident that we are not to think of
another divine revelation then given to Joshua in some other

[1] 'Commentary on St John,' pp. 58, 59. Clark.
[2] 'History of the Old Covenant,' vol. i., p. 189, etc.; vol. iii., pp. 175, 176.

way, as some interpreters suppose; because, in that case, the appearance of the Captain, who only now gives command to Joshua, would have been without an object. In chap. v. the directions would be wanting; in chap. vi. we should have no report of the appearance.'[1]

And this glorious Being now comes as Captain or Prince of the army of the Lord. But by the army of the Lord we are not to understand, as some have done, the Israelites; for they are never called *the* army, or *the* host, of the Lord. The army of the Lord is the heavenly host; whence the Lord is called *Jehovah Sabaoth,* or *the Lord of hosts.*[2] As *their* Captain did this august Being now appear, to lead them, as it were, to the conflict in which Joshua was now about to engage, and thus to discomfit all his enemies. How would Joshua be inspirited as he heard these words! He would perceive that this glorious personage before him had come with the omnipotent help of Jehovah, and of all the forces of heaven, to drive out the heathen before him, and to give to the Israelites the conquest over all their foes; and if previously he had any doubts or fears, now they would be dissipated, and now his confidence would be more firm than ever.

With equal confidence may the Church rely upon her Saviour now; for as the Captain of the heavenly hosts He was seen by John in the apocalyptic vision. 'And I saw heaven opened, and behold a white horse; and He that sat upon him was called Faithful and True; and in righteousness doth He judge and make war. His eyes were as a flame of fire, and on His head were many crowns; and He had a name written, that no man knew but He Himself: and He was clothed with a vesture dipped in blood: and His name is called The Word of God. And the armies which were in heaven followed Him upon white horses, clothed in fine linen, white and clean,' etc.[3] With such a leader, what have the

---

[1] 'Christology of the Old Test.,' vol. i., p. 121. Clark.
[2] See Keil *in loco.* [3] Rev. xix. 11, 16.

servants of Christ to fear? Their foes may be numerous, but more numerous are their friends. Their adversaries may be mighty, but their Captain is mightier than they all. 'Out of His mouth goeth a sharp sword, that with it He should smite the nations; and He shall rule them with a rod of iron: and He treadeth the wine-press of the fierceness and wrath of Almighty God. And He hath on His vesture and on His thigh a name written, KING OF KINGS, AND LORD OF LORDS.'

In what mode, and for what object, this Angel now revealed Himself to Joshua, we have already intimated. It was not in a dream or by an inward vision that this personage appeared to him, but by an actual manifestation to his outward sight; and the design of the manifestation was to give Joshua instructions as to the mode in which Jericho should be taken.[1] In the succeeding chapter the Angel Jehovah addresses him, and says, 'See, I have given into thine hand Jericho, and the king thereof, and the mighty men of valour;' and then He proceeds to instruct him what to do, and assures him that the plan, strange as it might appear, would be followed by complete success. Joshua had been wondering how he was to take the city, walled as it was and straitly shut up, and had perhaps been devising some plan of his own, when he was thus informed that God Himself would interfere miraculously, and that neither stratagem nor force would be required. And Joshua believed the word of Jehovah. His faith took hold upon the promise, and, with his mind relieved and his courage strengthened, he returned back to the camp to make preparations for the compassing of the city.

It is highly probable that the ancient Jericho occupied the site of the modern village Riha, taking in the great fountain 'Ain es Sultan, formerly called the fountain of Elisha. Bursting forth

---

[1] The division of the chapters just here is most unfortunate, and breaks the continuity of the whole narrative. Ver. 1 of chap. vi. is merely a parenthetical remark; and ver. 2 stands in close connection with ver. 15 of chap. v.

at the eastern foot of a double group of mounds, more than a mile in front of the Quarantana, this fountain pursues its course, joined by other streams, through the Wady Kell to the Jordan, spreading beauty and fertility of such extraordinary richness as almost to 'recall the scenery of an English park.' Such is the case even now; but in the days of Joshua the neighbourhood must have been far more beautiful, for then an extensive forest of palm-trees, relics of which were seen by Mariti and Shaw, but the last of which has recently disappeared, then lay between Gilgal and the city, recalling to the mind of Israel's leader 'the magnificent palm-groves of Egypt, such as may now be seen stretching along the shores of the Nile at Memphis.'[1] This forest, according to Mr Stanley, 'was nearly three miles broad and eight miles long,' and, majestic as the palm-tree is, must have presented to the Israelites a most enchanting spectacle; whilst above it they would behold Jericho itself, 'high, and fenced up to heaven,' and behind it 'the jagged range of the white lime-stone mountains of Judea, here presenting one of the few varied and beautiful outlines that can be seen amongst the southern hills of Palestine.'

Among the solemn feasts instituted by the law of Moses, was the Feast of Tabernacles, during which the Israelites were to dwell seven days in booths, constructed of the boughs of goodly trees, branches of palm-trees, and willows of the brook. And no sooner have they entered the land of promise than they see before them a whole forest of palm-trees, by which they perceive that it will not be difficult to obtain a supply of palm branches, either for the Feast of Tabernacles or any other occasion. Of this beautiful production of nature, the varieties are numerous, and the uses many. There is the cocoa-nut palm (*Cocus nucifera*), with its

---

[1] See Stanley's 'Sinai and Palestine,' pp. 304–5; Robinson's 'Researches,' vol. i., p. 554, etc.; Thomson, 'The Land and the Book,' p. 617; and Van de Velde's Map, with the Memoir.

unbranched stems, crowned with leaves and clusters of fruit, every particle of whose substance—stem, leaves, fruit, sap—may be turned to good account, so that it is said that this tree is applied to at least a hundred useful purposes. There is the talipot-palm (*Corypha umbra culifera*), the stem of which sometimes attains a height of a hundred feet, and the magnificent fan-like leaves of which, when laid upon the ground, will form a semicircle of 16 feet in diameter, and cover an area of nearly 200 superficial feet. There is the Palmyra palm (*Borassus flabelliformis*), which grows in profusion in North Ceylon, and which yields to the inhabitants palm-wine, oil, and sugar; whilst its leaves serve as a substitute for paper, as well as for a covering for the roof of dwellings. There is the Piriguao palm, whose smooth stem, nearly 70 feet in height, is adorned with delicate flag-like leaves, having curled margins, and which bears a large and beautifully coloured fruit, which, in its yellow and crimson tints, much resembles the peach. And to mention but one other species, there is the date-palm (*Phœnix dactylifera*), the Tamar of the Scriptures, remarkable for its erect and cylindrical stem, its feather-like leaves, and its much-esteemed fruit, the date.[1] It was no doubt this last species which grew in such abundance on the plains of Jericho; and as 'the first opening shoot of the date-palm announces the coming of balmy spring,' the forest must now have presented to the Israelites a most beautiful and luxuriant aspect. The fruit, however, would not be ready, as it does not ripen until August or September.[2]

Of all the remarkable sieges described in history or celebrated in song, that of Troy is one of the most famous and romantic. It took place, according to the Arundelian Marbles, about 1184 years B.C., and consequently upwards of 250 years after the events

---

[1] See on the subject of the palm, Sir E. J. Tennent, 'Ceylon,' vol. i., pp. 109–111. Humboldt's 'Views of Nature,' p. 223, etc. Bohn.

[2] See Humboldt's 'Cosmos,' vol. ii. Bohn. Rohr's Palestine, p. 67.

we are now relating. Homer has immortalized it in the Iliad; and Virgil, catching some of the fire of Homer's genius, has given another aspect of the story in the Æneid; and so long as poetry of the highest order has charms for the human mind, will these two productions of the Greek and Roman bards be read both by young and old. But far more glorious was the siege now to be related: and nobler far was Joshua than Agamemnon; Caleb than Achilles; and other leaders of the host of Israel, though their names are not conspicuous, than were Ajax, Patroclus, Nestor, or Ulysses. That was a siege against an unoffending city—save that a woman had been carried captive thither by Paris; this was a siege, undertaken at the command of the Most High, against a people who had filled up the cup of their iniquity; and, whilst the siege of Troy occupied ten years, and terminated only by the city being betrayed, that of Jericho lasted but seven days, when God Himself gave victory to the besiegers, in such a way as a victory was never won.

We may picture to ourselves the scene. On the vast plain east of the city, the hosts of Israel are encamped. And now Joshua, having received his instructions from the Angel Jehovah, appears in the midst of the camp, and, summoning the priests, commands them to take up the ark of the covenant—that sacred symbol of the Divine presence—and, preceded by a number of armed men, and by seven priests bearing rams' horns, to pass on toward the city. The procession is thus formed:—It consists, first, of the armed men of the tribes of Reuben and Gad, and the half tribe of Manasseh; next, of the seven priests, with the rams' horns; then of the ark of the covenant borne by other priests; and lastly, of the whole of the warriors of the other nine tribes and a half. And, leaving the women, the aged, and the young upon the plain, it advances towards the high-walled town. All is still. Jericho is straitly shut up. Its inhabitants are full of terror and alarm, and no one ventures beyond the gate. Perhaps

there are watchmen on the walls; and, doubtless, in the city there
is many an inquiry relative to the approach of the expected foe.
And the foe comes on, and on, and on; at first silently, without
shouting, without noise; until at length is heard the loud blast
of the rams' horns, which becomes louder, and still louder; and
continues to sound—alas! it is the death-knell of the inhabitants
of the city—as the vast procession encompasses the walls. But
that procession, having gone round the city, now retires, and
presently the watchers on the walls report that their enemies
have disappeared.

What strange thoughts and feelings must have occupied the
minds of the people of Jericho that night! 'Is this all that these
Israelites can do?' some would probably say; 'and do they
think that they will get possession of our city by such paltry
means as these?' But there would, doubtless, be others more
shrewd and far-seeing, who, remembering what Jehovah had
already done for His people, would view the conduct of the foe
as ominous of their victory; and would be all the more afraid,
because of the calm and confident manner in which that mysterious
procession had gone round the city.

But the morning dawns; and, at an early hour, the foe is seen
advancing towards the city again: on, and on, in the same order,
and again the city is encompassed, and again the foe retires.
And for seven days in succession this scene is witnessed from the
walls of Jericho, by some, perhaps, with laughter and derision;
but by others, with increasing dread. But why was not a single
march round the city sufficient? Why was it repeated these
several times? Why does the number seven appear so conspicuous in their arrangements? In reply to the latter question, it is
observed by Keil, that ' the number seven, amongst the Israelites,
was the seal of the covenant between Jehovah and Israel; and
by this march of seven days, and the repetition of it seven times
on the seventh day, together with the seven priests walking before

the ark of the covenant, and blowing seven trumpets, the host
of Israel were to show that they were the people of the covenant ;
and that, as the gracious presence of God was bound up with
the ark of the covenant, they had in the midst of them their
God and Lord, and were fighting in His name.'[1] But was the
repetition of the march intended as a challenge to the inhabitants
of Jericho to come out and fight with Israel? The very command of Joshua, 'Ye shall not shout, nor make any noise with
your voice,' seems to indicate the contrary; for, if the Israelites
had intended to challenge the inhabitants of Jericho, they would
surely have called upon them to come and meet them in the field.
The one design of the several days' march was, to exercise the
faith of the Israelites in the faithfulness and power of God.
'God orders them,' says Calvin, 'to make one circuit round the
city daily, until the seventh day, on which they are told to go
round it seven times, sounding the trumpets, and shouting. The
whole looked like nothing more than child's play; and yet it
was no improper test for trying their faith, as it proved their
acquiescence in the Divine message—even when they saw in the
act itself nothing but mere disappointment.' ''There was an
additional trial of their faith, in the repetition of the circuit of the
city during seven days; For, what could seem less congruous
than to fatigue themselves with six unavailing circuits? Then,
of what use was their silence, unless to betray their timidity,
and tempt their enemy to come out and attack besiegers who
seemed not to have spirit enough to meet them? But as profane men often, by rash intermeddling fervour, throw everything
into confusion, the only part which God here assigns to His
people is, to remain calm and silent, that thus they may the
better accustom themselves to execute His commands.'[2]

Most true it is, that God's ways are not as our ways, nor
His thoughts as our thoughts. Very different would have been

[1] Commentary on Joshua, p. 159.   [2] Commentary on Joshua, p. 93.

the plan of besieging Jericho, had it been left to the Israelites, or
to their commander, Joshua.   But what plan of man's devising
could have been successful?   The walls of the city were strong
and lofty; the Israelites had no siege train or battering-rams
with which to attack them, such as appear on the monuments
of Nineveh; and to have reduced the city to a famine, would
have occupied several months.   God's plan, then, was the best;
and in quietness and confidence was the people's strength.
Severe was the test by which their faith was tried; for everything, down to the use of the rams' horns, instead of the silver
trumpets deposited in the sanctuary, seems to set aside human
strength and glory; whilst the lapse of a whole week, ere the
least sign appeared of any breach in the city's walls, was calculated to excite impatience and discontent.   But happily they had
learnt, by the experience of the past, *to wait and trust;* and 'the
happy fruit of their endurance teaches us, that there is nothing
better than to leave the decisive moments and opportunities of
acting at God's disposal, and not, by our haste, anticipate His
providence, in which, if we acquiesce not, we obstruct the course
of His agency.'

The seventh day has now arrived; and 'about the dawning
of the day,' the Israelites rise early, and again the procession is
on its march.   On and on it again advances; but instead of returning to the camp when they have encompassed the city once,
the men of war, the seven priests with the rams' horns, the priests
bearing the ark, and the warriors following them, go round the
city six times more.   They have just completed the seven circuits,
and during the whole day no noise has been heard but the sounding of the rams' horns; but now Joshua lifts up his voice and
says, 'Shout; for the Lord hath given you the city.'   In a
moment the war-cry rises from the mighty host; and the priests,
who for awhile had left off blowing the trumpets, once more
blow them, perhaps with a much louder blast, when instantly

the walls of the city fall down flat, and every man enters it straight before him.

'By faith the walls of Jericho fell down, after they were compassed about seven days.'[1] There was, of course, no connection between the shouting of the people and the falling down of the walls, nor was their faith *the cause* of the event; but, simultaneously with the shout, the miraculous power of God was exercised, and the confidence which had been reposed in Him was thus signally honoured. As for the attempt of rationalists to account for this event on natural grounds, they are utterly unworthy of a moment's consideration. It is evident that the writer of the narrative intended to relate a miracle; and if we give credence to his history at all, we must believe that a miracle was really wrought. To the Israelites themselves it was another proof that the Lord was with them. Without any exertion on their part, the first city of the land of Canaan was given into their hands. They had now in their possession one of the strongest of the fortified cities, and, moreover, the key to the whole country into which they had come: and what had they then to fear? A pledge was thus offered to them of yet further conquests, and they had but to rely on the arm of the Omnipotent, and Canaan would, ere long, be theirs.

Jericho, like the cities of Canaan generally, had long been a wicked and rebellious city. Its crimes are not told, but they were doubtless of a heinous character, and, even as those of Sodom and Gomorrah in earlier times, had often cried for vengeance from on high. And vengeance, slow of step, but of keen and piercing eye, had come at last. 'The city shall be accursed,' said Joshua, 'even it and all that are therein, to the Lord;' and, with the exception of Rahab and her family, all that were in the city, both man and woman, young and old, and ox, and sheep, and ass, were destroyed with the edge of the sword. 'The word

---

[1] Heb. xi. 30.

חֵרֶם, in ver. 17, signifies the ban, which was the devotion of either persons or things to Jehovah, as irreclaimable and irredeemable property, in the execution of which men and animals were killed, and other things either completely destroyed, or set apart for ever for the purposes of the sanctuary.'[1] 'All the dreadful things that can possibly be thought of are included in this *one* word,' says Hengstenberg. It is rendered in the margin of our version *devoted*, but it is not applied to a holy or devoted thing generally, but to a thing which is holy in the sense of being devoted to God *by being destroyed*, for 'the temporal destruction of anything which does not serve God, makes known His praise.'[2] In some instances the *Cherem* was pronounced upon the *persons* of the Canaanites only; and their cities and possessions the Israelites took for themselves; but, in the case of Jericho, whatever was not destroyed—the silver and the gold, and vessels of brass and iron—were consecrated unto the Lord.

Terrible must have been the scene when the Israelites entered the banned city. 'The men of Jericho fought against them,'[3] but the strength of the men of Jericho was paralysed, and they fell on every hand, smitten by the conquerors' sword. Nor was any mercy shown either to the aged or the young, to women or to children; but all were indiscriminately put to death. Well may it be asked, On what principle can this be accounted for? and we admit that the subject is not without its difficulties. But let us look at it in the light of analogy and reason. It is involved in another and still wider question, namely, 'What right had the Israelites to the land of Canaan?' And to this question, therefore, we must first reply.

Palestine was not originally the land of the Hebrews, and the right of the Israelites to that land could not, therefore, as

[1] Keil, *in loco;* and see Num. xxi. 1-3; Deut. xiii. 16-18.
[2] See Hengstenberg's 'Christology,' vol. iv., p. 227 Clark.
[3] Joshua xxiv. 11.

some have represented, be founded on immemorial claims. This notion was entertained by the learned Michaelis, and has found several advocates in more recent times. But the hypothesis is quite untenable. The earliest possessors of the soil of Palestine appear to have been the Rephaim, a race of giants, or very tall people, two of whose tribes, the Emim and Zamzummim,[1] were conquered and nearly exterminated by the Moabites and the Amorites; and others of whom, who lived on the west of the Jordan, the Canaanites, or descendants of the fourth son of Ham, partly conquered and drave out. It is true that some of the pasture lands of the country remained unoccupied by the Canaanites; so that, when Abraham and Lot came out of Ur of the Chaldees, they were allowed the use of some of those lands wherein to feed their flocks. But such use of the unoccupied territory did not imply a claim to the land as an inheritance, and hence Abraham looked upon himself as a *stranger* in the land;[2] and when he wanted a burial-place for Sarah, he secured the right of a parcel of a field by *purchase*. He knew—for God had told him—that the land would *hereafter* be the inheritance of his seed; but he laid no claim even to a sepulchre in it, ere he had paid its full value, for he was but a sojourner in the country until a brighter day should dawn.[3]

Nor was the claim of the Israelites to Canaan founded simply upon *might*, as others have represented, under the idea that, in those early times, the rights of property were not strictly defined. There is no doubt that those rights were as strictly defined then as they are now, for they are founded on the immutable principles of justice and of truth; so that the Israelites would have been as guilty in dispossessing the Canaanites of the soil of Palestine, had they done it merely because they had the power to do it, as were the Spaniards in making war upon the inhabitants of

---

[1] Gen. xiv. 5; Deut. iii. 11.   [2] Gen. xxiii. 4, xxvi. 3.
[3] Gen. xxiii. 4–16.

Mexico and Peru. 'It is founded,' says Hengstenberg, 'in the arrangements of Providence,—of which the recognition is implanted in every human breast,—that every land, that, in short, everything, which hitherto has had no owner, from the instant that a nation takes possession of it, becomes their lawful property. From that instant it is to be regarded as a gift of Divine Providence, so that, whoever seeks to deprive them of it, fights against God.'[1]

But, when a nation which has obtained possession of a land, whether in this or in any other way, becomes notoriously wicked and increasingly rebellious against the government of the Most High, God has a right, and that not a mere arbitrary one, but a right founded upon the eternal principles of justice, to sweep away that nation by famine, by pestilence, or by the sword. Now, what had been the conduct of the Canaanites? They had themselves made war upon the aboriginal possessors of the soil, and partly driven them out; and when they had thus obtained authority over the land, instead of fearing and honouring the true Jehovah, they had pursued a course of flagrant transgression against the law written upon the heart, had become worshippers of idols, had changed the truth of God into a lie, and had given themselves up to vile affections, to work all manner of uncleanness with greediness. Long had they been spared, for they were in the land in the days of Abraham; but God then said of them, 'the iniquity of the Amorites is not yet full,'[2] and for upwards of five hundred years they were dealt with leniently, and time and opportunity given them for repentance. All, however, was in vain; and now their iniquity was full to the very brim. God, therefore, was utterly weary of them, and the land itself groaned for deliverance from their hated presence. What was to be done? Destroyed they must be; and God chose, as the agents of His

---

[1] Authenticity of the Pentateuch, vol. ii., pp. 402–3. English trans.
[2] Gen. xv. 16.

vengeance, not the waters of a deluge, not fire and brimstone, not pestilence and famine, but the people whom He had brought up out of the land of Egypt. Was there anything unjust in this? Was it less righteous in God to use the sword for their extermination, than it would have been to use fire, or water, or wild beasts, or the plague? And that God *did* employ the Israelites as the agents of His vengeance, that He *did* command them to destroy the Canaanites, is evident from the entire narrative of the conquest. Had they invaded Canaan on their own authority, they would no doubt have been justly ranked with the vilest banditti, and the worst of all murderers; but they were bidden to do all, and more than they accomplished: and, moreover, God Himself went before them, so that 'they got not the land in possession by their own sword, neither did their own arm save them;'[1] but the right hand of the Lord, and His mighty arm, wrought for them the victories they achieved.

If it be asked, But why did not God destroy the Canaanites by an immediate judgment from heaven? We reply with Hengstenberg, that 'no man reaches Canaan without struggling for it;' and that 'had God led the Israelites into a land already emptied of inhabitants, they would soon have forgotten that He had made it so: they would have ascribed the operation to natural causes.'[2] Nor is it true that their being employed in such a work would necessarily render them cruel and ferocious; for they were not bidden to torture their enemies, but to kill them: and they knew that they were but the executors of God's wrath upon a wicked people, and that, moreover, they would themselves merit a similar punishment if they became guilty of similar crimes. But were they not themselves as wicked as the Canaanites? and is it not strange that God should commission them to punish their companions in sin? They were not as wicked as the Canaanites; for whatever they had been during their sojourn in

[1] Ps. xliv. 3.   [2] Authenticity, etc., vol. ii., p. 412.

f

the wilderness, they were now a submissive and obedient people, and had recently, as we have seen, been readmitted into covenant relationship with the Lord Jehovah.[1] Individuals among them were perhaps vile enough; but, as a whole, they were now a very different people from what they had ever been, and were now, therefore, well fitted to accomplish God's design, in executing summary vengeance on a guilty race.

Such, in brief, we hold to be a satisfactory reply to the objections which have been advanced against the justice of this procedure,—an ample vindication of the wisdom and the righteousness of God in destroying the Canaanites, and in doing it by such means. 'It is our Lord Himself who expresses the general principle, of which the extinction of the Canaanites was only a special application: " *Where the carcase is, there will the eagles be gathered together;*"—where sin has become rank, there will the Divine punishments fall.' It has been so in very many instances already; it will be so, we fear, in many others, in days and years to come. Nations are employed to chastise nations; and though we may long for the day when wars of every kind shall cease, yet we must own, in many of the conflicts which from time to time occur, that God still sitteth above the water-floods, and reigneth King for ever.

Terrible, then, as was the scene of slaughter when the Israelites entered the city of Jericho, it was but the righteous infliction of a punishment which its inhabitants had long merited; and the Israelites had no alternative but to execute the Divine commands. Their feelings of humanity might have induced them to spare the women and the unoffending children; but they had learnt that the sins of fathers were often visited on their posterity, and spare they could not, because they were forbidden. Yet there was an exception. The promise given to Rahab by the spies was faithfully fulfilled; for at Joshua's command the two young men went

---

[1] See Judges ii. 7.

in, and brought out Rahab, and her father, and her mother, and her brethren, and all that she had; and they brought out all her kindred, and left them without the camp of Israel. A petty objection to the narrative has sometimes been advanced, on the ground that Rahab's house was on the town-wall, which is represented as having fallen down; but 'it troubleth me not to conceive,' says Fuller, 'how the rest of the wall falling flat, Rahab's house, built thereon, should stand upright; seeing Divine power, which miraculously gave the rule, might accordingly make the exception.[1]

It was not lawful for males who were uncircumcised, or for females who had not made a public profession of the Jewish religion, to enter the camp; and if Rahab and her family had been admitted there at once, they would probably never have become conscious of their own impurity. That the Israelites might not, then, be defiled with their society, and that they themselves might be induced to lay aside the heathenism in which they had been brought up, they were placed in a state of safety, but apart from the congregation of God's people, until such time as they were prepared to renounce the religion of the Canaanites, and to acknowledge the Lord God of the Israelites. It was a wise arrangement, and there is reason to believe that it was followed by the desired result; for of Rahab herself it is said by the writer, 'She dwelleth *in Israel*, even unto this day,' and, as we formerly observed, she subsequently became the wife of Salmon, and thus an ancestor of the house of David.

The city of Jericho is now destroyed; but that it might be a perpetual memorial of God's power and justice, Joshua completed the ban by pronouncing this adjuration: 'Cursed be the man before the LORD, that riseth up and buildeth this city Jericho: he shall lay the foundation thereof in his first-born, and in his youngest son shall be set up the gates of it.' That

[1] 'Pisgah Sight of Palestine,' p. 252.

this curse was not to light on any one who should merely build houses on the site of Jericho, is evident from the fact that the city was allotted by Joshua to the tribe of Benjamin,[1] and is subsequently spoken of as an inhabited place.[2]   Rather was it to fall upon the man who should build a wall around it, and erect gates, and thus constitute it what it had been, a fortified city.   Upwards of five hundred years afterwards, or in the reign of Ahab, king of Israel, the attempt was made by Hiel the Beth-elite, and was followed by the consequences which Joshua foretold.   He laid the foundations of the city, and lost his first-born son, Abiram; he set up the gates thereof, and lost his youngest son, Segub.[3]   'Strange that, seeing his first son drop away, he desisted not from that design; but such the precipice of bad projects, once step in, and seldom stop in the way of wickedness.'[4]   Hiel was not unacquainted with the ban pro-nounced by Joshua on the city, but the fear of God had vanished from his mind; and perhaps he thought—if, indeed, he thought at all—that, seeing so long a period had elapsed since the curse was uttered, it was not likely to be fulfilled.   But it is not the manner of the Lord Jehovah to forget either His promises or His threatenings; and hence the daring conduct of this Beth-elite met with the punishment it deserved.   Whether during the building of the city all his sons perished, from the first even to the last, or whether he lost the eldest and the youngest only, we are not able to decide; but if only the two fell, it was a stroke which no father in Israel would consider light, and Hiel would have the bitter reflection that his two sons were taken from him because he rebelled against an express command of the Most High.

---

[1] Joshua xviii. 21.   [2] Judges iii. 13; 2 Sam. x.
[3] 1 Kings xvi. 34.   [4] Fuller.

CASTING DUST ON THE HEAD.

CHAPTER VI.

THE SIN AND PUNISHMENT OF ACHAN.

IN the progress of our history, the curtain now rises on a solemn and impressive scene. It is eventide; and Joshua and the elders of Israel, with their clothes rent, and with dust upon their heads—the well-known signs of deep sorrow and distress—are prostrated before the ark of the covenant of the Lord. And the noble-minded warrior addresses himself in prayer to God, and says:—

'Alas, O Lord God, wherefore hast Thou at all brought this people over Jordan, to deliver us into the hand of the Amorites, to destroy us? would to God we had been content, and dwelt on the other side Jordan! O Lord, what shall I say, when Israel turneth their backs before their enemies? For the Canaanites and all the inhabitants of the land shall hear of it, and shall environ us around, and cut off our name from the earth: and what wilt Thou do unto Thy great name?' (chap. vii. 7–9).

But what has happened to call forth such expressions, and to awaken fears so sad and distressing as these? Jericho has been conquered; and never was Joshua more honoured and beloved than now. Yes; but part of his army has suffered a defeat, and six-and-thirty of his men have been smitten by the people of the land.

West of Jericho was a city called Ai, the site of which we shall indicate hereafter; and to this city Joshua had sent spies, saying to them, 'Go up and view the country.' They had obeyed, and returned with the information that the inhabitants of Ai were but few; and that, therefore, two or three thousand men would be sufficient to take it. This number had been sent, but, to Joshua's utter surprise, they had fled before their enemies; and the men of Ai had smitten thirty-six of them, and had chased the rest from the gate, so that the hearts of the people had melted and become as water.

That this defeat was not to be attributed to the smallness of the force which had been sent against the city, Joshua was well aware. Perhaps it was too small, and perhaps there was a want of foresight in not despatching a superior army; but God could save by many or by few; and Israel's leader, having the most perfect confidence in God, never anticipated a defeat of any kind. Ordinary commanders reckon upon what are called 'the chances of war;' but Joshua had no idea of such chances, but supposed that every battle would be followed by a victory—every siege by a speedy capture. Thus early, however, he was disappointed, and his prayer was indicative of the real state of his mind. He was greatly discouraged; he was apprehensive that this defeat would lead to others; he was jealous of the honour of God's great name. What could he do but take the matter to the Lord? True, he might have made a second attempt to capture Ai, by sending against it a much larger force; but he had not courage to do this: all he could do, was to humble himself in the dust and pray.

And it was well he did; for immediately his prayer was heard. 'Get thee up,' was the answer; 'wherefore liest thou on thy face?

Israel hath sinned, and they have also transgressed My covenant which I commanded them: for they have taken of the accursed thing, and have also stolen, and have dissembled also, and they have put it even among their own stuff,' etc. (ver. 10, 11).

When the people were about to enter Jericho, this was the express command which was given them: 'And ye, in any wise, keep yourselves from the accursed thing, lest ye make yourselves accursed when ye take of the accursed thing, and make the camp of Israel a curse, and trouble it.' Everything in the city, as we have already seen, was placed under the ban, and was therefore to be destroyed, or to be consecrated to the service of the Lord. Whoever, then, should appropriate to himself any of the spoils, would be guilty of theft; for he would be robbing God of that which He had already claimed as specially His own. Through every part of the camp would the prohibition be made known; so that no one might be able to excuse himself for a breach of it on the ground of ignorance; and little, perhaps, did Joshua think, that there was one among the people that would be so daring as to violate it, accompanied as it was with a warning so terrible. But what will avarice not dare? what will covetousness not take? The cupidity of a man will sometimes lead him to violate every law of honour, truth, and justice; and not only to risk the welfare and the life of others, but even to sacrifice his own. There *was* a troubler in the camp. There *was*, even after all the disciplinary training through which Israel had passed, one who could take of the accursed thing. And, so long as the sin remained unpunished, the guilt of it rested on the whole of the people. 'Israel hath sinned,' said God; 'therefore they could not stand before their enemies, but turned their backs before their enemies, because they were accursed; neither will I be with you any more, except ye destroy the accursed from among you' (ver. 12).

It may be asked, On what ground could the sin of one man

be laid to the charge of the whole nation? And to this inquiry there is but one satisfactory reply: 'The participation of the people in the guilt of Achan,' says Keil, 'can only be explained on the ground that Achan was a member of the nation, and that the sin of one member affected the entire body,—robbing it of the purity and holiness with which it ought to appear in the presence of God, and withdrawing from it the favour of God, which the nation enjoyed, as being God's pure and holy church. However truly the whole Scriptures speak of each man as individually an object of divine mercy and justice, they teach just as truly that a nation is one organic whole, in which the individuals are merely members of the same body, and are not alone isolated from one another and the whole. The state is thus treated as a divine institution, founded upon family relationships; and intended to promote the love of all to one another, and to the invisible Head of all.' There was then no injustice done to Israel, or to the three thousand who were defeated by the men of Ai. The whole camp was one, and, by the sin which had been committed, the whole camp was under the curse of the violated law.

What, then, could be done? God might have revealed to Joshua the name of the guilty individual, just as easily as He revealed to him the general fact that some one had taken of the spoil. But the people must be proved. They must themselves search out the man who had rebelled. They must voluntarily become parties to a strict and rigorous investigation. 'Up, sanctify the people,' said God to His servant, 'and say, Sanctify yourselves against to-morrow; for thus saith the Lord God of Israel, There is an accursed thing in the midst of thee, O Israel: thou canst not stand before thine enemies, until ye take away the accursed thing from among you.' Joshua was also informed how to proceed, and was required to state to the people the plan by which the culprit would be brought to light; and, moreover, the punishment that must be inflicted upon him. It was a sad event; and as Joshua heard these words, his noble spirit would doubtless be oppressed with deep and poignant grief.

That very evening, the intelligence spread through the camp —'There is an accursed thing among us; some one has taken of the spoils.' And oh, how the hearts of many would tremble, lest the offender should be one of their own tribe or family. To Achan himself, that must have been a night of utter wretchedness; and it is surprising that he did not at once go and throw himself at the feet of Joshua, and make confession of his crime. Had he done so, who can tell but that there might have been some mitigation of his punishment? But he was probably still deceived by the hope that he might perchance escape detection; and thus blinded by the god of this world, he ventured to await the approaching ordeal.

The morning dawned, and the heads of the tribes and families of Israel were called into the presence of their leader, Joshua. Though the lot is not expressly mentioned, yet this was no doubt the method employed to discover the guilty individual. The use of it was easy, inasmuch as there had grown up among the Israelites, from patriarchal times, a natural division of the people into tribes, clans, families, and households. The tribes were founded by the twelve sons of Jacob and the two sons of Joseph; these were again divided into clans,[1] which were founded by the sons or grandsons of the twelve patriarchs; and these again were subdivided into fathers' houses, or groups of families,[2] which were once again divided into households, which were named and numbered according to the men. When, therefore, the lots were cast, the heads of the people were present; and we may suppose that, first the names of the tribes being written upon small stones, and these stones cast into an urn, some one would be appointed to draw out one of the stones, it being understood that in the

---

[1] מִשְׁפָּחָה. See Num. xxvi. 20, etc.

[2] בֵּית אָבֹת. See Exod. vi. 25; Josh. xxi. 1; and see Keil *in loco*.

tribe whose name was written upon it, the guilty party would be found. This was done, and the tribe of Judah was taken. Next the names of the clans of that tribe would be written on stones in like manner, and one of these stones taken out of the urn. It contained the name of the clan of the Zarhites. Then the names of the several households of that clan would be written, and in the same way it would be found to whose household the guilty one belonged. The household of Zabdi was taken. Thus gradually was the circle reduced within which the culprit lay, as it were, concealed, until at length this breach of the command was brought home to a certain family. The scene must have been a deeply impressive one. At first anxiety would be depicted on every countenance, and, as the process went on, whilst some would be relieved in part, others would become more anxious still. At length the moment comes when the individual himself would be marked out as the transgressor. Man by man of Zabdi's household passes through a similar ordeal, and Achan the son of Carmi is taken.[1] When, in a similar way, but for a very dissimilar end, Saul the son of Kish was taken, he could not be found, having hidden himself among the stuff; and perhaps Achan, lashed by a guilty conscience and trembling for the issue of the terrible investigation, was not immediately within sight; but he would soon be discovered, and conducted from his hiding-place into Joshua's presence, for no one would dare to attempt to screen him, lest he should share in his guilt and punishment.

[1] 'The exact process followed in casting the lot,' says Dr Kitto, 'is not known, nor is the matter of much importance; but we incline to the opinion of those who conceive that tickets, marked with the names of the twelve tribes, were put into an urn, and the lot fell upon the one that was taken out; that then they cast as many tickets as there were ancestral families, or clans, in the tribe whose name was drawn; then as many as there were households in that family, and lastly as many as there were heads in that household.'—*Daily Readings*, vol. ii., pp. 281, 282.

God had given a 'perfect lot,' and there could be no doubt, in the mind of Joshua, of Achan's actual gilt; yet he addresses him, and says, 'My son, give, I pray thee, glory to the Lord God of Israel, and make confession unto Him; and tell me what thou hast done; hide it not from me.' How gentle are these words! There is no harshness, no severity, but a true paternal pity for the man who has placed himself in so fearful and perilous a position. 'By this example,' observes Calvin, 'judges are taught that, while they punish crimes, they ought so to temper their severity as not to lay aside the feelings of humanity, and, on the other hand, that they ought to be merciful without being reckless and remiss; that, in short, they ought to be as parents to those they condemn, without substituting undue mildness for the sternness of justice.'[1] Few things are more unbecoming than stern severity, on the part of an administrator of the law, towards one who has broken it; and the judge who weeps as he passes sentence on a prisoner, will be far more likely to lead him to repentance, than he would were he to address him in terms of harshness. That this was the effect of Joshua's appeal, however, can scarcely be affirmed. Achan ingenuously confessed his crime, but it is to be feared that it was somewhat as Judas did when he had betrayed his Master,—from terror, rather than from true repentance. There is, in fact, no virtue in a man's confessing his sins when they can no longer be hid. Had Achan acknowledged himself the transgressor prior to his detection by the lot, we might have indulged the hope that he had truly repented, and was deeply sorry; but it was not until he was dragged into the light, and his guilt exposed, beyond the possibility of being further concealed, that he uttered a word relating to the matter.

But let us hear his words and learn the extent of his crime. 'Indeed,' said he, 'I have sinned against the Lord God of Israel,

[1] 'Commentary on Joshua,' pp. 114, 115. Calvin Translation Society.

and thus and thus have I done : When I saw among the spoils a goodly Babylonish garment, and two hundred shekels of silver, and a wedge of gold of fifty shekels weight, then I coveted them, and took them ; and, behold, they are hid in the earth in the midst of my tent, and the silver under it.'

Jericho was a city of considerable wealth. It seems to have had commercial intercourse with the far-famed Babylon, and to have obtained some of its treasures. The Babylonish garment or cloak, called by the LXX. ψιλὴ ποικίλη, and by the Vulgate *pallium coccineum*, was probably a superior work of art, composed of various coloured materials. Josephus calls it 'a royal garment interwoven with gold.'[1] It is observed by Dr Kitto, that the literal rendering of the words of the text would be, 'a mantle of Shinar, of which Babylon was, in after times, the famous and dominant capital.'[2] But Shinar was, in fact, the earlier name for Babylon,[3] so that the rendering of our version is strictly correct ; and we know that, in later times at least, Babylon became celebrated for its sumptuous robes, one of which coming into the possession of Cato by inheritance, he commanded it to be sold, his simple habits being opposed to all luxuries. Recent discoveries in the ruins of ancient Nineveh, have brought to light remarkable illustrations of the state of the arts of weaving and embroidering on the banks of the Tigris and the Euphrates ; and the probability is, that this Babylonish garment was somewhat similar to one, in which a king appears clothed, on a slab described and pictured by Mr Layard. 'The dress of the king,' he observes, 'consisted of a long flowing garment, descending to the ankles, and elaborately embroidered and edged with fringes and tassels. It was confined at the waist by a girdle, to which were attached cords with large tassels, falling down almost to the feet. Over this robe, a second, nearly of the same length, but open to the front, appears to have been thrown. It was

---

[1] Antiq. v. 1, 10.   [2] Pict. Bible *in loco*.   [3] Gen. x. 10.

also embroidered and edged with tassels.'[1] The two hundred shekels of silver would probably be worth from L.20 to L.25; and the wedge, or tongue, of gold, which some suppose was a golden ornament, weighing fifty shekels, would be valued at from L.90 to L.100.

These valuable articles Achan first saw, then coveted, and then took. 'When lust hath conceived, it bringeth forth sin; and sin, when it is finished, bringeth forth death.' Herein was Achan's guilt; not that he saw, but that he coveted, or gave way to the lust of the eye, and that then he took what he knew was not his own. And these articles he had hid in the earth, in the midst of his tent, the silver being put under them, or under the Babylonish garment. Thus, as God had said (ver. 11), he had 'stolen and dissembled also,'—dissembled, that is, in concealing the stolen property; thus saying, in effect, that he had not taken it. But now he was compelled to confess his crime, now his base and sacrilegious conduct was fully brought to light. So true it is, as Lord Bacon says, that 'dissimulation is but a faint kind of policy;' on which aphorism Archbishop Whately observes, 'Nothing but the right can ever be the expedient, since that can never be true expediency which would sacrifice a greater good to a less.'[2] Too late did Achan learn, as it is to be feared many do, that by grasping at a little he lost all, and that his attempt to conceal his fault only rendered it the more disgraceful.

According to the Mosaic law, two witnesses were sufficient to establish a person's guilt; and, now that Joshua had the evidence of the lot and Achan's own confession, he might have proceeded at once to the execution of the sentence. But he acted the part of a kind and generous judge; for, anxious to be sure of Achan's guilt, and to present the evidences of it before

[1] 'Nineveh, and its Remains,' vol. ii., p. 319. See also Vaux's 'Nineveh and Persepolis,' p. 293.
[2] 'Bacon's Essays, with Annotations,' by Archbishop Whately, p. 81.

the people, he sent messengers to the tent to search for the stolen goods. There they found them, 'and they took them out of the midst of the tent, and brought them unto Joshua, and unto all the children of Israel, and laid them out before the Lord.' Probably before the ark of the covenant of the Lord, and in the presence of the elders of the people, the Babylonish garment, the two hundred shekels of silver, and the wedge of gold, were laid down, as a sign that they belonged to Jehovah, and ought to have been destroyed; and also as a witness of Achan's guilt, and of the desert of the punishment which he was about to suffer. Deep must have been the impression made upon the spectators' minds. They would see the folly of transgressing God's commands. They would learn that it was impossible to hide anything from Him. They would perceive how hateful sin was in His sight, the act of one man having brought sorrow on the whole congregation of Israel. And they would be prepared to acknowledge the justice of the penalty which was to fall on the transgressor, and also to take part in the speedy execution of it.

And now the hour of vengeance has arrived. Into a valley not far from Jericho, Joshua and all Israel took Achan, together with his sons and daughters, his oxen, his asses, his sheep, his tent, and the silver, and the garment, and the wedge of gold, and all that he had; and there Joshua addressed him, and said, 'Why hast thou troubled us? the Lord shall trouble thee this day.' Troublers of others, and especially of the Church, generally bring trouble on themselves. Achan had brought the ban upon all Israel; now it is to be removed from them, and to fall with tremendous violence on himself. No mercy could be shown him, for his crime was of an aggravated character, and had already cost the people the shame of a disastrous defeat.

Stoning was the legal method of inflicting the punishment of death upon criminals. 'Thou shalt bring forth,' said the law, 'that man or that woman which have committed that wicked thing, unto thy gates, even that man or that woman, and shalt stone them with stones until they die.'[1] It was by no means a cruel mode of dealing with a culprit, for death would ensue immediately that a heavy stone fell upon the head or upon the chest; nor was it ever accompanied with torture or mutilation, such as the seven brothers and their mother suffered, by command of Antiochus, in the times of the Maccabees;[2] or such as some poor victims of Papal wrath suffer even in our day, in the dungeons of the Inquisitions of Italy and Spain. No; the law of God, stern and inexorable as it doubtless is, gives no authority even to magistrates to inflict tortures of this kind on criminals of any class. It sanctions capital punishments; but it does so, not that revengeful passions may be gratified, but only for the benefit of the state.

Achan and all his were first stoned, and then burned with fire; after which a great heap of stones was raised on their remains. Even the gold and the silver were consumed: for, as Calvin observes, God 'would not allow the sanctuary to be polluted by the proceeds of theft;' and, therefore, although such things found in Jericho were to be consecrated to the Lord, and to be brought into His treasury, these He could not accept. Stolen property can never be offered to God with His approval, even for the benefit of the poor or for the service of the Church. To obey is better than sacrifice. Justice must be done before deeds of charity are wrought. It is to be feared that many a sacred edifice has been built with money which has been obtained by fraud or by oppression; but it is impossible that the God of truth and righteousness can smile upon such deeds. No offerings can be acceptable to Him on which the ban or curse of the law rests; and, therefore, none can be acceptable but such as are gained by honest means.

---

[1] Deut. xvii. 5; and see Num. xv. 32–36.   [2] 2 Macc. vii.

By throwing stones upon the spot where Achan was consumed, the people expressed their detestation of his crime; and there they heaped stones as a memorial to posterity of the sad event, and perhaps, as Calvin suggests, 'to prevent any one from imprudently gathering particles of gold and silver on the spot.' Nothing that belonged to Achan was hereafter to be touched by any of the people; and hence, everything was done that could be, to obliterate them from the sight of man.

But are we to understand that the sons and the daughters of Achan, together with his oxen, his asses, and his sheep, shared the same fate? To some, this has appeared so unreasonable and so unjust, that they have endeavoured, in various ways, to prove that it was not so; or that, if it was, God Himself did not so order it. Recourse has been had to verbal criticism: and as in vers. 25 and 26 the singular pronoun is used—'All Israel stoned *him* with stones;'—'and they raised over *him* a great heap of stones'—it has been supposed that only Achan himself suffered, and that his children were brought down to the valley merely to witness the execution of the sentence.[1] But, as Keil observes, this by no means follows, as the singular suffix is used interchangeably with the plural;—because Achan was the person most prominent in the punishment, he is therefore repeatedly mentioned alone. Again, it has been supposed that the members of Achan's family were included in his doom, 'by one of those sudden impulses of indiscriminate popular vengeance to which the Jewish people were exceedingly prone; and which, in this case, it would not have been in the power of Joshua to control by any authority which he could, under such circumstances, exercise.'[2] But in the 15th verse, God says expressly, 'And it shall come to pass that he that is taken with the accursed thing, shall be burnt with fire,

---

[1] See Dr A. Clarke's 'Commentary' *in loco*, where it is denied that his children suffered with him; whereas Josh. xxii. 20 certainly implies that they did.

[2] See Kitto's 'Cyclopædia of Bib. Lit.;' art. 'Achan.'

he and all that he hath.' Nor is there any indication in the narrative of a sudden outburst of popular feeling; but, on the contrary,
the sentence appears to have been executed with the greatest
calmness and solemnity.

Yet the law of Moses enjoined, that 'the fathers should not be
put to death for the children, nor the children for the fathers;'[1]
and we cannot suppose that God would now order a violation of
His own commands: for He visits the sins of the fathers upon
the children unto the third and fourth generation *of them that hate
Him;*[2] not upon children who love Him, and are obedient to His
commands. Hence, though no mention is made of the fact, we
must suppose either that Achan's children had been accomplices
in his deed, or that they had become accessories to it *ex post facto,*
and had assisted him in concealing the property in his tent. As
innocent persons, they could not be put to death. 'They shared
in the corrupt nature and *desires* which prompted their father to
the act.' They were his children not in a corporeal sense only,
but morally and spiritually. And God knew their hearts: He,
from whom no secret can be hid, was perfectly acquainted with
their inmost thoughts, and saw how they had connived at their
father's conduct, and thus made themselves partakers of his guilt.[3]
God is love; and, under the Old Testament dispensation as well
as under the New, ever dealt righteously with men, and was
more disposed to mercy than severity,—when mercy could be
exercised with safety to His government. 'Thou showest loving-
kindness unto thousands,' said the prophet Jeremiah, 'and recom-
pensest the iniquity of the fathers into the bosom of their children
after them: the Great, the Mighty God, the Lord of Hosts, is
His name; great in counsel, and mighty in work: for Thine eyes

---

[1] Deut. xxiv. 16; comp. 2 Kings xiv. 6; 2 Chron. xxv. 4.
[2] Exod. xx. 5, xxxiv. 6, 7.
[3] See Keil and Hengstenberg's 'Authenticity of the Pent.,' vol. ii., p. 448,
etc.

are open upon all the ways of the sons of men, to give every one according to his ways, and according to the fruit of his doings.'[1]

Thus we vindicate this procedure, believing it to have been most just and righteous. It was, however, a terrible judgment. ' The actor alone doth not smart with sacrilege ; all that concerns him is enwrapped in the judgment. Those that defile their hands with holy goods are enemies to their own flesh and blood.'[2] ' It is a fearful thing to fall into the hands of the living God.' Loudly too, does this narrative speak against the sin of covetousness. ' The love of money is the root of all evil; which while some coveted after, they have erred from the faith, and pierced themselves through with many sorrows.'[3] Yet, with all the solemn warnings which they have before their eyes, men continue to bow down to and to worship mammon ; and numbers there are who, if they cannot obtain wealth by honest means, will obtain it by dishonest : for wealth they must and will have, though their gold and their silver become cankered, and the rust of them witnesses against them, and eats their flesh as it were with fire.

Men's names are sometimes expressive of their character.[4] Achan is derived from *achor*, which signifies trouble or disturbance ; and a great disturber of the happiness of Israel had this man been. And now his name was transferred to the valley in which he suffered, ' for the name of the place was called the valley of Achor unto this day.' It is elsewhere mentioned in Isa. lxv. 10, and Hos. ii. 15, and in both instances with reference to this event. But its situation cannot be accurately determined. ' Jerome says that it was situated on the north of Jericho, near to Gilgal, and that even in his day the inhabitants called it by its ancient name. But the assertion merely rests upon an uncertain tradition, which had its origin in the present chapter, and does not accord with chap. xv. 7. According to this passage,

---

[1] Jer. xxxii. 18, 19.   [2] Bishop Hall.
[3] 1 Tim. vi. 10.   [4] See Gen. xxvii. 36.

the northern boundary of the tribe of Judah ran through the valley of Achor; 'and, therefore, the valley must have been on the south or south-west of Jericho, since this town was not within the territory of Judah.'[1] Whether, then, it was a gloomy valley, or one of considerable loveliness and beauty, we cannot tell; but a valley of trouble it certainly was, partly to Israel, but especially to Achan himself, the troubler. And yet it was changed into a door of hope; for the Lord turned from the fierceness of His anger, and the ban was removed from the congregation of the people. Let a nation or a church upon whom the displeasure of God has fallen, put away from it the accursed thing, and His anger against it will soon cease; but if, as in the church at Corinth in early times,[2] sin is committed, and the members of the church are puffed up, and fail to excommunicate the wicked person, and thereby make themselves sharers of his guilt, God cannot smile upon them, but will take away their candlestick out of its place. A diseased member must be cut off, or the whole body will be infected, and will perish.

There are Achans in almost every camp. Men there are, both in the State and in the Church, who, under a fair exterior, pleasing manners, and a smooth tongue, hide a selfish and covetous disposition; and whilst professing, perhaps, and that loudly, to be anxious to promote the welfare of others, are, in fact, secretly plotting to secure their own. Such men are the gangrene of society, and, were it not for the checks they meet with, would eat out its moral and spiritual life. But the eye of the Omniscient One is upon them; and though they may continue to deceive their fellow-men for a while, Him they cannot deceive. Nor will He fail to bring them to the light. Not by means of the lot is the Church to search them out, for that mode of discovering offenders has no longer the Divine sanction; but God Himself will, in His own time, take off the mask they wear, and

---

[1] Keil, *in loco.* [2] 1 Cor. v.

make them known, and then will they be covered with shame and ignominy, and their doom will be worse than that of Achan.

For the punishment of Achan did not necessarily involve the destruction of his soul. His repentance, though late, was ingenuous, and perhaps sincere; and this may have been one of those cases which are delivered 'unto Satan for the destruction of the flesh, that the spirit may be saved in the day of the Lord.' But if he that despised Moses' law died without mercy under two or three witnesses, of how much sorer punishment shall he be thought worthy, who sins against clearer light, and richer privileges, and a superior economy, and thus treads under foot the Son of God, and counts the blood of the covenant, wherewith he was sanctified, an unholy thing, and does despite unto the Spirit of grace? It is impossible for one favoured with the blessings of the Christian dispensation to be no more accountable to God than one who lived under the law of Moses; and it is impossible, therefore, that the guilt of both should be viewed in the same light, even though they violate one and the same law. An Achan under the New Testament economy would be a worse man, and liable, therefore, to a sorer punishment, than an Achan under the Old Testament economy; and hence, whatever became of the soul of the Achan of our narrative, the Achans of our own day may well tremble for the consequences of their covetousness and dissimulation; and the sooner they take vengeance on their sins, and destroy them utterly, as the real troublers both of themselves and others, the greater hope there will be that they will escape the wrath which is to come. But if they think of a death-bed repentance, let them know, as Jeremy Taylor says, that 'no man can in a moment root out the long contracted habit of vice, nor upon his death-bed make use of all that variety of preventing, accompanying, and persevering grace, which God gave to man, because man would need it all;' and that, therefore, to procrastinate so great a work, is to render it all but certain that it will never be accomplished at all.

EBAL AND GERIZIM.

CHAPTER VII.

THE DESTRUCTION OF AI.

S when a dense cloud charged with the elements of destruction, which has for some time hung over a country, is suddenly dispersed, and the sun's bright beams once more gladden all nature, so now were the Israelites relieved from the apprehensions they had suffered since the sin of Achan had placed them under the ban. They had wiped their hands of his crime, they had put away from them the accursed thing; and now the cloud of the Divine displeasure had rolled away, and a ray of hope again gleamed upon the camp.

'Fear not, neither be dismayed,'[1] said God to Joshua, when He called him to accept the leadership of His people. 'Fear not, neither be dismayed,'[2] was the word of encouragement with which he was again addressed. And this word was followed by an assurance that Ai and her king would be given into his hand; that as He placed Jericho and her king under the ban, and had destroyed them, so should He do also to Ai and her king; and that, in this case, the people would be permitted to take the spoil and the cattle, as a prey, unto themselves. Who can conceive the joy and gladness with which the valiant commander of God's people would hear these words? Afraid he had been, and considerably dismayed; but all his fears were now given to the winds, and with reanimated courage he proceeded a second time to attack the city.

Ai is described as 'beside Beth-aven, on the east side of Beth-el.'[3] Both Ai and Beth-el existed in the time of Abram; for when Abram entered Canaan, and had passed through the land to the plain of Moreh, it is said 'he removed from thence unto a mountain on the east of Beth-el, and pitched his tent, having Beth-el on the west and Hai (Ai, הָעַי) on the east.'[4] According to Gen. xxviii. 19, the original name of Beth-el was Luz, and its later name (בֵּית אֵל, the house of God) appears to have been given to it by Jacob, first, after he had seen the vision of the ladder, and again on his return from Padan-aram (Gen. xxxv. 7). It is mentioned by Jerome as situated twelve miles from Jerusalem, on the right hand of the road to Shechem; and here, on a hill, Dr Robinson found some ruins, which cover a space of three or four acres, called by the Arabs Beitin. 'There is little room for question, that both the name and the site of Beitin are identical with those of the ancient Beth-el;'[5] and on one of these

---

[1] Josh. i. 9; Deut. xxxi. 6, 8.
[2] Josh. viii. 1.
[3] Josh. vii. 2.
[4] Gen. xii. 8, 9, xiii. 3.
[5] Robinson's 'Researches,' vol. i., p. 449.

heights Abram no doubt built his altar, and called upon the name of the Lord.[1] Dr Keil, however, does not agree with this identification; but, following Thenius, contends that Beth-el must have stood on or near Sinjil, three miles further north, and he then identifies Ai with Turnus Aya, a village situated upon a low mound a little east of Sinjil. Here, however, says Van de Velde, 'there is no deep valley, and Michmash, which, according to 1 Sam. xiii. 5, was near to Ai, is at least three or three and a half hours south of Turnus Aya.'[2]

Where, then, was Ai? Dr Robinson found a village called Deir Diowân, in an uneven rocky basin, one hour south-east of Beitan (Beth-el), 'the position of which,' he observes, 'would answer well to that of Ai.' But there are no ruins here, nor does its position agree exactly with the scriptural account of the position of Ai. Hence even Dr Robinson himself seems doubtful, and Van de Velde fixes upon another spot, discovered by Mr Finn, called by the natives Tell-el-haja, that is, 'the Mount of Stones.' It is an isolated mount, thirty-five minutes east of Beth-el, and answers exactly to the scriptural requirements for Ai, whilst an old cistern and huge heaps of stones indicate the site of an ancient town.[3]

This identification we are disposed to adopt, as by far the most probable solution of the difficulty; and we will now attempt a description of the siege.

On the former occasion the expedition against Ai consisted of but 3000 men, but now Joshua was commanded to take with him 'all the people of war;' for, their courage having been damped, it was necessary to consult their weakness, and to animate them

---

[1] Van de Velde, 'Syria and Palestine,' vol. ii., p. 282; Stanley, 'Sinai and Palestine,' pp. 215, 216.

[2] Memoir accompanying the map, p. 283. Narrative, vol. ii., p. 278.

[3] Van de Velde, 'Syria and Palestine,' vol. ii., p. 279, etc.; comp. Stanley, p. 202, 204.

for the attack, by the thought that they were numerous. It is not necessary, however, to suppose that 'all the people of war,' meant all who were capable of bearing arms, but, as Keil observes, 'a proportionate number' from the several tribes, and that the actual number employed was the thirty thousand mighty men of valour, mentioned in verse 3.

By God Himself, Joshua was commanded to lay an ambush behind the city (ver. 2), and to take it by means of stratagem. And is it lawful, then, ask some, to employ wiles and stratagems in war? If war is lawful at all, undoubtedly it is; for war consists not merely in the use of physical force, but in seeking to obtain victory by skilful manœuvres. 'Those are the best commanders,' says Calvin, 'who accomplish more by art and counsel than by mere violence.' Laws, then, are to be observed in warfare, which no true soldier will on any account violate; but it has never been understood, either in former or in later times, that, to take a besieged city, the besiegers were not at liberty to have recourse to stratagem, and hence stratagem has been employed whenever it was thought needful.

But who formed the ambuscade? It would seem, from the narrative, that it was composed of the thirty thousand mighty men; yet it is difficult to conceive how so numerous a force could be employed in such a service without attracting the attention of the inhabitants of the city. Hence several methods have been proposed of meeting the difficulty; some suggesting an emendation of the text, and others that there were two ambuscades, one of 30,000 concealed at a distance from the town, and another of 5000 in the immediate neighbourhood. But the most plausible interpretation is that of Keil, who observes that it is characteristic of Semitic historians, to announce as far as possible, at the very outset of a narrative, the termination of the whole affair, and then to complete the historical sketch by proceeding with their description of the intermediate occurrences. The writer does this in the account before us. He tells us what arrangements were made by Joshua for marching against Ai (ver. 3–8), and then he informs us that they were carried into execution (ver. 9). Afterwards follow the details of the story (ver. 10–20); and it is from this point that we are to mark the progress of the narrative.

Having received his instructions from the Lord, Joshua selected 30,000 men, and rose up with all the people of war to advance towards Ai, and that night he lodged among the people. Early in the morning he reviewed his troops, and then set them in motion in the direction of the city. The distance from Jericho to Tell-el-hajar is about twenty miles; so that they would reach the spot where they encamped, on the north side of the city, towards the evening of that day. Immediately on their arrival, Joshua sent five thousand to lie in ambush between Beth-el and Ai, on the west side of the city, saying to them, 'Behold, ye shall lie in wait against the city, even behind the city; go not very far from the city, but be ye all ready: and I, and the people that are with me, will approach unto the city; and it shall come to pass, when they come out against us, as at the first, that we will flee before them, (for they will come out after us,) till we have drawn them from the city; for they will say, They flee before us, as at the first: therefore we will flee before them. Then ye shall rise up from the ambush, and seize upon the city: for the Lord your God will deliver it into your hands,' etc. (ver. 4–8).

'Beth-el,' says Van de Velde, 'though lying quite near, in the direction of west by north, cannot be seen from Tell-el-hajar; two rocky heights rise between both places, just as the laying of an ambush to the west of Ai would require.' Here, then, the five thousand take their position, hid from the observation of the inhabitants of Ai, and waiting the signal which is to call them to the attack. Meanwhile, Joshua remains with the five and twenty thousand on the eminence north of the town, and during the night conducts his army into the midst of the valley, 'a deep and steep-sided glen,' which lies between him and the fated city. The morning dawns, and the king of Ai observes his enemies in the valley, and immediately sallies forth with all the men of the city to attack the Israelites on the plain. They offer no resistance, but, as if they are afraid of them, they fly towards the wilderness, so that all the male inhabitants of the city are allowed to follow them; whilst those of Beth-el[1] also, who see the flight of the Israelites, but do not see the ambuscade that threatens them, rush forward to share in the victory.

The Israelites reach an elevated spot north-east of Ai, where they can be seen by the ambuscade stationed in the valley. And now the preconcerted signal is given. Joshua, at the Divine command, stretches out his spear[2] towards Ai; and the men in ambush rush into the city, whose gates are left open, and hastily set it on fire. At the same time, the Israelites turn round upon their pursuers, who, seeing the smoke rising from their dwellings, are seized with consternation, and have no power to flee this way or that. Terrible is the slaughter. Numbers fall before the sword of Joshua, and others, who rush towards the city, are met by the five thousand who have caused the conflagration; so that now the men of Ai are between two companies of the Israelites, and escape is utterly impossible. Not a man survives. In the field or in the wilderness all are slain, the king only excepted;

---

[1] From Judges i. 22, 23, we learn that Beth-el, which was a walled city, was taken subsequently by the tribe of Joseph. Its king, however, may have been slain on this occasion (Josh. xii. 16), and it is probable that its fighting men had already come to Ai as allies.

[2] This was probably a long spear with a small flag attached to it, by which it would be rendered conspicuous at a distance. Calvin says, 'It is scarcely possible to believe that the spear was seen by the ambuscade, when we consider the long space that intervened, and more especially that Joshua was standing in a valley.' But there is no evidence that he was standing in a valley, and there may have been persons stationed at different posts to watch for the signal, and to convey it to the men in ambush.

and now the entire army of the Israelites enter Ai, when the rest
of the inhabitants—the women and the children—are also slain,
and 12,000 people thus fall a sacrifice to the avenging sword.

'The cattle, and the spoil of the city, Israel took for a prey
unto themselves.' We are not then to understand, by their setting
the city on fire, that they did so with the design of consuming it
utterly, for then there would have been no spoil left.   'The fire
was indeed applied so as to let both armies know that the city
was in possession of the Israelites, but it was not actually destroyed by fire.   It was not practicable in a moment of time to
seize and carry off the booty, nay, to bring the vessels and a
large part of the property without the walls; and it would have
been absurd voluntarily to destroy spoil which God had granted.
We see, then, that the first fire was not kindled for the purpose
of destroying the whole city, but was merely a partial conflagration, giving intimation of its capture, and that the Israelites had
entered at the open gates without bloodshed or struggle.   This
is confirmed shortly after, when the burning is ascribed to Joshua
himself, not only because it was burnt under his command, but
because he was careful, after returning from the battle, to see
that it was utterly destroyed; as it is immediately added that
he made it a heap of stones, in order that it might be a perpetual
desolation.'[1]

Of Joshua it is said, that he 'drew not his hand back wherewith he stretched out the spear, until he had utterly destroyed
all the inhabitants of Ai.'   Intrepid warrior!   'As if his hand
had been fastened to the spear, he exhorts the soldiers to look
to God alone, to whom he resigns the success of the battle.'
There was, however, no mystical power in the spear of Joshua,
as there was in the elevation of the hands of Moses during the
battle with the Amalekites.   Rather is the fact mentioned as
illustrative of the noble spirit of perseverance displayed by Israel's

[1] Calvin, *in loco.*

commander, for he was a man who feared neither toil nor danger so long as duty called him to the work. Would that all God's servants were like him! But how many are there, who, long before the battle is won, draw back the hand, and sheath the sword, and retire from the conflict, leaving their enemies in possession of the field! Let the reader be upon his guard. Called to contend with spiritual adversaries, let him buckle on the armour, and take the spear or the sword, and resolve never to lay it down until the victory is sure. Joshua is a noble example for the Christian warrior; and our own national history presents other noble examples which we shall do well to imitate. Nelson, Wellington, Havelock, and others we might name, were men who drew not back their hands, but went on bravely, in spite of weariness and pain. Perseverance was their motto. *Nil desperandum* was their constant watchword. Look at Havelock before Cawnpore. With a thousand British soldiers and three hundred Sikhs, who had marched twenty miles in the hottest day of the hottest season of the year, he encountered a force of five thousand native troops, well trained and disciplined; and when his horse was shot he mounted a common hack, and, before a withering fire, led forward his noble band, and bore down upon the enemy with irresistible force. Cawnpore was won—won by courage, faith, and perseverance; and these are the principles which every Christian warrior should cultivate, if he intends to carry off the prize before him. Men who draw back their hands are not the men to conquer in the great battle which we are called to wage against sin and Satan. Victory is awarded to those who, like an eminent modern traveller, think that, if God is served at all, it should be done in a manly way, and who are determined to succeed or perish in any great enterprise to which they may be called.

The kings of the Canaanitish cities were treated with greater severity by Joshua than their subjects, for they were doubtless

the leaders and instigators of the people in their career of crime.
The king of Ai was spared in the general overthrow; but subsequently he was put to death, and then hung upon a tree or
stake until the evening. As we have already seen, the mode of
executing the sentence of death adopted by the Israelites was
that of stoning, so that we are not to suppose that the king of
Ai was hung alive. He was, in all probability, either stoned or
slain with the sword; and being under the ban, he was afterwards
hung upon the stake. But the law required that bodies thus
hung should not remain upon the tree all night, but should be
buried the same day;[1] and Joshua, therefore, gave orders that
the carcase of the king should be taken down before the setting
of the sun, buried at the entrance of the gate of the city, and
covered with a heap of stones.[2] All this was done, and the city
itself was burnt, and became, like Jericho, a scene of desolation.
The word *Ai*, or *Ha-ai*, signifies 'ruins;' and the name *Tel-el-
Hajar* means 'the Mount of Stones,' which, says Dr Stanley,
'certainly agrees well with the curse on Ai,—*Tel* being the same
word used to express "the heap" which was to take the place of
the city, and the "Hajar," or mound of stones, corresponding to
the cairn over the dead king.'[3]

Under the name of Aija,[4] this city is spoken of after the
captivity, but it appears to have been rebuilt at an earlier
period; for it is said by Isaiah, that, when the Assyrian army
was advancing towards Jerusalem, they came to Aiath, passed
on to Migron, and laid up their carriages at Michmash.[5] Yet
the ruins of the former city may have remained, and the new city
may have been erected at a short distance from them. Now
however, the very name itself has disappeared, and Ai seems

---

[1] Deut. xxi. 22, 23.   [2] Josh. viii. 29.
[3] 'Sinai and Palestine,' p. 202, note.
[4] Neh. xi. 31; comp. vii. 32, and Ezra ii. 28, where it is called Ai.
[5] Isa. x. 28.

doomed to be what Joshua designed it should become—'a perpetual desolation, a heap for ever.'

The siege and capture of Ai taught the Israelites some valuable lessons. It taught them that, whilst they honoured God by a strict obedience to His commands, He would honour them, and not forsake them; it taught them that they had nothing to fear from the inhabitants of the land, for that God could always find a way to baffle and overcome them; and it taught them that to obtain the conquest of the country, they must put forth their own efforts, and not expect that God would always work miracles on their behalf. Lessons such as these naturally suggest themselves to our own minds, and it is highly probable that they would be presented to the minds of many of these people. They were still being trained for the service of the Lord Jehovah; and the battles they were called to fight, together with the victories they won, were part of the discipline which God employed to fit them for greater and nobler work.

Ai having been destroyed, and the inhabitants of the land sufficiently awed to deter them from attempting to attack the Israelites, the way was now opened for the assembling of the tribes on a spot which Moses had mentioned before his death, commanding the people there to set up great stones, and to build an altar unto the Lord their God. To the commands of the illustrious lawgiver Joshua paid due regard, *as soon as it was practicable*, after they had crossed the Jordan; and into the valley between Ebal and Gerizim he now led the mighty host.

Mounts Ebal and Gerizim still retain their names.[1] The former name is thought by some to signify, 'stript of leaves;' the latter name is supposed to have been derived from an ancient

---

[1] Gerizim is now called by the inhabitants of the neighbourhood Jebel-et-Sur, but the Samaritans know it by its ancient name. The modern name of Ebal is Jusad-ed-Deen, the 'pillar of religion.'

tribe, called the Gerizi, or Gezerites, who are mentioned in Scripture only once (1 Sam. xxvii. 8). From Beth-el (Beitin) to these mounts the distance is upwards of thirty miles; whence it has been affirmed that the event now before us is not recorded in the order of time, but must have occurred at a later period: for how, it is asked, could the whole body of the Israelites journey so many miles through a country still in the undisputed possession of the enemy? To meet this difficulty, the Septuagint inserts the episode, if such it may be called, after the account of the league of the Amorites given at the commencement of chapter the ninth. But this, says Keil, ' is merely another example of the arbitrary manner in which the translators made transpositions in the text to suit their own taste;' nor is the difficulty insurmountable after all. Other victories may have been obtained over the inhabitants of the intervening territory, though they are not recorded; or it may have been, as we have intimated above, that the people were so terrified by the destruction of Ai, as to retire before the advancing host, and leave to Joshua an open path, by which he could proceed to the locality he wished to reach.

Two days' march northwards from Ai, through the Wady-el-Lubban, and then over the great plain of Mukhna, would bring the Israelites to the valley of Nabulus (Shechem), out of which Mount Gerizim and Ebal rise in steep rocky precipices, to about nine hundred feet in height. Gerizim, which lies to the south of the valley, has been described as fruitful and picturesque; Ebal, on the contrary, as desolate and sterile. Dr Robinson, however, speaks of them both as equally naked and barren, the only exception in favour of Gerizim being a small ravine opposite the west end of Nabulus, which is full of springs and trees. On the summit of Gerizim is a table-land, stretching to the west and south-west, from one point of which there is a commanding view of the valley, and of Mount Ebal on the opposite side of it, the top of which also spreads into a table-land, but more rocky and broken, and less susceptible of cultivation.[1] The breadth of the valley, from the foot of Mount Ebal to that of Mount Gerizim, is not more, in one spot at least, than five hundred yards wide, extending from south-east to north-west ; and here, probably, the elders of the people were assembled, whilst the vast masses occupied the adjacent slopes. Eusebius, and after him Jerome, objected to this locality as the scene of the events, on the ground of the wide interval between the two mountains, and maintained that the Ebal and Gerizim of Joshua were near to Gilgal : but the interval is not so great ; and though Deut. xi. 30—where it is said, 'Are they not on the other side Jordan, by the way where the sun goeth down, in the land of the Canaanites, which dwell in the champaign over against Gilgal '—would lead us to look for the mountains in the neighbourhood of Jericho, yet the mention in the same passage of the terebinths of Moreh,[2] which, according to Gen. xii. 6, were near to Sichem, renders it certain that the common view is correct.

The first act of Joshua, on arriving at this spot, was to erect an altar unto the Lord God of Israel on Mount Ebal. It was written in the law, ' And if thou wilt build Me an altar of stone, thou shalt not build it of hewn stone : for if thou lift up thy tool upon it, thou hast polluted it.'[3] It was therefore built of whole stones, over which no man had lifted any iron tool ; for ' had the stones been hewn, they would not have represented earth in its elementary state, and would not therefore have tallied with the essential meaning of an altar, since every bloody sacrifice was immediately connected with sin and death, by which man, the creature of earth, is brought to earth again.'[4] How false, in this light, is the character of the altars so called, elaborately

---

[1] Robinson's Researches, vol. ii., p. 278, etc. ; Olin's Travels, vol. ii., 346, etc.
[2] See Stanley, p. 286, note ; Smith's Dictionary of the Bible, Art ' Ebal.'
[3] Exod. xx. 25.   [4] See Keil, in loco.

wrought of the most costly marble, erected in the cathedrals of the Church of Rome. But, in fact, they are not altars, nor should the Lord's table be ever so designated; for Christianity has but one altar—the cross of Christ, on which He offered up Himself *once for all.*

On this altar 'they offered burnt-offerings, and sacrificed peace-offerings.' The burnt-offerings were symbolical of the solemn dedication of the people to the Lord; and the peace-offerings, with which thank-offerings were associated, and a sacrificial feast, indicated the joy of the congregation on this renewal of the covenant, all the blessings of which they would now again have a right to claim. Most impressive must have been the scene when, upon that lofty eminence, and in sight of the vast multitudes assembled on the plain below, the priests presented these offerings on the altar, and the smoke of the burnt-sacrifices ascended up to heaven. Many a heart would beat with deep emotion, and that of Joshua himself would, we may be sure, be the seat of extraordinary joy. For what had God done for him since he became the commander of the people? He had enabled him to surmount the greatest difficulties; He had given him the victory over powerful enemies; and now He had brought him into the very midst of the land which was to be the inheritance of the sons of Jacob. Well, then, might Joshua rejoice; and well may we conceive that that day was one of the happiest of his life.

But another duty Joshua had also to perform. 'And it shall be,' said Moses, 'on the day when ye shall pass over Jordan unto the land which the Lord thy God giveth thee, that thou shalt set thee up great stones, and plaster them with plaster. And thou shalt write upon them all the words of this law, when thou art passed over; that thou mayest go in unto the land which the Lord thy God giveth thee, a land that floweth with milk and honey; as the Lord God of thy fathers hath promised thee. Therefore

h

it shall be, when ye are gone over Jordan, that ye shall set up these stones, which I command you this day, in Mount Ebal, and thou shalt plaster them with plaster.'[1] This important work Joshua accomplished; for 'he wrote there, upon the stones, a copy of the law of Moses, which he wrote in the presence of the children of Israel.'[2]

Were these stones the stones of the altar, as Josephus and others represent? This is by no means likely; for the stones of the altar would be comparatively small; and, moreover, they were left in their natural state, and not covered over with plaster. These stones were no doubt additional to the stones of the altar, and were probably set up on the sides of it. But what was written on them? Not, as some have supposed, the whole of the Thorah, or law, moral and ceremonial; for that would have been far too lengthy: nor, as others, the blessings, and the cursings, of Deut. xxvii.; for they were not the law, but only motives added to impel or adjure the people to keep it: nor yet the Decalogue, as the substance of the law; for the Decalogue is not specially referred to either by Moses or in the narrative of Joshua. Calvin supposes that, by 'the law' here, is meant the substance and sanctions of the law; and Hengstenberg, Keil, and others, understand by it, 'the so-called second law,' contained in the book of Deuteronomy, from chap. iv. 44 to chap. xxvi. 19. This, it is true, may appear a large portion to write on stones; but when we look at the extent of the writings on the immense slabs recently dug out of the mounds of Nineveh, and when we consider especially that this writing was not on the stones themselves, but on the plaster which covered them, we can easily conceive that the whole of that portion of Deuteronomy was written upon them; for the stones were large, and the number of them was not limited.

But, was the law written upon the plaster? or was it en-

---

[1] Deut. xxvii. 2–4.　　　　　[2] Josh. viii. 32.

graven on the stones, and then covered with plaster, that the inscriptions might remain uninjured, and at a later period, when the plaster should fall off, appear to view for the first time? A device of this kind was adopted by Sostratus the architect, who, being ordered to engrave the name of the king of Egypt on a block of marble, engraved his own name first, then covered it with plaster, and upon that inscribed the name of the king; so that soon the king's name perished, whilst his own continued on the block. But there is no foundation for the opinion that Moses commanded anything of this sort to be done. It is evident, from the text quoted above, that the law was written upon the plaster with which the stones were coated. Such writing was common in ancient times. 'I have seen numerous specimens of it,' says Dr Thomson, 'certainly more than *two thousand years* old, and still as distinct as when they were first inscribed on the plaster.'[1] 'In this hot climate, where there is no frost to dissolve the cement, it will continue hard and unbroken for thousands of years, which is certainly long enough. The cement on Solomon's Pools remains in admirable preservation, though exposed to all the vicissitudes of the climate, and with no protection. The cement in the tombs about Sidon is still perfect, and the writing on them entire, though acted upon by the moist, damp air always formed in caverns, for perhaps two thousand years. What Joshua did, therefore, when he erected the stones at Mount Ebal, was merely to write *in* the soft cement with a stile, or, more likely, *on* the polished surface when dry, with red paint, as in ancient tombs. If properly sheltered, and not broken away by violence, they would have remained to this day.'

Here, then, on this lofty eminence, were these stones erected; and for many years afterwards, in all probability, they stood as a monument of the fidelity of Joshua, but especially as witnesses

[1] 'The Land and the Book,' p. 471.

for the Lord Jehovah.   Many a traveller, attracted to the spot,
would read there the most solemn and impressive words; and,
had those stones been listened to, what calamities would the
Israelites, as a people, have escaped!

We must linger around Ebal for a little while longer, that
we may witness a scene which, for grandeur and solemnity,
has not been equalled since the giving of the law upon Mount
Sinai.   In the valley which lies between Ebal and Gerizim
stands the ark of the covenant of the Lord; half the people
being on the one side of it towards the former mount, and
half of them on the other side towards the latter.   And not
only are the elders of the people there, with the officers and the
judges, but all the congregation of Israel, with the women, the
little ones, and even the strangers that walked among them—the
descendants, perhaps, of the mixed multitude that came with
them out of Egypt, or such as, like Rahab and her family,
had already become proselytes from among the inhabitants of
Canaan.   All are there, for all must understand the obligations
of the covenant into which they have been admitted, and learn
to fear its curses and to aspire after its benefits and blessings.
Beautiful is that valley, and beautiful is the whole scene.   On a
carpet of most lovely green, the tints of which are deepened here
and there by the shadows of the mountains, thousands of men,
women, and children are reclining, in expectation of some great
event.   Lovely melodies are caused by the gentle movements of
numerous olive trees, and by the rippling of the waters of a
hundred little rills; and a delightfully cool and pleasant atmosphere pervades the spot, and renders it a welcome resting-
place for Israel's hosts.[1]   The Levite priests take their stand
upon Mounts Ebal and Gerizim: and beneath those who stand on
the former mount are the tribes of Reuben, Gad, Asher, Zebulon,

---

[1] See the description of this vale by Van de Velde, 'Syria and Palestine,
ii. 293.

Dan, and Naphtali; beneath those who stand on the latter mount are the tribes of Simeon, Levi, Judah, Issachar, Joseph, and Benjamin. The vast multitude is silent, all nature is calm and still, and first the deep voices of the Levites who stand upon Mount Ebal utter the words—

'*Cursed be the man that maketh any graven or molten image, an abomination unto the Lord, the work of the hands of the craftsman, and putteth it in a secret place.*'

And from the tribes at the foot of the mount there arises a loud AMEN—SO BE IT, which is repeated at the close of each curse uttered from above.[1]

Then the voices of the Levites who stand upon Gerizim are heard saying—

'*If thou shalt hearken diligently unto the voice of the Lord thy God, to observe and to do all His commandments which I command thee this day, it shall come to pass that the Lord thy God will set thee on high above all nations of the earth: and all these blessings shall come on thee, and overtake thee, if thou shalt hearken unto the voice of the Lord thy God. Blessed shalt thou be in the city, and blessed shalt thou be in the field. Blessed shall be the fruit of thy body, and the fruit of thy ground, and the fruit of thy cattle, the increase of thy kine, and the flocks of thy sheep. Blessed shall be thy basket and thy store. Blessed shalt thou be when thou comest in, and blessed shalt thou be when thou goest out.*'[2]

And as each blessing is pronounced, the Amen rises louder and yet louder from the tribes at the foot of Mount Gerizim, until at length the last Amen is heard, and dies away on the air.

---

[1] Deut. xxvii. 15–26. That the curses should be pronounced from the mount on which the altar was erected, appears to some incongruous; and the Samaritan text of the Pentateuch represents the altar as erected on Gerizim.

[2] Deut. xxviii. 1–6. It would seem that all these words were uttered on Mount Gerizim; but whether the whole chapter was repeated by the Levites may be considered doubtful. If it was, part of it—vers. 15–68—must have been uttered from Mount Ebal.

Deep was the impression which this event must have produced upon the minds of that vast assembly. God had promised ample rewards to His servants who should obey the law. On the other hand, curses were denounced in order to deter transgressors. 'Each is now forced to subscribe to his own condemnation, while an amen is the response to every single sentence. For in this way they not only hear themselves condemned by the mouth of God, but, as if they had been heralds sent by Him, they denounce the punishment which may await themselves. A similar promulgation was made in the plain of Moab beyond the Jordan; but now they are bound more solemnly, and acknowledge on what condition they are to dwell in the land of Canaan. It added no little weight to the whole, that the children also were admitted as witnesses.'—(Calvin.)

HEWERS OF WOOD.

CHAPTER VIII.

THE GIBEONITES.

NEARLY half-way between Beth-el and the vale of Shechem, on the road leading from Jerusalem to the latter, is a village now called Jiljilia, which stands on a lofty eminence, and affords an extensive view over the great plain to the Mediterranean Sea.[1] The name Jiljilia corresponds with the ancient name Gilgal; and there is little doubt that it was here, and not at the Gilgal near to Jericho, that Joshua encamped after the scene which occurred at Mount Gerizim. For that, after advancing so far into the interior of the country, he would retrace his steps, and bring that vast multitude back to

[1] 'Robinson's Researches,' ii., p. 265.

the Gilgal on which they first encamped, is altogether improbable; whilst Jiljilia, which was but a few miles south of Gerizim, was a most eligible spot from which to direct his future operations. 'Who can believe that this commander, after he had long left the valley of the Jordan, and penetrated so far into the mountainous country, would retire with his whole army behind Jericho into the Jordan vale, in order to undertake further operations? To so improbable a supposition it was necessary to yield, only if another Gilgal had not existed in Palestine,—if Gilgal over against Ebal and Gerizim had not already been made known to Moses.'[1] But another Gilgal is mentioned in Deut. xi. 30; and we meet with it again, at a later period, in the history of the prophet Elijah, of whom it is said, that, being at Gilgal with Elisha, he 'went down to Beth-el,'[2]—an expression which would be wholly incorrect if the Gilgal referred to was that near Jericho, but not if it were the Gilgal now pointed out; for the former is considerably lower than Beth-el, whilst the latter is somewhat higher.

Here, then, Joshua and his army are encamped (Josh. ix. 6), when a confederacy is formed against him by several of the kings of the country, who, having partly recovered from the panic occasioned by his victories, are resolved to give him battle, and to prevent, if possible, his further progress. This was natural, and by no means surprising. There was, however, one tribe that did not join in the confederacy, but, to secure their own welfare, took a very different course; and before the historian proceeds to narrate the circumstances of the conflict with the hostile nations, he pauses to describe the plan adopted by this one tribe, together with the results that followed (chap. ix. 3–27).

---

[1] Keil's Commentary on Kings, vol. i., p. 340, note; Clark. See also his Commentary on Joshua, p. 232; and Van de Velde's Map and Memoir, p. 316.

[2] 2 Kings ii. 2.

Gabaon, or Gibeon, which signifies literally *a high hill,* was one of the royal cities of Canaan, and was situated, according to Josephus, fifty stadia, or rather more than six Roman miles, from the city of Jerusalem.[1] Somewhat farther from Jerusalem than this, is a village situated on the summit of a hill, called el-Jib, respecting which Dr Robinson observes, 'It is not difficult to recognise in el-Jib and its rocky eminence the ancient *Gibeon* of the Scriptures, the Gabaon of Josephus; although the specifications which have come down to us respecting the position of that place are somewhat confused. There is, however, enough in connection with the name to mark the identity of the spot. The name *Jib* in Arabic is merely the abridged form of the Hebrew Gibeon; and presents perhaps the most remarkable instance that occurred to us, in which the *'Ain* of the Hebrew, that most tenacious of letters, has been dropped in passing over into the Arabic.'[2] Such then was the site of the city of the Gibeonites, who seem to have been accounted a brave people,[3] and who formed part of a republic, governed by elders, which also embraced the towns Chephirah, Beeroth, and Kirjath-jearim. Chap. ix. 17.

These were the people who stood aloof from the confederacy. The other tribes resolved to resort to force in order to resist the progress of Joshua; the Gibeonites, on the other hand, had recourse to craft.

Having heard what Joshua had done to Jericho and to Ai, they went to work wilily, even as the sons of Jacob had done to some of their ancestors several centuries before.[4] Theirs, however, was a wiser and more righteous stratagem, and displayed no little tact, prudence, and foresight. 'I commend their wisdom in seeking peace,' says Bishop Hall; 'I do not commend their falsehood in the manner of seeking it.' What did they?

---

[1] Wars ii. 19, 1; comp. Antiq. vii. 11, 7, where it is said to be 40 stadia.
[2] 'Researches' i., p. 455.   [3] Josh. x. 2.   [4] Gen. xxxiv. 25-28.

Wait until the army of Joshua surrounded their cities, and then sue for peace? To have done that, would have been useless; for, whether they knew it or not, Joshua had no authority to spare any of the inhabitants of the land. At once, and notwithstanding the scorn and derision of their neighbours, who would probably charge them with treachery and cowardice, they resolved to send ambassadors to the camp at Gilgal, and to make such representations to the commander of the Israelites as they thought would be likely to excite his pity. Our version says, that 'they made as if they had been ambassadors,' but they were truly ambassadors; and 'hence,' says Keil, 'the whole passage should be translated, "they went and travelled as ambassadors," or, "they started on their journey as ambassadors."'

Observe them carefully, and take notice of their equipment. They are covered with old garments; on their feet they have old shoes strongly mended;[1] their bread is dry and crumbled;[2] and their asses they have laden with their provisions, in old worn-out sacks, and old leathern bottles[3] made of the skins of goats, torn and tied up. In this apparently miserable plight they commence their journey to Gilgal, where, as we have seen, Joshua's army is encamped. The distance is about fifteen Roman miles; so that in the course of two or three hours they arrive at the spot, and in their singular attire present themselves

---

[1] Or clouted, מְטֻלָּאוֹת.   [2] Or mouldy, נִקֻּדִים.

[3] *E.g.*, wine-bottles; but such bottles, used also for water and milk, were made of leather, or of skins prepared in the manner described by Dr Robinson, as follows:—'These are merely the skins of goats stripped off whole, except at the neck; the holes at the legs and tails being sewed up. They are first stuffed out full, and strained by driving in small billets and chips of oak wood, and are then filled with a strong infusion of oak bark for a certain time, until the hair becomes fixed, and the skin sufficiently tanned. This constitutes the whole process. Not less than fifteen hundred skins were lying, thus stuffed, in rows about the yard. They are sold at different prices, from fifteen up to forty piastres.'— *Researches* ii. 79. We have seen many such skins, similarly prepared, and others differently, in South Africa, where they are used chiefly as milk-sacks.

before Joshua and the elders of the people. Of their number we are not informed, but it was probably not large; yet at once they attract attention, and, addressing Joshua and the men of Israel, they say, 'We be come from a far country; now therefore make ye a league with us.' But 'peradventure ye dwell among us,' is the reply; 'and how shall we make a league with you?' That the Israelites should not form an alliance with any of the inhabitants of Canaan, was the express command of God. 'When the Lord thy God shall deliver them before thee, thou shalt smite them, and utterly destroy them; thou shalt make no covenant with them, nor show mercy unto them.'[1] Such was the injunction of the Most High; for, as we have already seen, the nations of Canaan had now filled up the measure of their iniquities, and were henceforth to be dealt with as incorrigible sinners. How, then, could the Israelites make a league with any of them? This was their difficulty. 'Who are ye? and from whence come ye?' said Joshua, therefore, to the Gibeonites. They answered, 'From a very far country thy servants are come because of the name of the Lord thy God: for we have heard the fame of Him, and all that He did in Egypt, and all that He did to the two kings of the Amorites, that were beyond Jordan, to Sihon king of Heshbon, and to Og king of Bashan, which was at Ashtaroth. Wherefore our elders, and all the inhabitants of our country, spake to us, saying, Take victuals with you for the journey, and go to meet them, and say unto them, We are your servants: therefore now make ye a league with us. This our bread we took hot for our provision out of our houses on the day we came forth to go unto you; but now, behold, it is dry, and it is mouldy: and these bottles of wine which we filled were new; and, behold, they be rent: and these our garments and our shoes are become old by reason of the very long journey.' Vers. 9–13. It was a strange story, and almost as full of false-

---

[1] Deut. vii. 2, comp. Exod. xxiii. 32, xxxiv. 12.

hoods as of words.   As to the 'very far country,' Joshua might have asked, Where is it?   Eastward it could not be; for from the other side Jordan, in that direction, the Israelites had themselves come.   Westward it could not be; for but a few miles distant was the coast of the Mediterranean, or Great Sea.   Could it then be southward?   What nations resided in that direction, beyond the boundaries of the land of Canaan?   They might possibly have come from the north; for there, among the mountains, there were perhaps tribes and nations beyond the borders of the land which God had given to His people; and perhaps Joshua thought that their home was really there.   But he might have asked again, 'If you dwell at so great a distance, why are you so anxious? for we are come, not to molest you, but only to drive out the inhabitants of the country we are now in.' Joshua, however, seems not to have thought of this; and these Gibeonites, anxious only to save their lives, supposed that if they only induced the Israelites to make a league with them, they would certainly be spared, even though it would ultimately appear that they had acted falsely, and had spoken lies.

The injunction given to the Israelites not to make a covenant with the nations, did not extend to those nations that dwelt beyond the boundaries of Canaan;[1] and of this fact the Gibeonites had probably become aware.   Joshua might, then, supposing that their story was true, very innocently receive them into his service; and this he did, for 'the Israelites took of their victuals, and asked not counsel at the mouth of the Lord.   And Joshua made peace with them, and made a league with them, to let them live: and the princes of the congregation sware unto them.'

[1] Deut. xx. 10, 11: 'When thou comest nigh unto a city to fight against it, then proclaim peace unto it.   And it shall be, if it make thee an answer of peace, and open unto thee, then it shall be, that all the people that is found therein shall be tributaries unto thee, and they shall serve thee.'   There can be little doubt that these directions related, not to the cities within the boundaries of Canaan, but to those without them.   See our former remarks in chap. v., p. 80.

'They took of their victuals,' not, as some have supposed, in sign of friendship, or as a ratification of the treaty; nor yet, as others think, to taste them, in order to ascertain whether they were really old; but they took them in their hands, credulously believed their story, and looked closely at their provisions, instead of asking 'counsel at the mouth of the Lord.'

It is surprising how the usual foresight and sagacity of Joshua failed him here. His duty was, in a case like this, to have recourse to the Urim and Thummim of the high priest, and thereby to ascertain whether the account these strangers gave of themselves was true or not. And had he entertained any doubt respecting them, this he would certainly have done. But he and the elders of Israel were too ready to listen to their story; and ridiculous, and even absurd as it really was, gave to it at once their implicit credence. Though it is not well to cultivate a suspicious temper of mind, yet to be over-credulous is also dangerous. Too confident and trustful in the word of God we cannot be; but in the word of man, deceitful and cunning as he often is, we may be. We do not, it is true, like to be suspected of falsehood or of hypocrisy ourselves, and therefore we ought not, on slender grounds, to suspect others. But in dealing with perfect strangers, of whose character we are wholly ignorant, prudence would dictate that we should not give them our entire confidence hastily, but suspend our judgment for a while, until we have had sufficient time to form a correct one. Joshua might have said to the ambassadors, 'The account you give of yourselves seems plausible; but we cannot at once comply with your request, until we see whether or not you are inhabitants of the land.' But he did not wait even one day, but at once confided in their word.

His great error was, however, in not asking counsel of the Lord. It was his special privilege, as the leader of God's people, to take every matter of difficulty to the high priest, who, by the Urim and Thummim in his breastplate, could inquire of the Lord respecting it, and receive such an answer as would wholly solve it.[1] How many evils arise from a similar neglect! Too often do we fail to ask counsel of the Lord, and hence we fall into innumerable errors. If, in seasons of perplexity and doubt, when our way is hedged up, and the dark clouds of adversity are hanging over us, and we know not what course to adopt, or what path to pursue, we were to carry our difficulties to the throne of grace, and ask the wisdom which is profitable to direct, we should doubtless escape a host of difficulties. But, instead of this, we either form and act upon a hasty decision of our own, or we take the advice of erring mortals like ourselves; nay, there are some amongst us who, like Saul, seem disposed to seek counsel of those who profess to have a familiar spirit, like the witch of Endor, who put confidence in clairvoyants, and media, and other such foolery, rather than in the living God! 'If any of you lack wisdom, let him ask of God, that giveth to all men liberally, and upbraideth not, and it shall be given him,' is a promise applicable both to secular and to sacred things; and facts innumerable go to prove that those who are in the habit of carrying the perplexities of daily life directly to the Most High, and asking counsel at His mouth, are often—may we not say invariably?—led aright. Not miraculously, not by an audible voice from heaven, but by the finger of Providence and the silent teachings of the Holy Spirit, do those who ask counsel of the Lord in humility and in faith obtain the counsel they ask; and, taught of Him, guided in every step of life by Him, they avoid many errors into which others fall.

But to return to the narrative : Joshua granted the Gibeonites peace, and made a league with them, to let them live; and this covenant was ratified by the solemn oath of the princes of the

---

[1] See 1 Sam. xxviii. 6; Ezra ii. 63; Neh. vii. 65.

congregation, so that the ambassadors would return to Gibeon satisfied that they had fully succeeded in their enterprise.

Three days elapsed, and then the Israelites discovered that they had been deceived. It was scarcely possible that the truth of the matter could be hidden long, and perhaps the Gibeonites themselves were not desirous that it should; yet they were not the first to reveal it, for the Israelites came on the third day to their cities, Gibeon, and Chephirah, and Beeroth, and Kirjath-jearim, and then found that they belonged to the very people with whom they had made a league. The position of the first of these cities we have already pointed out. Chephirah was afterwards assigned to Benjamin, Josh. xviii. 26, and mention is made of it subsequent to the captivity.[1] 'It is now,' says Van de Velde, 'a ruin called Kefir, on the heights south of Wady Soleimon, about one hour east of Yâlo.'[2] Yâlo Dr Robinson regarded as the ancient Aijalon, and he observes, 'At Yâlo we were told of a ruin in the mountains, on the east, said not to be far off, called Kefir. It was, however, now too late for us to visit it from Yâlo; nor were we able afterwards to make an excursion to it from Jerusalem. But in the name Kefir it is impossible not to recognise the ancient Chephirah, a city of the Gibeonites, afterwards assigned to Benjamin, and after the captivity again inhabited by the returning exiles.'[3] It is about 7½ Roman miles west of Gibeon, and 15 south-west of Gilgal. Beeroth was identified by Dr Robinson with the modern el-Bîreh, a village 10 miles north of Jerusalem, on the road to Shechem (Nâbulus), and five miles north of Gibeon. 'The correspondence of the names,' says Robinson, 'is in itself sufficiently decisive. And further, according to Eusebius, Beeroth was seen by the traveller in passing from Jerusalem to Neapolis, at the seventh Roman mile. This road was the present camel-path

---

[1] Ezra ii. 25; Neh. vii. 29.   [2] 'Memoir,' p. 303.
[3] 'Researches,' vol. iii., p 146.

from Jerusalem to Ramleh, passing near el-Jib. And to this day the description of Eusebius holds true.'[1] It is 'remarkable,' observes Dr Stanley, 'as the first halting-place of caravans on the northern road from Jerusalem, and therefore, not improbably, the scene of the event to which its monastic tradition lays claim —the place where the "parents" of Jesus "sought Him among their kinsfolk and acquaintance; and when they found Him not, turned back again to Jerusalem."'[2] Kirjath-jearim, or 'the city of forests,' called also Kirjath-baal, or 'the city of the sanctuary,' is now represented by a village named Kuriet el-Enab, 'the city of grapes,' situated nine Roman miles from Jerusalem, on the way to Ramleh and Lydda.[3] It was a frontier city of Judah and Benjamin;[4] and at a later period was the place to which the ark of the covenant was brought from Beth-shemesh.[5]

Thus all the cities of the Gibeonites have been identified, and they all lay within a comparatively narrow circuit. The children of Israel did not destroy them, or even injure them, 'because the princes of the congregation had sworn unto them by the Lord God of Israel.' But were they then bound to stand by a treaty which they had entered into under false impressions? This is a question of considerable importance, and has perplexed commentators not a little. Some have supposed that legally they were under no obligation to keep the treaty, inasmuch as it was made with the understanding that the Gibeonites did not belong to the tribes of Canaan; whilst others think that, inasmuch as no proviso was introduced into the treaty, to the effect that it should be binding only if the story of the Gibeonites was found true, the Israelites could not violate it without gross injustice. The former is undoubtedly the more correct view of the case; for though there was no such proviso in the exact terms of the

---

[1] 'Researches,' vol. i., p. 452.   [2] 'Sinai and Palestine,' p. 211.

[3] Robinson, vol. ii., p. 11.   [4] Josh. xviii. 14; Judg. xviii. 12.

[5] 1 Sam. vi. 21.

treaty, yet such was the representation of the Gibeonites, and *on that representation* the treaty was framed. The Israelites might, therefore, have said, 'We did indeed form a league with you, and promise you, with an oath, that we would not injure you; but it was, as you yourselves must acknowledge, under the false impression that you came from a distance. We are not, then, bound to fulfil our promise, for we have no authority to make peace with any of the nations of Canaan; and you, as well as the rest, must fall before the avenging sword.'

At the same time, there is something so solemn in the nature of an oath, that even when 'a man sweareth to his own hurt' he ought not to change, unless, by standing to his word, he injures not himself only, but society at large. Perhaps it will be said that this was just a case of that kind, and that the princes of the congregation, by honouring their treaty, were dishonouring their own people, and placing them in great jeopardy. Hence 'all the congregation murmured against the princes,' for they doubtless felt afraid that the Gibeonites would become a plague to them, or that some such calamity would occur, as happened when Achan took of the spoils in disobedience to God's command. Very different was the murmuring of the Israelites, on this occasion, from the murmurings of their ancestors against Moses and against God. These murmurings were founded on the fact that Joshua and the princes had spared a nation which the divine mandate required them to destroy; the earlier murmurings were those of an ungrateful and discontented race, whom it was almost impossible to please. For *these* murmurings, then, the Israelites are not to be condemned; yet the princes said in reply, 'We have sworn unto them by the Lord God of Israel: now, therefore, we may not touch them;' and, inasmuch as they felt their oath so sacred, neither in this respect are the *princes* to be condemned. They did wrong in giving credence to the story of the Gibeonites without asking counsel of the Lord; and they

i

did wrong in making a league with them, and ratifying that
league by swearing to them in the name of the Lord Jehovah.
But as they conscientiously believed that their oath was binding
on them, now that it was made, they did right in observing it;
and their doing so was not, as Calvin affirms, a fresh violation
of the will of God, for even an oath imprudently taken cannot be
violated without sin, if the conscience of a man tells him that he
ought to keep it; and they were afraid that, if they did disregard
their oath, the divine wrath would fall upon them for their sin.[1]

But what, then, could be done? Could the Gibeonites, now
that their falsehood was found out, be permitted to live among
the Israelites in perfect freedom, and to retain possession of
their lands and cities? No. They had sinned, and their sins
deserved punishment, as both the people felt and the princes
themselves acknowledged. The latter, therefore, said, 'Let them
live; and let them be hewers of wood, and drawers of water, unto
all the congregation:' and this being agreed to, the Gibeonites,
or their ambassadors, were summoned into Joshua's presence to
hear their doom. They came, and with mingled feelings of
satisfaction at the thought that they had saved their lives,
yet perhaps of fear, if not of terror, lest their fate should be
even worse than death itself, they stood before the illustrious
commander of the Israelites. With becoming dignity he addresses them, and says, ' Wherefore have ye beguiled us, saying,
We are very far from you; when ye dwell among us? Now
therefore ye are cursed; and there shall none of you be freed
from being bondmen, and hewers of wood, and drawers of water,
for the house of my God.' They listen, and this is their reply:
' Because it was certainly told thy servants, how that the Lord
thy God commanded His servant Moses to give you all the land,
and to destroy all the inhabitants of the land from before you,

---

[1] See Calvin's 'Commentary' *in loco*, where this question is discussed at
length; and compare the remarks of Keil.

therefore we were sore afraid of our lives because of you, and have done this thing. And now, behold, we are in thine hand: as it seemeth good and right unto thee to do unto us, do.'

We have already seen how intelligence of the conquests gained by the Israelites had spread through the land of Canaan; and this intelligence having reached the ears of the Gibeonites, they were, and well might be, afraid of their lives. It was for their lives that they devised this stratagem: for all that a man hath will he give for his life. Liberty is precious, and men will sometimes risk their lives to secure it, and perish in the attempt; but give a man, or give a people, the choice between bondage and death, and it is all but certain that the former will be preferred. The love of life is instinctive in us all; and only when the hope of another and a happier life is implanted in the breast, are we disposed to surrender it without a struggle. No wonder, then, that the Gibeonites, ignorant as they were of the higher principles of morality, should have recourse to stratagem and falsehood for the security of their lives. They were willing, however, to submit to whatever task might be imposed on them; and they became henceforth hewers of wood and drawers of water for the congregation, and for the altar of the Lord.

Hewers of wood and drawers of water are both very useful servants in the East; but the work is often laborious, and is generally assigned to the lowest class of menials. The hewers of wood have to fetch it from the forest, and then to cut it up into pieces suitable for burning. The drawers of water have to go to the rivers or to the wells outside the town, and bring it in vessels on their heads, or in prepared goat-skins on their backs, or on the backs of camels or of asses. 'In a time of public calamity,' says Dr Kitto, 'the water-carriers are the last to discontinue this; and their doing so is a sure indication that the distress has become intense and imminent, and is, indeed, a great calamity in itself. The writer remembers that, when this happened in the time when a severe plague was raging, Europeans, who were quite alive to the importance of maintaining a strict quarantine in their own houses, were, nevertheless, obliged to go out from the town to fetch water for themselves from a distant river.' To have abundance of coal with which to supply our fires, instead of having to hew wood for the purpose, is a great advantage; and to have water conveyed by pipes through our streets and into our houses, is one of the benefits of modern civilisation, the value of which, even as a saving of labour only, it is impossible to over-estimate; whilst to see drinking fountains at every few yards' distance, as we now do in some of our populous towns and cities, is a sight most refreshing to the eye, and a blessing for which many a thirsty one will give thanks.

It is a mistake, however, to suppose that the Gibeonites were made domestic slaves to the Israelites, and thence to derive an argument in favour of such slavery as existed a few years ago in some of our British colonies, or as now exists in the Southern States of America, and elsewhere. No! though, as descendants of Canaan, the son of Ham, they were under the curse, and though they had forfeited, by their crimes, their liberties and even their lives, yet they were not made slaves to the Israelites, as the Israelites had been slaves to the Egyptians, but were appointed to relieve the congregation in the work of hewing wood and drawing water for the service of the sanctuary. Somewhat onerous would this service be, during the great festivals of the nation especially; but the Gibeonites appear to have discharged their task with considerable fidelity: and it is a remarkable fact, that at Gibeon, which became one of the Levitical cities, the tabernacle was set up for many years under the reigns of David and Solomon, the ark of the covenant being at Jerusalem; for David left 'Zadok the priest, and his brethren the priests, before the tabernacle of the Lord, in the high place that was at Gibeon, to offer burnt-offerings unto the Lord upon the altar of the burnt-offering continually morning and evening, and to do according to all that is written in the law of the LORD, which he commanded in Israel.'[1] It was here that Joab laid hold on the horns of the altar in the tabernacle, and at Solomon's command was slain;[2] and it was here that, shortly after, Solomon went up to sacrifice—for it was the great high place—a thousand burnt-offerings upon the altar before the Lord, and that the Lord appeared to him in a dream by night, and said, 'Ask what I shall give thee,' and, at Solomon's request, gave him a wise and understanding heart.[3] Dr Stanley is of opinion that 'the great high place' above mentioned, on which the tabernacle stood, was 'the lofty height of Nebi-Samuel, towering immediately over the town El-Jib;' and if the fact that this height is more than a mile from El-Jib, is not a valid objection to this view, we may consider it as at least highly probable. And how imposing, in that case, must have been the scenes here witnessed! From the city itself, which lay always where its modern representative lies now, on the lower eminence, the Gibeonites 'hewed the wood' of the adjacent valley, and 'drew the water' from the springs and tanks with which its immediate neighbourhood abounds, and carried them up to the sacred tent; and there attended the 'altar of the Lord,' which, from its proud elevation, overlooked the wide domain of Israel.[4]

That the Israelites were bound to observe their engagement with the Gibeonites, appears from the fact that there was famine in the days of David three years, year after year, and that when David inquired of the Lord, the Lord answered and said, 'It is for Saul, and for his bloody house, because he slew the Gibeonites.' We have no account of Saul's doing this in the history of his reign; but it appears that, in his zeal for the children of Israel, and perhaps with a view of taking possession of the landed pro-

---

[1] 1 Chron. xvi. 39, 40, and see 2 Chron. i. 3, 4.   [2] 1 Kings ii. 28.
[3] 1 Kings iii 5–13.   [4] 'Sinai and Palestine,' p. 214.

perty of the Gibeonites, he slew a considerable number of them, and devised a general massacre of the rest. It was a cruel, unjust, and daring act, and, as yet, it had not been avenged upon his house. David, therefore, called the Gibeonites, and said, 'What shall I do for you? and wherewith shall I make the atonement, that ye may bless the inheritance of the Lord?' They might have accepted a fine of the house of Saul, but they had a right to demand blood for blood; and their request was, that seven of Saul's sons should be delivered up to them to be slain; and David said, 'I will give them.' It is not improbable that these persons had participated in their father's crime, for, according to the Mosaic law, the children were not to be put to death for their father's sin; and from the expression, 'Saul and his bloody house,' we should infer that his family was a wicked one, and deserved to die. Jonathan, the best of them, and David's friend, had been already slain, and for his sake David spared Mephibosheth his son; but the two sons of Aiah, whom she bare unto Saul, and the five sons of Michal the daughter of Saul, and therefore Saul's grandsons, he delivered into the hands of the Gibeonites, who first slew them, and then hanged them in Gibeah of Saul, where they remained until the drought ceased, and 'water dropped upon them out of heaven.'[1] The Gibeonites, however, were no doubt reprehensible in allowing the bodies to hang so long, as the sight of them would be highly exasperating to the Israelites. Yet no one interfered, save one lone woman; and all that she could do was to sit down upon the rock, on which she had spread a piece of sackcloth, and there protect the bodies from the birds of the air by day, and the beasts of the field by night. Yes, such was the noble conduct of Rizpah, the daughter of Aiah, and the mother of two of the slain; and when David heard of it he had the bodies taken down, and, together with the bones of Saul and Jonathan his son, buried in Zelah, in

[1] 2 Sam. xxi. 1–10.

the country of Benjamin.[1] How deep and tender is a mother's love! Who does not admire this remarkable display of it? and who can help sympathizing with the sorrowing Rizpah, as she sits and watches these corpses dangling in the air? Poor woman! and could *she* defend them from the beasts of the field? She thought she could, and at least she was resolved to try.

Of the Gibeonites at a later period we know but little. One of David's mighty men, Ismaiah, was a Gibeonite; so also was Melatiah, who assisted Nehemiah in repairing the wall of Jerusalem after the captivity: so that the race appears to have been perpetuated for at least several centuries, and did not become extinct even during the captivity in Babylon.

Not without its lessons is this remarkable episode; and to some of these we have adverted in the preceding pages. The only one we would further mention is, that if, to save their lives, the Gibeonites would submit to any servitude, and stoop to the meanest and most abject labour, we surely ought to be willing to accept any conditions which God may impose, in order that we may save our souls from death;—to be willing to sacrifice property, ease, rank, honour, or whatever else we may possess, and to become 'hewers of wood' or 'drawers of water' in the Church of Christ, if such is the position assigned us, counting it a privilege to have any place, however humble, in His sanctuary, if we may but hope to be admitted hereafter to a higher sphere. And many whose lot in this life is comparatively mean, who are now little better, to all appearance, than menials in the Church, will doubtless, if they are faithful, and if they perform their work with a cheerful and ready mind, be one day kings and priests unto God and the Father, and be raised to the noble service of the temple of the skies.

[1] 2 Sam. xxi. 10-13.

VALLEY OF AJALON.

CHAPTER IX.

THE DEFEAT OF THE FIVE KINGS.

JOSHUA had returned to Gilgal, leaving the Gibeonites in quiet possession of their cities, until a fitting opportunity should occur to employ them in the services they were hereafter to fulfil, when, one day, their ambassadors again stood before him, and, with deep anxiety, said, 'Slack not thy hand from thy servants; come up to us quickly, and save us, and help us: for all the kings of the Amorites, that dwell in the mountains, are gathered together against us'—chap. x. 6.

And such was, in fact, the case. Adoni-zedek, the king of Jerusalem, having heard that Joshua had conquered Ai, and

that the Gibeonites had made peace with the invaders of the
land, was greatly alarmed; for Gibeon was a large city, and its
inhabitants were renowned as mighty men. He probably, and
very naturally, thought that, if a royal city like Gibeon, whose
people, he knew, were brave and courageous, feared so much the
armies of the Israelites as to sue for a dishonourable peace,
there would be little probability of his being able to defend
himself against so formidable an enemy; and that, therefore,
the sooner he entered upon an offensive movement the better.
But what could he do? He had not courage to go and offer
battle, in the first instance, to the Israelites themselves; but he
might attack the Gibeonites, who, as he thought, had basely
and meanly cringed at the feet of Joshua, and, by becoming his
allies, had shut themselves out from the brotherhood of the
surrounding tribes. Yet, even on this expedition, he was afraid
to enter alone; and he therefore 'sent unto Hoham king of
Hebron, and unto Piram king of Jarmuth, and unto Japhia king
of Lachish, and unto Debir king of Eglon, saying, Come up
unto me, and help me, that we may smite Gibeon: for it hath
made peace with Joshua, and with the children of Israel.'

Canaan, as we have already seen, was, at this time, divided
into a number of petty states, each one governed by its own independent king. Five of these are here mentioned. Adoni-zedec,
whose name signifies, lord of righteousness (equivalent to Melchi-
zedec, king of righteousness[1]), was the king of the Jebusites,
whose capital was Jerusalem, and whose kings were so called just
as the kings of Egypt were called Pharaohs.[2] The most ancient
name of Jerusalem was Salem, or Shalem[3] (שָׁלֵם), which signifies
peace; but when it came into the possession of the Jebusites, it
was called Jebus, or Jebusi,[4]—that, probably, being the name of
the third son of Canaan.[5] On the import and derivation of the

[1] Gen. xiv. 18. [2] Comp. Judges i. 5. [3] Gen. xiv. 18; Ps. lxxvi. 2.
[4] Judges xix. 10, 11. [5] Gen. x 16.

name Jerusalem, there is a diversity of opinion : Gesenius, who is followed by many, says it signifies 'the foundation,' or 'the house of peace;' Hitzig, 'the district or territory of Salem.' But Hengstenberg maintains that it is a compound of ירוש, possession, and שלם, peaceful, and signifies, therefore, 'the peaceful possession;'[1] and it appears to have received this name even before the days of Joshua. Its situation, says Stanley, 'is in several respects singular amongst the cities of Palestine. Its elevation is remarkable, occasioned, not from its being on the summit of one of the numerous hills of Judea, like most of the towns and villages, but because it is on the edge of one of the highest table-lands of the country. Hebron, indeed, is higher still, by some hundred feet; and from the south, accordingly, the approach to Jerusalem is by a slight descent. But from every other side the ascent is perpetual; and, to the traveller approaching Jerusalem from the west or east, it must always have presented the appearance, beyond any other capital of the then known world—we may add, beyond any important city that has ever existed on the earth—of a mountain city; breathing, as compared with the sultry plains of the Jordan, or of the coast, a mountain air; enthroned, as compared with Jericho or Damascus, Gazer or Tyre, on a mountain fastness.'[2] Its distance from Gibeon was rather more than five Roman miles.

HEBRON, of which Hoham was the king, was a celebrated city in the history of the patriarchs, and, previous to its capture by the Israelites, was called Kirjath-arba, or the city of Arba, the father of the Anakim.[3] Like the modern city, *el-Khulil—i.e.*, 'the friend,' so called from Abraham, the friend of God—it was situated in a deep valley, twenty-two Roman miles south of Jerusalem, which, in the present day, abounds with vineyards, the grapes of which are the finest in Palestine. JARMUTH, where

---

[1] Hengstenberg on the Psalms, vol. ii., p. 436; and Keil on Joshua. p. 245.
[2] 'Sinai and Palestine,' p. 168.   [3] Josh. xiv. 15, xv. 13.

Piram reigned, was situated in the lowland country, on the road between Jerusalem and Eleutheropolis, and is now represented by a village called Yarnûk. LACHISH, the capital of Japhia's territory, is supposed by many, though Robinson doubts it, to have been situated on a site now called Um-Lakis, between Gaza and Beit-Jibrin, thirty-eight Roman miles distant from Jerusalem. And EGLON is no doubt identical with Aiglan, a heap of ruins not far distant from Lachish.

These five kings dwelt, then, within a comparatively small circle; and hence Adoni-zedec would be able to communicate with Hoham, Piram, Japhia, and Debir in the course of a few hours. And this was his request: ' Come up with your forces, and help me to take vengeance on the Gibeonites, who have made peace with our enemies, the invaders of the land.' They immediately complied; and from some lofty eminence might have been seen the armies of these kings gathering together to a place of rendezvous, for the purpose of preparing for a general attack upon their former friends. It was a melancholy display of envy, malice, and revenge; yet, heathens as they were, we are not surprised that they should engage in such an enterprise : nor is their conduct without its parallels in the history of later times. And now, what could the Gibeonites do but have recourse to Joshua? They had a claim on his protection. They had a right to expect his immediate succour. Nor do they ask for it in vain. Generous and noble-minded as he was, he could not see these Gibeonites attacked, and make no attempt to defend them. At once, and without delay, he summoned his army; and, by a forced march from Gilgal 'all night,' arrived ' suddenly' on the spot, ere the allied forces had time to commence their attack upon the city. The rapidity of his movements was a proof of his skilful generalship. To delay, at such a moment, might have been fatal to his purpose; and therefore, not trusting to the superiority of his forces. nor yet to any miraculous aid from heaven, Joshua made haste and rushed to the rescue of the Gibeonites with the utmost speed.

But was he indeed under any obligation to assist them? Which of us would not have thought Joshua had a good pretence for his forbearance, and have said, 'You have broken your league with me: why do ye expect help from him whom ye have deceived? All that we promised you was a sufferance to live; enjoy what we promised, we will not take your life from you. Hath your faithfulness deserved to expect more than our covenant? We never promised to hazard our lives for you; to give you life with the loss of our own.' But that good man durst not construe his own covenant to such an advantage. He knew little difference between killing with his own sword and the sword of an Amorite: whosoever should give the blow, the murder would be his. Even permission in those things we may remedy makes us no less actors than consent: some men kill as much by looking on, as others by smiting. We are guilty of all the evil we might have hindered.[1]

It is probable, however, that Joshua felt this enterprise to be a perilous one, and that he set out with no little anxiety respecting the result. He took with him ' all the people of war, and all the mighty men of valour.' Not knowing what forces the allied kings had mustered, or what was the military character of their armies, he would be unable to judge of his ability to conquer them. But it was in no arm of flesh that he relied. Whilst he employed such means as were at his command, he placed not his confidence in them alone, but trusted, as he had ever done, on the arm of God. And if, for a moment, he felt any fear, that fear was soon dispelled by the repetition of the divine word, 'Fear them not;' and by the promise which accompanied it, ' I have delivered them into thine hand; there shall not a man of them stand before thee.' It was a seasonable and reanimating

---

[1] Bishop Hall's 'Contemplations,' Book ix. 1.

word; and as he heard it the courage of our hero would be renewed, and he would rush to the conflict with the certainty of complete success.

No ordinary commander, however skilful, can be quite sure of the victory. His forces may be numerous, and his soldiers brave; the foes he has to encounter in the field may have already been disheartened by losses and defeats, and he may appear to possess every advantage requisite for a successful battle; yet such are the chances of war, that some minute circumstance or other, wholly unforeseen, may turn the tide against him in a moment, and he may be compelled to fly from before the face of his enemy. But Joshua's victory was already certain; and so, also, is the victory of every soldier of the cross: for God has said to him likewise, 'Fear not,' and has given him the promise of a glorious triumph, conditioned only on his fidelity to the cause he has espoused.

The morning dawns, and finds Joshua and his army near to Gibeon, whilst right before him are the forces of the allied kings. Little, perhaps, did those kings expect that the Gibeonites would obtain such succour, or they would not have ventured on their foolish expedition; and now they would doubtless have returned if possible; but their doom was sealed, and nothing remained for them but to defend themselves as best they could. How feeble was their defence! How terrible was their overthrow! 'The Lord discomfited them before Israel, and slew them with a great slaughter at Gibeon, and chased them along the way that goeth up to Beth-horon, and smote them to Azekah, and unto Makkedah.' 'The LORD discomfited them,' and yet He used the sword of Joshua for the purpose; for, as Calvin observes, 'Joshua did not abuse the divine promise by making it an excuse for sluggishness, but felt the more vehemently influenced after he was assured of a happy issue. Many, while they ostentatiously express their faith, become lazy and slothful from perverse

security. Joshua hears that victory is at hand, and, that he
may gain it, runs swiftly to the battle. For he knew that the
happy issue was revealed, not for the purpose of slackening his
pace or making him more remiss, but of making him exert
himself with greater zeal. Hence it was that he took the
enemy by surprise.'

There is no reason to suppose, as some have done, that in
the tenth verse other means of discomfiture, not particularly
described, are alluded to, as lightning or thunder of a very
terrible kind. An attack was, doubtless, made by Joshua, and
that attack was signally successful; but its success depended on
the special aid afforded by the Lord Jehovah, who, doubtless,
animated Joshua's army with courage, whilst their enemies were
seized with fear. Hence it is said, 'the Lord discomfited
them;' for all the glory of the victory belonged to Him, and the
Israelites were but instruments in His hand, which He could
as well, had it pleased Him, have done without.

Ten miles distant from Gibeon was the higher Beth-horon—
'the house of the cavern'—now Beit 'Ur el-Foka, which was
separated from the lower Beth-horon by a pass, called both the
ascent and descent of Beth-horon, leading from the region of
Gibeon (el-Jib) down to the western plain.[1] Dr Robinson
describes the ascent as very rocky and rough; and says, that
'the rock has been cut away in many places, and the path
formed into steps, showing that this is an ancient road.'[2]
Down this path Joshua chased the allied armies, and smote
them until they reached Azekah and Makkedah. According
to 1 Sam. xvii. 1, Azekah was near to Shochoh (Shurveikeh);
and between these two places was Ephes-dammin, which Van
de Velde identifies with a ruined city called Khirbit Damûn,
on the route from Beit-Jibrin to Jerusalem. A mile and

---

[1] Comp. Josh. xviii. 13. 14; 1 Macc. iii. 16, 24.

[2] Researches, vol. iii., p. 250-1.

a half north of Damûn, he found a village on a hill-top
called Ahbek; and this he identifies as Azekah, its position
answering exactly with that where the Onomasticon places
Azekah, and corresponding perfectly with the scriptural requirements.[1] Makkedah is probably identical with Summeil, a considerable village on an elevation in the plain, about two hours
and a half north-west of Beit-Jibrin, where Van de Velde was
assured that there was a large cavern, though he himself was
unable to visit it.

Observe the progress of the battle. It began at Gibeon,
and, at the first onslaught, the allied armies were smitten before
the Israelites, when, seized with terror, they fled precipitately
towards Beth-horon-the-upper. Many of them fell by the sword,
but the rest, gaining upon their pursuers, rushed madly down
the pass towards Beth-horon-the-lower. And now a fearful
storm overtook them; for the Lord cast down great stones
from heaven upon them, which continued to fall until the five
kings themselves, with a few others, reached Azekah and Makkedah, in a cave in which latter place those kings sought refuge,
both from the pitiless storm and from the sword of Joshua.
To the allied kings and their armies it was a terrible day. Many
were slain by the hand of the Israelites, but still more by the
hailstones which fell upon them from heaven; yet these did no
injury to their pursuers, nor does it appear that Joshua lost in
the affray a single man.

Grotius, Calmet, and other commentators, are of opinion that
actual hail could hardly have killed so many men, and, therefore,
suppose that they were real stones that fell upon these armies
and destroyed them. Nor is the supposition beyond probability,
as, not only have single stones fallen from heaven at different
periods and in different countries; but showers of stones in
considerable quantities. Many remarkable phenomena of this

---

[1] 'Memoir,' p. 290.

kind are well authenticated; and one especially, which occurred
at Crema, on the shores of the Adda, is described, says Humboldt, 'with especial vivacity, but unfortunately in a rhetorical and
vague manner, by the celebrated Peterus Martyr, of Anghicra.'
'On the plain of Crema, where never before was seen a stone
the size of an egg, there fell pieces of rock of enormous dimensions and of immense weight. It is said that ten of these were
found weighing a hundred pounds each. Birds, sheep, and even
fish, were killed.' A fall of stones occurred at Benares, in Hin-
dostan, on the 13th of December 1798; another at Aigle on the
26th of April 1803; and another at Braunau on the 14th of
July 1847, when the stones were so hot that after six hours they
could not be touched without causing a burn.[1] Some have
supposed that such aerolites are concretions formed in the
atmosphere; others, that they are projected from volcanoes in
the moon, which, coming within the sphere of the earth's attrac-
tion, necessarily fall upon it. But the latter view cannot be
correct, as these aerolites do not consist of lava, but of iron,
nickel, copper, zinc, carbon, and several other elements. Is
there, then, in the regions of space, an inexhaustible number of
bodies, too small to be observed, moving round the sun, the
planets, and even the satellites of the planets, which occasionally
come in contact with our atmosphere, and are drawn with considerable velocity to the earth? Such is the most recent view
entertained by scientific men,[2] and hence the destruction of the
Amorites might have been effected by a shower of real stones
from heaven. Still, these stones are said, in verse 11, to have
been hail-stones, אַבְנֵי הַבָּרָד, Sept. λίθους χαλάζης, and such they
are called by Josephus, and nearly all the commentators. Hail-

---

[1] See Humboldt's Cosmos, vol. iv., p. 587; Dr Clarke's Commentary; and
the Pictorial Bible, on Joshua x., where other instances of the kind are
mentioned.

[2] See Humboldt's Cosmos, vol. i., p. 117. Bohn.

storms are often exceedingly violent, and instances are on record of hail-stones having fallen as large as pigeons' or even hens' eggs. 'The masses and blocks of ice which have not unfrequently fallen,' says Mrs Somerville, 'appear to have been formed of hail-stones of large size frozen together;' and, 'when large, true hail is pear-shaped, and consists of a nucleus of snow coated with ice, and sometimes of alternate layers of snow and ice.' Such, we doubt not, was the nature of the storm which fell upon the fugitives; and though it did not transcend the laws of nature, yet, like the hail of Egypt, it was brought about by the miraculous providence of God, for it fell with tremendous violence on the Amorites, whilst to the Israelites it did no harm. The power of the Lord Jehovah is resistless. Who can thunder with a voice like His? Who can stand before His cold? 'The Lord also thundered in the heavens, and the Highest gave His voice; hail-stones and coals of fire. Yea, He sent out His arrows, and scattered them; and He shot out lightnings, and discomfited them.'[1] Thus did He discomfit the five kings and their armies; and thus, at a later period, did He discomfit the Philistines: nor is He ever at a loss for means whereby to deliver His own people, and to destroy the foes by whom they are assailed.[2]

In a celebrated battle fought by the Emperor Theodosius, in A.D. 394, a violent tempest, such as is often felt among the Alps, suddenly arose from the east, which blew a cloud of dust into the faces of the enemy, disordered their ranks, wrested their weapons from their hands, and diverted or repelled their inef-

[1] Ps. xviii. 13, 14.

[2] Of a hail-storm and its effects, which occurred at Constantinople in the summer of 1831, a most graphic account is quoted by Dr Kitto in the Pictorial Bible, from Commodore Porter, who says that large balls of ice fell from the heavens, which broke the tiles on the houses, shattered the windows, desolated the vineyards, killed two boatmen and wounded others, and that several pieces of ice weighed three-quarters of a pound, and some a pound each. See also Kitto's 'Daily Readings,' vol. ii., p. 293; and Bush on Joshua, *in loco*.

k

fectual javelins, whilst the army of Theodosius was sheltered by their position from the impetuosity of the wind. The event was looked upon as a special interference of Divine Providence on the Emperor's behalf; it was celebrated in verse by the poet Claudian, and Ambrose compared it to the miraculous victories of Moses and of Joshua. That the hand of God was in that storm we do not doubt, but we should by no means be disposed to attribute it to any very special agency of Providence; nor can we think, for a moment, of placing it in the same category as the storm which destroyed the enemies of the Israelites. Far more evidently providential was the storm which shattered many of the ships of the Spanish Armada as they approached the shores of Britain; but neither was that event miraculous, but simply the employment of the ordinary laws of nature to defeat an object which, had it been successful, would have changed perhaps the destinies of Europe and of the world. All nature is under God's control, and, either by a temporary suspension of those laws, or by a special guidance and direction of them, He can render them tributary to His own extraordinary purposes, whenever He has such purposes to fulfil.

But we must resume the narrative, for it records an event far more extraordinary than the hail-storm, and one which, assuming its literality, transcended every law of nature with which we are acquainted, even after all the discoveries that modern science has opened to our view. 'Then spake Joshua to the Lord, in the day when the Lord delivered up the Amorites before the children of Israel, and he said in the sight of Israel, Sun, stand thou still upon Gibeon; and thou, Moon, in the valley of Ajalon. And the sun stood still, and the moon stayed, until the people had avenged themselves upon their enemies. Is not this written in the book of Jasher? So the sun stood still in the midst of heaven, and hasted not to go down about a whole day. And there was no day like that before it or after it, that the

Lord hearkened unto the voice of a man: for the Lord fought for Israel. And Joshua returned, and all Israel with him, unto the camp to Gilgal,'—vers. 12–15.

Now, is this the record of an actual fact? or is it a poetical adornment of the narrative of the battle, designed to celebrate the greatness of Joshua? So long as the Ptolemaic system of astronomy, which represented the earth as the centre of our system, and the sun and all the planets as revolving round it, held sway, no doubt was entertained on this subject; but it was believed that the sun and moon did actually stand still, as the text taken literally declares, and this passage in sacred history was for a long time one of the grand stumbling-blocks in the way of the reception of the Copernican system, which is now universally admitted to be the true one. But in the light of the modern astronomy, the difficulties that present themselves are neither few nor small; and hence the whole subject demands the most careful consideration.

Now, it is expressly stated in the text, that the account of the miracle is 'written in the book of Jasher;' and we have first, therefore, to inquire into the character of this book, and whether it was a book of authentic history. We know, however, but little about it; for it is mentioned but in one other place in the Scriptures, viz., 2 Sam. i. 18: 'Also he bade them teach the children of Judah the use of the bow: behold, it is written in the book of Jasher.' But, from its title—Sepher Hayyashar, סֵפֶר הַיָּשָׁר, which, according to the best authorities, signifies ' the Book of the Just'—it was, ' in all probability, a collection of odes in honour of theocratic heroes, to which fresh contributions were made at different times;' so that it may have existed prior to the days of Joshua, and may have contained songs in honour of the patriarchs and of Moses, to which this song, if song it may be called, was added in honour of Joshua; and, at a later period, the elegy of David on the death

of Jonathan. Josephus makes no mention of the book of Jasher;
but he is supposed, by some, to allude to it, where he appeals to
certain 'books laid up in the temple' for confirmation of the
fact, that 'the day was lengthened at this time longer than
ordinary.'[1]

Is, then, the whole of the passage—verses 12 to 15—a quotation from this book? or does the quotation end with the words,
' Is not this written in the book of Jasher?' The latter view is
maintained by most authorities; but Keil advocates the former,
especially on the ground that verse 15 seems otherwise out of
place; for, that Joshua returned into the camp to Gilgal prior
to the slaughter of the five kings at Makkedah, cannot be supposed.[2] But, whichever view is the correct one, the question
necessarily arises, Does the passage thus quoted record a simple
historical truth? or did the writer merely intend to express, in
highly imaginative terms, the fact that Joshua uttered the wish
that the day might not end until the defeat of the enemy was
complete? Certainly the *entire passage* is not poetical. All that
can be considered poetry is the following :—

' Sun, stand thou still upon Gibeon ;
And thou, Moon, in the valley of Ajalon.
And the sun stood still,
And the moon stayed,
Until the people had avenged themselves upon their enemies.

What follows is pure prose, like the termination of the song

---

[1] Antiq , vol. i., p. 17. The views of the Talmudists and others respecting
the book of Jasher, will be found in Smith's Dictionary of the Bible, Art.
' Jasher ;' and in Horne's Introduction, vol. iv., p. 741, etc., eleventh edit., a
minute account is given of a spurious book, called the book of Jasher, an English edition of which was printed at Bristol in the year 1829. Of Dr Donaldson's
' Book of Jasher,' which is a mere compilation of its author's, to which he was
pleased to give that title, nothing need be said, except that it attracted far more
attention than it deserved.

[2] The verse is arbitrarily omitted by the LXX.; others would fain alter
the text.

of Moses—Exod. xv. 19; and, according to some critics, may be thus rendered: 'Is it not written in the Sephar Haiashar? So the sun stood still midway in the heavens, and tarried to go down, as if he had tarried the entire day.' There must, then, have been some ground for the insertion of the passage into the book of Joshua, and, indeed, for the origin of the passage itself. What was that ground? an ordinary event, or a miraculous one? That the sun and moon literally stood still, as the early fathers of the Church, and even many later ones maintained, cannot be supposed; but Joshua, who knew nothing of the modern system of astronomy, spoke after the manner of men, and indeed after the manner in which we ourselves speak to this day. Had he spoken otherwise, he would not have been understood; for it was, no doubt, the universal belief, at that time, that the apparent motion of the sun is a real one—that it literally performs a journey round the earth in four-and-twenty hours. But was the earth, by whose diurnal motion on its axis the phenomena of day and night are really caused, arrested in its course? and was it by this means that the light of the sun continued to shine upon the field of battle? Such is the opinion of not a few; and one popular commentator, Dr A. Clarke, maintains that the sun's rotation on its own axis is in part the cause of the daily revolution of the earth, that Joshua said to the sun, 'Be silent, restrain thy influence,' that the sun ceased to revolve round its axis, and that, therefore, the earth did the same! Whether such an explanation of the case will satisfy any inquiring mind, we know not; it certainly does not satisfy ours. We believe that, were the earth's diurnal motion to be stopped, even for a moment, the utmost confusion would ensue upon its surface; whilst, at the same time, the whole of the planetary system would be thrown into disorder. Doubtless the power of God could prevent this if He chose. 'We are not even perplexed,' says Keil, 'by the difficulty that, if the earth was thus suddenly stopped in its rotation upon its axis, all the work of men's hands which existed anywhere upon its surface would be destroyed, and the earth itself, with its satellite the moon, would be thrown out of its orbit; for we know that the almighty hand of God, which not only first created the stars, and so arranged them that they move with unvaried regularity in their orbits, but which continues to move, preserve, and govern all things in heaven and on earth, would not be too weak to ward off any such disastrous consequences.' But in this case how stupendous a miracle it must have been! All the miracles of Moses were as nothing in comparison with it. Before it, the plagues of Egypt, the passage of the Red Sea, and the drying up of the Jordan, sink into the shade. And yet, whilst these miracles are repeatedly referred to in subsequent portions of the sacred Scriptures, not the slightest allusion is anywhere made to this, either in the Old Testament or the New.[1] Besides which, can we suppose it probable that, for an end so inadequate as the routing of an army already conquered, God would in such a way interfere with the general laws by which the universe is sustained? Is He so lavish of miracles as this supposes? Have not miracles, when wrought at all, been wrought for some grand and lasting purpose?

These objections apply, though with considerably less force, to another conjecture—that the sun's course was retarded by means of refraction, or that its disc appeared above the horizon long after it had actually set. 'We must explain the miracle thus,' says Peyrerius, as quoted by Keil: 'when the sun had already set, without any change in the celestial and natural order of things, the light of the sun, but not the sun itself, by a very great miracle, continued in the atmosphere, or in the region

---

[1] The miracle is mentioned by an Apocryphal writer, Jesus the son of Sirach, xlvi. 4; but the passages from the Old Testament which have been adduced as favouring it—Isa. xxviii. 21; Hab. iii. 11; Ps. xviii.— do no such thing, though the first does refer both to the battle and the victory. See the 'Journal of Sacred Literature,' October 1850, p. 466, etc.

of vapour which was in the midst of the sky and the air, above the city of Gibeon. The sunshine, however, fell upon the city of the Gibeonites in such a way, that the reflected rays lighted up the neighbouring valleys on all sides, and thus prevented the Amorites, who were routed and flying, from escaping the pursuit of Joshua, which, in fact, was the design of the miracle.' This is the explanation, variously modified, of Grotius, Jahn, Benj, Spinoza, Bush, Bishop Gleig, and others; and Gleig renders the words of Joshua, 'Solar light, remain thou upon Gibeon; and be thou, moon, stayed, or supported over the valley of Ajalon.' 'To the apprehension of the Israelites,' says Dr Kitto, 'this would have all the effect of staying the career of the sun, and to ours that of arresting the earth's revolution on its axis; and this is all that the sacred text requires—all that Joshua required—all that we need require.'[1]

Not so, however, thinks Keil, the latest and the ablest commentator on Joshua, and by no means of the rationalist school of interpreters. He enters into a careful examination of the passage, and the following are the results at which he arrives: It was the early part of the day, and during the engagement before Gibeon itself, the sun and the moon were both visible in the heavens—the former above Gibeon, the latter over the valley of Ajalon; and Joshua, lifting up his hand, said, in the sight of Israel, 'Sun, wait at Gibeon; and Moon, in the valley of Ajalon, till the people avenge themselves on their enemies,'—not, however, intending to express a desire that God would work a miracle, and make the sun and moon stand still; but simply an anxious wish that the victory should be decided before the sun went down. And decided it was; so that in the succeeding words the poet announces the fact that the sun waited, and the moon stood still, until the people had avenged themselves upon their enemies. True, it is said in verse 14, that 'there was no day like that

---

[1] 'Daily Readings,' vol. ii., p. 295. See also the Pictorial Bible, *in loco.*

before it or after it, that the Lord hearkened unto the voice of a man;' but this does not necessarily imply that the day was supernaturally lengthened, but refers only to the miraculous hailstorm by which 'the Lord *fought* for Israel.' Truly there was no day like that before it, or after it up to the time that the book of Joshua was written; for whilst the miracles of Moses were wrought by divine command, this—the discomfiture of Israel's enemies by the storm—was wrought in answer to the prayer of Joshua.

'The stars in their courses fought against Sisera,' said Deborah in her song; 'He bowed the heavens, and came down, and darkness was under His feet,' said David in the eighteenth Psalm; and Isaiah prayed and said, 'O that Thou wouldst rend the heavens, that Thou wouldst come down, that the mountains might flow down at Thy presence!' But none of these expressions are to be interpreted literally; and neither, as Keil thinks, is the address of Joshua, but only as a poetic form of representing the rapidity of his victory over the Amorites, and the fact that he was specially and remarkably assisted by the Lord Jehovah.[1]

Such, in substance, is Keil's interpretation of this very remarkable passage; and that it removes a difficulty which has long been felt, especially in recent times, will be generally acknowledged. Hence it has met with favour from some of the most eminent writers of the day;[2] and though others hesitate to accept it,[3] they evidently feel that it would be a great relief to their minds to do so. If, however, they cannot receive it, let them at least be charitable, and not charge those who do with favouring rationalism, or something worse; for surely, on a question of this kind, there may be diversity of opinion, without any

---

[1] See Keil on Joshua, and also articles by J. von Gumpach in the 'Journal of Sacred Literature' for January 1849 and October 1850.

[2] See Ayre's edition of Horne's Introduction, vol. ii., p. 620, and Rawlinson's Bampton Lecture, p. 383.

[3] See Lee on Inspiration, p. 409, note, 2d edition.

injury to the doctrine of the inspiration of the Scriptures. I would say further, that if the idea of a miracle must be maintained (and I do not, by any means, assert the contrary), the *modus operandi* must be left unexplained; for it is evident that every attempt to explain it hitherto has failed, whilst some such attempts appear perfectly ridiculous.[1] Doubtless God has means at His disposal by which He could lengthen a day for several hours, without interfering with the established order of things; but it is no more possible for us to explain those means, than it is for us to explain the means by which Christ multiplied the loaves and fishes. Leaning to the side of Keil's interpretation, I nevertheless hold, that if it were positively affirmed that the day was lengthened, there is nothing at which we need to stumble here, since the power of God is adequate to accomplish whatever He pleases and whatever He will.

The valley of Ajalon was so called from a city of that name which was subsequently given to the tribe of Dan. Dr Robinson identifies the city with a village called Yalo, and describes the valley to the north, now designated Merj Ibn Ömeir, as a broad and beautiful valley which runs out west by north, quite through the tract of hills, and then bends off towards the great western plain.[2] Memorable region this! It reminded Judas Maccabeus that 'the victory of battle standeth not in the multitude of an host, but strength which cometh from heaven;' and, animated with this thought, and with the recollection of Joshua's victory, he, in the same locality, met and defeated Seron and his army, and 'pursued them from the going down of Beth-horon unto the plain, where were slain about eight hundred men of them; and the residue fled into the land of the Philistines.'[3]

---

[1] See Gausen's 'Theopneustia,' Baxter's edition, p. 192.

[2] 'Researches,' vol. ii., p. 253; and see also 'The Land and the Book,' pp. 533, 669.

[3] 1 Macc. iii. 19-24.

In the chalk and limestone cliffs of Palestine there are many large caverns, some excavated, but others natural; and in one of these, at Makkedah, now probably either Dhikkin or Sûmeil, the five kings, who had evaded their pursuers, hid themselves, with the hope of saving their lives. But it was a forlorn hope. Joshua was informed that they were there, and he commanded great stones to be rolled upon the mouth of the cave, and men to be set to watch it; and when, at length, he had smitten the hindermost of his enemies, and the last of the fugitives fell before the sword, he and all the people returned to Makkedah in peace. And now the mouth of the cave was opened, and the five kings were dragged into the presence of the conqueror. No quarter could be given them, for they had been the leaders of the expedition against Gibeon; besides which, they, like the rest of the inhabitants of Canaan, were under the ban of an avenging God. They were, therefore, sentenced to be slain; and first, in the presence of 'all the men of Israel,' Joshua said to the captains of the men of war, 'Come near, put your feet upon the necks of these kings,'—a piece of barbarism, some, perhaps, will be ready to say; but it was not so, but only a symbolic action intended to intimate to the people how complete should be the subjection of all their enemies.[1] And, indeed, it was a common form of expressing victory over enemies, as the sculptured rocks of Egypt, Media, and other countries intimate. 'When,' says Mr Roberts, in his 'Oriental Illustrations,' 'people are disputing, should one be a little pressed, and the other begin to triumph, the former will say, "I will tread upon thy neck, and after that beat thee." A low-caste man insulting one who is high, is sure to hear some one say to the offended individual, "Put your feet on his neck."' Such, then, was the treatment of these five kings, who were then slain, and whose bodies were afterwards hung on five trees until the evening. They were then cast into the cave

[1] Comp. Ps. xviii. 40, cx. 1.

in which they had been hid, and thus terminated this never-to-be-forgotten conflict.

' So let Thine enemies perish, O Lord; but let them that love Thee be as the sun when he goeth forth in his might.' ' This whole history,' says Calvin, ' holds up to us, as in a mirror, how, when the Lord is seated on His tribunal, all worldly splendour vanishes before Him, and the glory of him who seemed to excel is turned by His judgment into the greatest disgrace.' Joshua is here especially a type of the true Deliverer, whose foes, though numerous, shall all be scattered ; whose enemies, though mighty, shall lick the dust ; who still goes forth conquering and to conquer, and who shall ultimately wield the sceptre of justice and of mercy over all the kings and princes of the earth. Conqueror, not of Canaan only, but of the world, Christ shall reign from sea to sea, and from the river unto the uttermost parts of the earth; and of those who refused to submit to His authority, He will say, ' These Mine enemies, that would not that I should reign over them, bring hither, and slay them before Me.'

SIDON

CHAPTER X.

FURTHER VICTORIES.

THE most celebrated military commanders have generally been distinguished for the rapidity of their movements. They have not, after obtaining a signal victory, sat down to enjoy repose; but they have taken advantage of their position, and, as quickly as possible, pushed forward their forces to new efforts and to new conquests, until their latest foes have been driven from the field.

But never, perhaps, was the spirit of enterprise and perseverance more signally displayed than in the conduct of Joshua, the son of Nun. Six cities in succession—Makkedah, Libnah, Lachish, Eglon, Hebron, and Debir—were, in succession, rapidly besieged and taken, and all their inhabitants smitten by the sword; for 'Joshua smote all the country of the hills, and of the south, and of the vale, and of the springs, and all their kings: he left none remaining, but utterly destroyed all that breathed, as the Lord God of Israel commanded'—chap. x. 28–40. All the cities here named were situated in the south of Canaan; and some of them, as we shall see hereafter, were given to the Levites. Makkedah was situated in the plain, and is probably identical with a village now called Sûmeil, two and a half hours north-west of Beit-Jibrin. Libnah is identified by Van de Velde with the Tell of Arak-el-Menshiyeh, between Sûmeil and Um-Lakhis. Lachish is, no doubt, represented by the latter spot—Um-Lakhis—midway between Gaza and Beit-Jibrin. Eglon is now Ajlan, 'a low mound, with a few scattered building stones, one hour east of Lachish.' Hebron, or Kirjath-arba, now el-Khulil, was the well-known city in which Abraham dwelt; and Debir is probably identical with a ruin called Dibbeh, on the summit of a hill two hours south-west of Hebron. All the cities, then, were comparatively contiguous, so that Joshua's conquests can easily be conceived. He is said also to have defeated and slain Horam, king of Gezer, who came up to help Lachish; but it is nowhere said that he took Gezer; for, in fact, it was too far out of his way, somewhere near the coast towards Ashdod.[1]

Of the five kings who were confederate against Joshua, and whom he slew at Makkedah, three belonged to as many of these cities,—to Lachish, Eglon, and Hebron: hence the kings of Lachish and of Eglon are not here mentioned; but of the kings of Makkedah, Libnah, and Debir, it is said that he did unto them as he had done unto the rest. In verse 37 the king of Hebron is spoken of; but the words may have been interpolated, or a successor to the former king may be referred to here.

[1] See, on all these places, Van de Velde's Map and Memoir.

It is not to be understood that in this expedition Joshua depopulated the whole territory. He did not search out the hiding-places of those who fled, but destroyed only those who fell in his way. Hence Hebron and Debir were at a later period in the hands of the Anakim, who were driven out of the former by Caleb, and out of the latter by Othniel;[1] yet he smote the country from Kadesh-barnea, in the desert of Sin,[2] even unto Gaza, the most southerly city of the Philistines, and all the country of Goshen, so called from a city of that name in the same neighbourhood,[3] even unto Gibeon, 'at one time,' or in one campaign, 'because the Lord God of Israel fought for Israel.'

But now, Joshua having returned unto the camp to Gilgal, another confederacy was formed against him, headed by Jabin, king of Hazor, who had heard of these things, and who was, no doubt, considerably alarmed. Hazor was situated in the north of Canaan, near Lake Merom, and was 'the head of all the kingdoms' in that part of the country; so that there Jabin was probably what Adoni-zedek was in the south—the most prominent and influential chieftain of the neighbourhood. And as Adoni-zedek headed an alliance with the kings in his vicinity, so Jabin sent to those near him, to the king of Madon, the king of Shimron, the king of Achshaph, 'and to the kings that were on the north of the mountains, and of the plains south of Chinneroth, and in the valley, and in the borders of Dor on the west.' Nay, his messages went further still, 'to the Canaanites, east and west; to the Amorite, the Perizzite, and the Jebusite in the mountains, and to the Hivite under Hermon in the land of Mizpeh'—chap. xi. 2, 3.

Of this extensive tract of country it may be well to take a brief survey, that we may be the better able to form a conception of the gathering together, from so many quarters, of the

---

[1] See chap. xi. 21, xiv. 12, xv. 15–17.   [2] Num. xx. 14.   [3] Chap. xv. 51.

hosts who were now about to do battle with the Israelites.
Beginning at the north, there towers before us, the lofty Hermon, or the Jebel-esh-Sheikh, which rises to the height of ten
thousand feet above the Mediterranean Sea, and is partially
crowned with perpetual snow, which lies in ravines, and presents at a distance the appearance of radiant stripes. It is the
most southerly point of the chain of Anti-Libanus, and from its
south-eastern base, 'a low broad spur or mountainous tract
runs off towards the south, forming the high land which shuts
in the basin and lake of the Huleh on the east.'[1] This is none
other than 'the land of Mizpeh,' and now bears the name of
Jebel Heish. It is a magnificent country, and was, in all
probability, thickly populated in the days of Joshua, even as it
now is by tribes who have recently been at deadly war. On from
this region southwards to the plains of Chinneroth, or to the Sea
of Galilee, thence far away to the west on the heights of Dor,
which stood upon 'the great sea' below the promontory of Carmel, and thence eastward over the mountain and across the plain
of Esdraelon to the valley of the Jordan,—was the territory
whence Jabin gathered 'much people, even as the sand upon
the sea-shore in multitude, with horses and chariots very many.'
The sites of Madon, Shimron, and Achshaph are unknown; but
that of Hazor is identical, according to Dr Robinson, with a
prominent Tell called Khuraibeh, a little north-west of the
waters of Merom, where he found stones which had apparently
been built up into houses at different epochs, and other signs of
the handiwork of man. The site agrees with the statement of
Josephus, that Hazor was situated over the Lake Samochonitis ;
and it equally agrees with the narrative before us, as the capital
of Jabin would naturally form the rallying point of the hosts he
mustered.

Here, then, was the battle-field ; for 'when all these kings were met together, they came and pitched together at the waters of Merom, to fight against Israel.' This was the Lake Samochonitis, now el-Huleh, which is about four or five miles long, and nearly as broad, and through which the Jordan, after uniting its several branches six miles northward, runs towards the sister Lake Gennesaret. The plain and marsh above it are about ten miles square: and the former, being sufficiently dry for cultivation, is the great granary of the surrounding country.[1] 'On the east and west the lake is bounded by mountain slopes; and it was probably on the rising ground on the western side that the allied kings pitched their tents, for we find them, in verse 7, *above* the waters of Merom.'

This locality was an ancient battle-field; for here it was that Abraham and his little band came upon the forces of Chedor-^aomer and his allies, who had carried away captive Lot and his family from the vale of Sodom. The spoilers were utterly defeated, and Abraham brought back all that they had taken, leaving the king of Elam and his confederates dead upon the field.[2] It now becomes the scene of a more terrible conflict. Vast multitudes are here gathered together, 'even as the sand that is upon the sea-shore in multitude, with horses and chariots very many.' Their intention is to proceed towards Gilgal, and there to attack the camp of the Israelites; but Joshua is aware of their movements and designs, and resolves not to wait their coming, but to act on the offensive, and to proceed at once towards the place of their encampment.

Several days must have been occupied in the movements of the armies; but Joshua stealthily advanced from Gilgal to Lake Merom, and, on the day before the battle, pitched perhaps in some valley where the enemy did not observe him. And here he received encouragement to proceed. The forces he was about to meet were more formidable than any he had yet encountered,

---

[1] See 'The Land and the Book,' p. 214. [2] Gen. xiv. 1–14.

consisting of infantry, cavalry, and chariots of iron; and, as the Israelites had no cavalry, it required extraordinary courage to do battle with such a host. The LORD therefore said unto Joshua, 'Be not afraid because of them; for to-morrow, about this time, will I deliver them up all slain before Israel: thou shalt hough their horses, and burn their chariots with fire.' '*I* will deliver them up.' What is it that Omnipotence cannot do? If God be for Joshua, who can be against him? If Jehovah fight for Israel, who will be able to injure or molest them? Yet the Israelites were not to be mere spectators of the victory, but were to attack the enemy, to render their horses useless, and to destroy their chariots. Moses had left instructions for the future king of Israel that he should not multiply horses to himself,[1] lest he should be led, like other kings, to trust in horses and in chariots, rather than in the living God; 'it was necessary, there-fore,' as Calvin observes, 'to render the horses useless for war, by cutting their sinews, and to destroy the chariots, in order that the Israelites might not become accustomed to the practices of the heathen.'

The morning dawned, and suddenly, ere the mighty hosts of Jabin had time to get ready for the battle, nay, even before they were aware that the foe they were intending to attack was near them, Joshua and all the people of war fell upon them, 'above the waters of Merom, and smote them.' 'The mighty shout strikes terror into every heart. The shock is irresistible. Jabin, with his confederate kings, wakes only to join the universal rout. This vast theatre of plain and marsh, and valley and mountain, is covered with fugitives and their wild pursuers. Those whose homes lay beyond the mountains, to the north and east, sought them by the great wady of the Upper Jordan, now Wady et-Teim, or out east of Hermon, in the Hauran, the land of Mizpeh. Those from the sea-coast of Acre and Carmel

---

[1] Deut. xvii. 16.

l

fled over those hills, and down south-west by Hazor to Misrephoth-maim, on the north border of the plain of Acre, now called
Musheirifeh. Thence they dispersed to their homes along the
sea-board as far south as Dor. Joshua himself chased a third
division along the base of our mountain northward, past Abel-
Beth Maachah, through the plain of Ijon, down the tremendous
gorge of the Litany to the ford at Tamrah, or the bridge at the
Khutroch, and thence over the wooded spurs of Jebel Rihan
toward Great Zidon, behind whose lofty walls the flying host
alone could find safety. Returning southward, he recrossed the
Litany, stormed Hazor, the capital of king Jabin, and utterly
consumed it with fire.'

Such is Dr Thomson's vivid description of the victory, but
it is desirable that we should look at it still more minutely.
Brief as the narrative is, it is remarkably graphic and full of life.
The laws of modern warfare were not then in force; and Joshua
was therefore under no obligation to wait until his enemies were
prepared to meet him, but might, without giving them a moment's
warning, attack them suddenly whilst they were slumbering in
their tents. And this he did. There, on the plains east of the
Lake Merom, lay the hosts of the allied kings, like grasshoppers
for multitude, when, with the heroism of one who knew that he
had Omnipotence on his side, Joshua led his comparatively small
army, perhaps in three divisions, into the very heart of the encampment; and such was the shout they raised, and such the
force of their attack, that the foe was smitten with terror and
confusion, and every man sought to fly with all the speed he
could command. Thousands probably fell at the very first onslaught; and thousands more, some in one direction and some in
another, fled before the face of the conquering Israelites. One
portion of the army sought refuge towards the north-west, and
were chased by their enemies unto Great Zidon, thirty miles distant, on the shores of the Mediterranean Sea. Zidon, or Sidon,

was then the metropolis of Phœnicia, and therefore designated Great; but, at a later period, its splendour was eclipsed by that of Tyre, which then became the first of Phœnician cities. Of Sidon mention is made in Gen. x. 19, xlix. 13; and we read of it in Homer, for among the prizes offered to the racers by Achilles—

> 'First, he produced
> A silver goblet of six measures: earth
> Own'd not its like for elegance of form;
> Skilful Sidonian artists had around
> Embellish'd it, and o'er the sable deep
> Phœnician merchants into Lemnos port
> Had borne, and the boon to Thoas given.'[1]

Its name is said to signify 'fishing,' or 'a fishery;' and it lay on the north-west slope of a small promontory, which jutted out obliquely into the sea, towards the south-west. It is now called Saida, and contains a population of seven thousand souls.[2]

But was Jabin, then, a Phœnician, or were any of the vast multitudes whom he had gathered together Phœnicians? It is not improbable that some of them were; for, whatever may have been the original home of the Phœnicians, there is little doubt that they were descendants of Canaan, the son of Ham. They settled along the coast of the Mediterranean, from Mount Lebanon to the promontory of Carmel, and were called Phœnicians by the Greeks, as some think, from the fact that they traded principally in purple (φοινος), but, as others suppose, from their sun-burnt complexion, the word φοῖνιξ signifying a red-brown colour. No mention is made of them, under this name, in the Pentateuch; but in later books of the Bible their principal cities are often spoken of, for they were not conquered by Joshua, but continued to exist as an independent people, were in friendly alliance with David and with Solomon, planted colonies in

---

[1] 'Iliad,' Cowper's trans., xxiii. 924.
[2] Robinson's 'Researches,' ii., p. 478, etc.; Kendrick's 'Phœnicia,' p. 17.

Carthage and elsewhere, and, for a time, were the most powerful rivals and enemies of Rome.

Whether, then, there were any Phœnicians or not in league with Jabin, the victory of Joshua, decisive as it was, did not materially affect them. It is, indeed, related by Procopius, that some of the nations of Canaan, on their expulsion by Joshua, fled to Northern Africa; and that in the neighbourhood of Tangiers there are two statues of white stone, engraved with Phœnician letters, and bearing the inscription, 'We are they who fled from the face of the robber Joshua, the son of Nun.' But, though the genuineness of this inscription was at one time admitted by several eminent scholars, there are, we believe, but few who now hold this to be a correct translation of the inscription.[1] 'Had the original conquest of Canaan by the Israelites, or their subsequent wars, given them possession of the towns of the sea-coast, we might have expected,' says Mr Kendrick, 'to find that the inhabitants, availing themselves of their fleets, had withdrawn from the extermination or slavery which awaited them, and settled in foreign countries.' But of this there is not the slightest evidence, for the oldest genuine inscription in the Phœnician character is not earlier than the fourth century; and we know that the inhabitants of the coast country were not driven out of the land, or even conquered, either by Joshua or by the kings of Israel.

But to return to the narrative. A second portion of the allied forces fled, and were pursued to Misrephoth-maim,—a word respecting which there has been no little diversity of opinion. The LXX. took it as a proper name; but many think that it signifies burnings, salt-pits, glass-houses, or smelting-houses,—there being in the neighbourhood of Zidon places of this kind in very early times. Literally, it is said to mean 'burnings by the

---

[1] See Kendrick's 'Phœnicia,' p. 68. Rawlinson, however, is in favour of the translation. 'Bampton Lectures' for 1859, pp. 381-2.

waters;' and it may refer either to Zidonian glass factories, to hot springs, or simply to the burning of Jabin's chariots. Dr Thomson, however, in the passage quoted above, supposes it to be identical with a place now called Musheirifeh, which he found on the north border of the plain of Acre. ' This Musheirifeh,' he observes elsewhere, ' with the noble fountains at the base of the same name, I am disposed to identify with the Misrephoth-maim (waters of Misrephoth) to which that part of the Canaanitish host which came from Dor, etc., fled from the battle of Merom; and I do this notwithstanding the contradictory renderings of these words in the margins of our Bibles, and all other philological criticism whatsoever. The ancient and modern names are nearly identical in form, and, I believe, in signification, and both were suggested by the bright and glowing colour of those magnificent cliffs which overhang the sea; and any one who will study the route which the division of Jabin's army that came from Dor must have taken to escape Joshua's troops and reach home, will see that this is the spot where they would most likely first find a safe and convenient halting-place on the shore. The difficult pass, commanded by a castle, where the present bay stands, would be an effectual barrier against their enemies, and the plain below, in possession of Achzib, which the Jews did not subdue, would afford a delightful place for them to refresh themselves after the fatigue of that disastrous day.'[1]

It is gratifying to meet with such identifications; and, with Dr Thomson, we say, ' Let Musheirifeh, therefore, stand for Misrephoth.' But if this be the case, then how much more is wrapped up in the brief narrative of the flight than at first appears ! Whilst one part of the discomfited allies fled, as we have seen, nearly due north, to Zidon, another fled, almost due west, to Misrephoth or Musheirifeh, which was situated at the distance of an hour from Achzib, the ancient Zib, and lies on the coast

---

[1] ' Land and the Book,' pp. 303–4; comp. Van de Velde's ' Memoir,' p. 335

north of the Bay of Acre. These had come from this part of
the coast; and whither, when they were defeated, should they
fly but to their homes? Even in the confusion which resulted
from the attack of Joshua, they would instinctively turn towards that part of the country in which their own habitations
lay; and, instead of following those who fled towards Zidon,
would hasten thither, where safety would appear more sure.
Many of them doubtless succeeded in their object: nor was
this part of the coast conquered by the Israelites; for though
it fell to the lot of the half-tribe of Manasseh, it is said in
Judges i. 27, 'Neither did Manasseh drive out the inhabitants
of Beth-shean and her towns, nor Taanach and her towns, nor
the inhabitants of Dor and her towns, nor the inhabitants of
Ibleam and her towns, nor the inhabitants of Megiddo and
her towns: but the Canaanites would dwell in that land.'
They became, however, tributary to the Israelites; and Solomon stationed at Dor one of his twelve purveyors, whose duty it
was to provide victuals for his household, each man his month
in a year.[1]

A third party of the fugitives took another direction, and
hastened towards 'the valley of Mizpeh eastward.' The word
Mizpeh signifies 'a watchtower,' and there were several places
which bore the name: but 'the valley of Mizpeh' here mentioned
lay beyond the Wady et-Teim, in the Hauran, east of Hermon.
Of this there can be no doubt, though the name has not yet been
found in that particular locality. It is an extensive and richly
watered country, and probably contained in the days of Joshua
a very considerable population. Thence had part of Jabin's
forces been gathered, and thither such of them as escaped the
sword, belonging to this neighbourhood, fled. Thus from the
field of battle were these warrior-clans scattered, northward,
westward, and eastward, whilst, for a while, the Israelites pur-

sued them in three divisions, till at length they reached their respective fastnesses.

A more decided victory Joshua had not gained. It was the death-blow to all the hopes of the Canaanites. It settled the question, whose shall the country be? And from the pursuit of the fugitives Joshua turned back, smote the cities of these kings, took possession of the cattle and the spoil, slew all the inhabitants, and set Hazor, Jabin's capital, on fire. The other cities he did not burn, but left them 'standing in their strength;' but Hazor, 'which was the head of all those kingdoms,' and in which Jabin himself had taken refuge, he did not spare, and the king he smote with the sword. It was a terrible retribution, and we dwell on these details not without pain; but we deny that there was any injustice in Joshua's proceedings, for he was but the agent of Divine Justice, sent to chastise a people whose crimes had long insulted Heaven and provoked the Majesty on high. Joshua had authority for what he did. He was actuated, not by cruelty, not by a spirit of blood-thirstiness and revenge, but by a stern sense of duty; for 'as the Lord commanded Moses his servant, so did Moses command Joshua, and so did Joshua: he left nothing undone of all that the LORD commanded Moses.'[1] Shall we then condemn him? We condemn him not. He was a brave soldier of the Lord Jehovah, and only did what he was commanded to do, mediately through Moses, or directly by God Himself.

Of Hazor it should be observed that it was probably rebuilt; and we read of another Jabin in the book of Judges, who was probably a successor of the Jabin of our narrative. Highly important was the position of Hazor as a defence against the eastern nations; and hence Solomon built a wall round it, as he did round Megiddo, Gezer, and Jerusalem. At a later period

[1] Josh. xi. 15; comp. Exod. xxiii. 27–33; Num. xxxiii. 52; Deut. vii. 1 xx. 16.

some of its inhabitants were carried captives to Assyria;[1] and, later still, Jonathan Maccabeus went to the plain of Nazor (Hazor) to meet Demetrius, whom, after some reverses, he put to flight.[2]

Joshua's victory over Jabin all but completed the conquest of the land, and verses 16 to 23 of chap. xi. contain a review of what he had effected, whilst in chap. xii. is given a list of the names of the kings subdued by Moses and by Joshua on both sides of the Jordan. 'A long time did Joshua make war with all those kings,' several years being occupied in the task;[3] but 'he took all that land, the hills, and all the south country, and all the land of Goshen, and the valley, and the plain, and the mountain of Israel, and the valley of the same; even from the Mount Halak, that goeth up to Seir, even unto Baal-gad in the valley of Lebanon, under Mount Hermon'—chap. xi. 16–23. First, he conquered the south of the land, as related in chap. x. 1–42, 'from a row of white cliffs,' here called Mount Halak, or the bald mountain, which ascends to Mount Seir on the south of the Dead Sea, and thence crosses the Arabah or great valley which lies between that sea and the Gulf of Akabah;[4] and thence his conquests extended to the land of Goshen, which probably lay on the coast between Gaza and Gibeon, to the valley and the plain beyond, that is, the line of coast from Joppa to Mount Carmel. Secondly, he conquered the north country as far as Baal-gad in the valley of Lebanon, under Mount Hermon, which Ritter and others suppose to have been situated in the neighbourhood of Hasbeiya, on the southern side of Jebel esh-Sheikh, but which Dr Thomson identifies with Baalbek, much farther north, where there are ruins of very high antiquity.[5]

Thus the whole land lay at Joshua's feet; for, though the war

[1] 2 Kings xv. 29.　　　　[2] 1 Macc. xi. 67, etc.

[3] Josephus says five (Antiq. v. 1, 19); the Rabbins say seven.

[4] See Keil *in loco*, and Robinson's 'Researches,' vol. ii., pp. 183–4.

[5] This view of the site of Baal-gad is, however, very doubtful.

was not one of utter extermination, since many of the tribes were still permitted to remain in it, yet virtually it was in the hands of Israel, and, save the inhabitants of Gibeon, not a city made peace with them or sought their friendship. This is surprising; but the explanation is, 'It was of the LORD to harden their hearts, that they should come against Israel in battle, that He might destroy them utterly, and that they might have no favour.' They had long hardened their own hearts, and now their hearts were hardened judicially by the Lord Jehovah ; and, as if reckless of the consequences, they rushed forward to the battlefield, and met their fate. Does this doctrine of the obduration of men's hearts seem harsh and mysterious? Let it be observed that it does not imply any immediate operation of the Divine will upon the human mind, but simply the withholding from men those gracious influences which they have forfeited by their neglect of them, so that they are left to themselves, and therefore become more obdurate and more averse to good. 'If a ray of divine light,' says Muller, 'has fallen upon one, he cannot, as many would like to do, pass away from it with quiet unconcern and indifference ; but if he closes himself up against the light, he becomes driven to bitterness and wrath against it. In relation to such an individual, the means of spiritual healing, the efficacy of which he has intentionally destroyed, not merely loses its saving power, but operates in a directly opposite character.'[1] Now, the Canaanites had had the light of nature and of conscience, and were, therefore, without excuse ; but that light they had rejected, that light they had repelled, that light they had wilfully shut out from their minds. Hence the light itself became darkness, and God gave them up to work all manner of uncleanness with greediness, until at length the measure of their iniquities was full, and justice doomed them to destruction.

And now the Israelites stood in the midst of a scene of ruin

[1] 'Doctrine of Sin,' vol. ii., p. 468. Clark.

and desolation, upon which they can scarcely have looked without sadness and distress. Well might the poet of the 'Christian Year' put into their lips such words as these,—

> Where is the land with milk and honey flowing,
>> The promise of our God, our fancy's theme?
> Here over shattered walls dank weeds are growing,
>> And blood and fire have run in mingled stream:
>>> Like oaks and cedars all around,
>>> The giant corses strew the ground,
> And haughty Jericho's cloud-piercing wall
> Lies where it sank at Joshua's trumpet call.

> ' These are not scenes for pastoral dance at even,
>> For moonlight ravings in the fragrant glades,
> Soft slumbers in the open eye of heaven,
>> And all the listless joy of summer shades.
>>> We in the midst of ruins live,
>>> Which every hour dread warning give;
> Nor may our household vine or fig-tree hide
> The broken arches of old Canaan's pride.'

But other tasks were now before them. 'There still remained very much land to be possessed' (chap. xiii. 1); and then the whole country must be divided and assigned to the different tribes, as Moses had commanded. It is said, indeed (chap. xi. 23), that Joshua took 'the whole land,' but the expression is not to be taken in its full and literal meaning; and from the first it was God's design to drive out the Canaanites 'by little and little,' to prevent the rapid increase of the wild beasts of the field, which would have taken place had the country been at once depopulated of all its original inhabitants.[1] 'Jehovah,' says Havernick, 'is described (in the books of Joshua) as giving to the Israelites the land of promise; and the work is so far completed by Joshua, that he is able to portion out the whole land. This does not, however, place the Israelites in such a position that they have nothing more to do. On the contrary, the strong-

[1] Deut. vii. 22; Exod. xxiii. 29, 30.

holds of the Canaanites are to serve as a test of the faith even
of future generations.   By means of these the question is to be
decided, whether Israel will henceforth continue to be what it has
been under the command of Joshua.'

What, then, had been done? what yet remained to be done?
The former of these questions has been already answered; but
chap xii. presents us with a brief summary of the victories
achieved.   On the other side Jordan, Moses had taken possession of the country from the brook Arnon, now the Wady Mudjib,
to Mount Hermon, and all the plain of the Jordan on the east;
and had slain Sihon king of the Amorites, and Og king of
Bashan, and given their lands to the Reubenites, the Gadites,
and the half tribe of Manasseh (vers. 1–6).   And on the western
side of the river, Joshua had smitten thirty-one kings, a catalogue
of whose names and cities is given (vers. 7–24), though some
of the cities were not taken until a later period.[1]   The second
question—what remained to be done? or what portion of the
land was not yet subdued?—is answered in chap. xiii. 2–6.   All
the borders of the Philistines, and all Geshuri, which lay in
the desert between Palestine and Egypt,[2] remained to be conquered.   This territory reached to Sihor, or the black river, supposed by some to be the Nile, but which was no doubt the brook
which flows into the Red Sea near Rhinocura, called elsewhere
'the waters of Egypt,'[3] and now the Wady el-Arish.   On the
north it extended to Ekron, now called Akir, a village of considerable size in a plain north of the Wady Surar; and it embraced the cities Gaza, Ashdod, Eshkalon, and Ekron, with the
land of the Gittites and the Avites.   The Avites, however, who
were no doubt Canaanites, are placed by the LXX. in the south

---

[1] On the alleged discrepancies in this chapter, see Keil, whose explanations
will satisfy every candid mind.

[2] 1 Sam. xxvii. 8.

[3] Num. xxxiv. 5· Josh. xv. 4; and comp. 1 Chron. xiii. 5.

of Philistia; and this part of the territory remained also to be conquered. Then, in the north-west, there remained Mearah, or the cave of the Sidonians, and thence the whole breadth of the country unto Aphek (now Fik, a village on the table-land east of the lake of Gennesareth), even to the borders of the Amorites. Further, there was Gebal, the country of the Giblites, or hewers of wood and stone, now Byblus, north of Beirout, and all Lebanon towards the sun-rising, from Baal-gad even to Mount Hermon, whose snowy peak glitters in the morning rays, and which stands at the entrance of Hamath, the river of which, the Orontes, rises at Lebweh, etc., under the lofty Lebanon,[1]

> ‘Whose head in wintry grandeur towers,
> And whitens with eternal sleet;
> While summer, in a vale of flowers,
> Is sleeping rosy at his feet.’

Such were the regions which were not yet in possession of the Israelites; but Joshua was now old and stricken in years, and, therefore, could not be expected to survive until the whole country was subdued. He had, however, done enough; and now he must proceed to divide the land, as if it were all conquered, and to assign the several portions of it to the different tribes, leaving those who came after him to contend with such of the inhabitants as might oppose them. He was not to exempt from the division even the unconquered territory; but, believing that God would give it to His people, to obey His commands without fear of disappointment, inasmuch as, whatever He promised to His people, He was able to perform. And, virtually at least, the whole country did ultimately become the possession of the Israelites; for the kingdom of Solomon embraced the whole country, and those of the Canaanites who were left in the land he laid under tribute and made his servants (1 Kings ix. 21).

---

[1] See Robinson's 'Researches,' vol. iii., p. 538, etc.; 'The Land and the Book,' p. 239.

We have thus reached a period in the history of Joshua, which to himself must have been one of joy and satisfaction.   Hitherto he had been called to wield the sword, and now he was to lay it aside, and to take up in its stead the instruments of labour and of skill.   The land was to be surveyed ; and he was to appoint, by lot, the territory of each tribe.   Three of the tribes had, however, received their inheritance on the other side Jordan ; and the Levites were to have no inheritance, but to dwell in cities scattered through the land.   For eight tribes, therefore, and the half tribe of Manasseh, Joshua had now to make provision ; and to this task he set himself with all the zeal and generosity of a real patriot.   But, first of all, his old friend and companion, Caleb, must be remembered as one deserving of special honour.

HEBRON. LOWER POOLS.

CHAPTER XI.

THE INHERITANCE OF CALEB.

IT is gratifying to see merit well rewarded. In the school-room and in the camp, in the Church and in the State, every generous mind looks on with pleasure, as one who has toiled hard and faithfully obtains at last the honour he deserves. We cannot fail, then, to read of Caleb's fortunes with peculiar interest, and to admire at the same time the readiness with which Joshua acknowledged his claims to special consideration.

Not without importance is the question of Caleb's genealogy. He is said to have been the son of Jephunneh,[1] who was a

___
[1] Num. xxxiv. 19.

descendant of Hezron, the son of Pharez, the grandson of Judah.[1]
But Jephunneh is called the Kenizzite, whence it has been supposed that he was descended on the father's side from the tribe of
that name, mentioned in Gen. xv. 19, who were, in all probability,
a clan of the Edomites. This is, however, a hasty conclusion;
for the term Kenizzite here means simply a descendant of Kenaz,
of whom we know nothing more, but who must have belonged
to the posterity of Judah, and was probably a distinguished
member of the family; for Othniel, the brother of Caleb, is
called his son,[2] and one of Caleb's own sons was named Kenaz.[3]

Seven years had elapsed since the entrance of the Israelites
into Canaan, when Caleb came to Joshua, and said, ' Thou
knowest the thing that the Lord said unto Moses, the man of
God, concerning me and thee, in Kadesh-barnea. Forty years
old was I when Moses, the servant of the Lord, sent me from
Kadesh-barnea to espy out the land; and I brought him word
again as it was in mine heart. Nevertheless my brethren that
went up with me made the heart of the people melt: but I
wholly followed the Lord my God' (xiv. 6–8). How deeply
-would Joshua feel as his mind was thus thrown back to former
days! and with what interest would he listen to his honoured
friend's appeal! Well did he know the truth of this statement.
Well did he know that there was in it no exaggeration of the
truth. He himself was Caleb's companion when he went to
search out the land; and he himself took part with Caleb when
' he stilled the people,' who, on the return of the spies, murmured at the report given by the ten. Yes, his brethren who
went up with him made the heart of the people melt; but he
followed the Lord wholly, and, confiding in His promised help,
said, ' Let us go up at once and possess the land; for we are
well able to overcome it.' All this Joshua knew. He had
never forgotten it, and never could. The conduct of Caleb on

[1] 1 Chron. ii. 5, 18, 25.　　　[2] Josh. xv. 17.　　　[3] 1 Chron. iv. 15.

that occasion was too noble, too generous, ever to be erased from his recollection; and to that conduct he owed not a little, as it encouraged him also to deny the report of the faithless and timid spies.

It is a great thing to follow the Lord fully. Not a few there are who enter upon the path of duty well, and who are brave and heroic enough when they first encounter the foes they have to meet, but who, ere long, become timid and fainthearted, and soon give up the contest in despair. To follow the Lord fully requires courage, zeal, and confidence more than ordinary; and happy is the man who, possessing these, does not let 'good beginnings vanish,' but in whom 'the last corresponds with the first.'

The veteran soldier proceeds to remind Joshua, that Moses sware unto him that day, saying, 'Surely the land whereon thy feet have trodden shall be thine inheritance, and thy children's for ever, because thou hast wholly followed the Lord thy God.' No record of any such oath is found either in Num. xiv. or in Deut. i.; all that we find there, is a promise given by God Himself, that Caleb should enter the land of Canaan, and that his seed should possess it. ' To him will I give the land that he hath trodden upon, and to his children, because he hath wholly followed the Lord.' On what, then, was the claim of Caleb to any particular portion of the country founded? There can be no doubt that, as Keil observes, 'the Lord God had made an express declaration to Moses with reference to His faithful servant, and that Moses had informed him of it, probably in the hearing of Joshua also.' And what if that promise had not been placed on the public records? Was it, therefore, to fail? was it, therefore, not to hold good? It could by no means fail; and now the time had arrived when Caleb saw that he might lay claim to the inheritance, and this was therefore his request.

' And now,' said he, ' the Lord hath kept me alive, as He

said, these forty and five years, even since the Lord spake this word unto Moses, while the children of Israel wandered in the wilderness ; and now also I am this day fourscore and five years old. As yet I am as strong this day as I was in the day that Moses sent me : as my strength was then, even so is my strength now, for war, both to go out, and to come in.'—' I am this day fourscore and five years old.' It was the second year after the Exodus that the events referred to by Caleb occurred ; and, as he says forty-five years had since elapsed, it has been inferred that thirty-eight of these years were spent in the wilderness, and seven in the conquest of the land of Canaan. Already, then, his life had been toilsome, and, with the exception of Joshua, he was twenty years older than the oldest of the people then alive ; and yet his ability for counsel and for action remained unimpaired. A green old age is pleasant to contemplate. Beautiful is the aged oak which, though gnarled and knotted, still throws out young branches, and is covered with luxuriant foliage ; but there is something specially attractive in an aged man who carries about with him the elasticity and buoyancy of youth, and whose manly frame seems as if it bade defiance to the ordinary ravages of time. When Ulysses returned home to Ithaca, after long sufferings, in the twentieth year, his strength was unimpaired ; and the bow, which others had attempted to bend in vain, he took, and with the utmost ease sent the arrow flying through the rings. And often have we heard of aged men who, in like manner, have put many younger to the blush by their bold and daring feats. Usually, however, it is otherwise. ' Men of age,' says Lord Bacon, ' object too much, consult too long, adventure too little, repent too soon, and seldom drive business home to the full period, but content themselves with a mediocrity of success.' But Caleb was of the opposite class. He was prepared to adventure as much now as when he was sent to spy out the land. He was as well able to drive the business home as when first he entered on the task. No mediocrity of success would satisfy him; but, if he might, he would expel the Anakim from the mountain, and take possession of it for himself and his posterity.

The mountain for which he asked was that of Hebron, but it was in possession of the giant race of the Anakim; for after they had been driven out by Joshua,[1] they had probably taken the advantage of his absence in the north to return and re-possess themselves of their former dwellings. Caleb knew that they were there; and knew, moreover, that to expel them would be no easy task. Yet, strong, vigorous, and healthy as he was, he would undertake the task, and *perhaps* the Lord would be with him, and would enable him to drive them out. This 'perhaps,' however, or 'if so be,' does not indicate doubt on Caleb's part. He distrusts himself, but he does not distrust the power of God. He knows the difficulty of the enterprise, but hope animates his breast; and not in his natural strength does he rely, but in the promised aid of the Lord Jehovah.

Some of the princes of Judah had accompanied Caleb into the presence of Joshua—ver. 6, and, as he belonged to that tribe, they doubtless seconded his request; for 'it was no less the interest of the whole people than of one private family, that that which as yet depended on the incomprehensible grace of God, and was treasured up merely in hope, should be bestowed as a special favour.' But was the lot of the children of Judah already determined? and did Caleb ask for this mountain because it was situated in the territory assigned them? There is no evidence of this. On the contrary, the lot of Judah was deter-mined subsequently; and in this the finger of God was manifest, that it fell in the south of the country, where Hebron itself was situated.

'It was fit,' says Matthew Henry, 'that this phœnix of his

---

[1] Chap. xi. 21.

age should have some particular marks of honour put upon him in the dividing of the land;' and ready enough was Joshua to comply with the request of his old companion and friend. 'Joshua blessed him,' and gave unto him Hebron with the surrounding country for an inheritance. His blessing him was a prayer for the successful issue of his efforts; and admirable was the spirit of Joshua in thus recognising Caleb's claims; nor would Caleb himself forget that interview, or fail to reciprocate Joshua's kindness. The whole scene must have been one of intense interest; and well might the painter exercise his skill in depicting it on the canvas in the highest style of art.

Beautiful was the territory thus assigned to Caleb, and beautiful is that territory still. Describing his approach to it, Dr Stanley says, 'The valleys now began, at least in our eyes, almost literally " to laugh and sing." Greener and greener did they grow; the shrubs, too, shot up above that stunted growth. At last, on the summit of farther hills, lines of spreading trees appeared against the sky. Then came ploughed fields and oxen. Lastly, a deep and wide recess opened in the hills; towers and minarets appeared in the gap, which gradually unfolded into the city of " the Friend of God "—this is its Arabic name: far up on the right ran a wide and beautiful upland valley, all portioned into gardens and fields, green fig-trees and cherry-trees, and the vineyards—famous through all ages; and far off, gray and beautiful as those of Tivoli, swept down the western slope the olive groves of Hebron.'[1]

Hebron was a very ancient city, having been built seven years before Zoan in Egypt, which was no doubt erected prior to the time of Abraham. Hence Hebron was a well-known town when Abraham entered the land of Canaan. 'Its name before,' says the historian, 'was Kirjath-arba; which Arba was a great man among the Anakims.' The Rabbins say that this

---

[1] 'Sinai and Palestine,' p. 99.

name signifies 'the city of the four,' and that the place was so called because the four patriarchs, Adam, Abraham, Isaac, and Jacob, were buried there! How foolish the story we need not stop to prove. But was Kirjath-arba really its original name? and did it now receive the name Hebron for the first time? This cannot be supposed; for the latter name occurs in the Pentateuch, and even as early as the days of Abraham.[1] We conclude, then, with Hengstenberg, that it was originally called Hebron; that subsequently it received the name Kirjath-arba, from a giant of the race of the Anakim who had conquered it; that it bore this name, as well as that of Hebron, up to the times of Joshua; and that then its more ancient name was restored to it, by which it was ever afterwards particularly distinguished.[2]

And did Caleb accomplish the task of driving out the Anakim from that mountain? He did, though not until after the death of Joshua. It will give unity to this chapter, and will not interfere with any subsequent portion of the work, if we here trace the fortunes of Caleb and his family, and mark the circumstances under which they obtained possession of the inheritance allotted to them.

These circumstances are narrated in Joshua xv. 14–19, and again in Judges i. 10-15. It has been supposed that the latter passage is a quotation of the former, or that the former is a quotation from the latter; but neither of these suppositions is correct. The writers of these two books derived their information from a common source,—probably the original documents of the period; and from the fact that the conquest of Hebron is narrated in Judges in connection with other events which did not take place until after the death of Joshua, that event itself could not have occurred before his death. Nor is it remarkable that this event should be narrated in the book of

---

[1] Num. xiii. 22; Gen. xiii. 18.
[2] See Hengstenberg's 'Genuineness of the Pentateuch,' vol. ii., p. 155.

Joshua also; for that book was written probably by one of the elders after Joshua's decease, whose design it was to complete the history of the division of the land among the tribes.[1]

Joshua, then, was dead; and soon after Joshua's death, Caleb, now an old man, verging towards ninety, put himself at the head of an army of his own tribe, and made an attack on the city of Hebron. The children of Anak were there—Sheshai, and Ahiman, and Talmai—who were of that race whose stature so greatly alarmed ten of the spies who went to search out the land. Whether the Anakim were really very tall men, or whether they only appeared such in the imagination of the spies, may admit of question; but that there were, in early times, men of gigantic stature, there can be little doubt; for the Scriptures allude to them in many places. The Greeks, too, had their real or their fabled giants in the Trojan wars, of whom the aged Nestor speaks in Homer thus:—

> 'Their equals saw I never, never shall:
> Exadius, Cæneas, and the god-like son
> Of Ægeus, mighty Theseus; men renown'd
> For force superior to the race of man.
> Brave chiefs they were, and with brave foes they fought,
> With the rude dwellers on the mountain-heights,
> The Centaurs, whom with havoc such as fame
> Shall never cease to celebrate, they slew.'[2]

Nestor was courageous, but his prowess was surpassed by that of Caleb; for Nestor fought when in his prime, Caleb when he was far advanced in life. A noble sight it must have been to have seen the veteran warrior advancing to the attack of Hebron, animating his companions to follow him up the mountain, and perhaps putting to shame, by his heroism and his valour, many that were considerably younger than himself. And his exploit was successful: Sheshai, and Ahiman, and Talmai were slain,

[1] See Keil, and also Calvin, *in loco*.
[2] 'Iliad,' Book i. 327. Cowper's translation.

and all their followers driven out of Hebron. Nor did Caleb stop when he had accomplished this object. On he went to Kirjath-sepher, one of the royal cities of Canaan, which Joshua had previously conquered, but which, like Hebron, had again become inhabited by the Canaanites. It must have been a noted place, as its name קִרְיַת־סֵפֶר, Kirjath-sepher, or קִרְיַת־סַנָּה, Kirjath-sanna, is said to signify 'the town of books,' or, 'the city of archives.'[1] What can have given rise to such a name? Were the inhabitants exclusively occupied with writing and the sciences? or was there in this city a famous library, like that of Alexandria at a later period? We need not have recourse to either hypothesis; yet books there must have been, and therefore the art of writing must have been known by the Canaanites as well as by the Egyptians. The books which the city contained were, however, probably few; and, as Dr Kitto conjectures, may have had reference to superstitious rites, or may have been 'records and covenants' of estates and territories. What became of them, it is useless to inquire; but it is scarcely probable that they would escape destruction when Caleb took possession of the city. 'It is by no means unlikely that old Caleb threw the entire bundle of books that formed the library of Kirjath-sepher into the fire.'[2] The city was also called Debir, which some think signifies 'a word,' or 'an oracle;' others, that it signifies 'coming after,' and that the city was so called because it stood behind the other cities towards the west.

[1] Both names are rendered by the LXX. πόλις Γραμματιῶν, 'the city of letters' Josh. xv. 16, 49.

[2] Dr Kitto's 'Daily Readings,' vol. ii., pp. 301–303. Thomas Fuller calls Kirjath-sepher, 'the City of a Book, conceived a Canaanitish university;' and observes, 'Although the giant Anakims dwelling hereabouts may be presumed but little *bookish*, yet civilised countreys, in all ages, have allowed such places for the education of youth, who are better unborn than unbred.'— *Pisgah Sight of Palestine*, p. 277.

About two hours south-west of Hebron, Dr Stewart found the ruins of a town, covering the hill to the north, called Birket el-Dilbeh, of which he says, 'An Arab of the place pointed out to me an aqueduct covered with large stones, which he said brought down a constant supply of water from a spring near the top. A stream of beautiful clear water was running in it. The ruins bore the same name as the wadi and birket. The whole valley was waving with corn. A little farther on, in the same wadi, we came to an ancient draw-well, built with hewn stones, the name of which is Bir el-Hugry. What may have been the name of this town in ancient days? If we consider the *Resh* to have been changed for the sake of sound into *Lamed*, we have in Dilbeh a sufficiently exact representation of the name DEBIR to permit us to conclude that this was the city taken by Othniel, Caleb's nephew, by which exploit he won his wife, and got it for her dower.'[1]

Not, we may be sure, to spare himself, but rather to animate others with a spirit of enterprise, Caleb said, 'He that smiteth Kirjath-sepher, and taketh it, to him will I give Achsah my daughter to wife.' Othniel, having perhaps some regard for Achsah, was animated by the promise to make the attempt: his courage was rewarded with success, and the daughter of Caleb became his wife. And who was Othniel? Some say, the nephew of Caleb, as, had he been his brother, such a marriage would have been illegal; and they read the words of Joshua xv. 17; Judges i. 13, 'Othniel, the son of Kenaz, Caleb's brother,'—making Kenaz Caleb's brother. But Keil observes, 'The objection offered by earlier expositors, that marriage with a brother's daughter was prohibited, is unfounded;' and certainly the meaning of the sacred text appears to be that Othniel was a descendant of Kenaz, and the younger brother of Caleb. Othniel afterwards became the first judge in Israel.[2]

But Achsah was not quite satisfied with her dowry; and, on

[1] 'The Tent and the Khan,' p. 224.   [2] Judges iii. 9.

arriving at her home, she urged her husband to ask of Caleb, her father, an additional field. Othniel perhaps hesitated to do this, though he no doubt approved of her wish; and hence she resolved to make the request herself; and having ridden to her father, she lighted quickly from her ass, so that her father, fearing that something was amiss, said, 'What wouldest thou?' 'Give me a blessing,' was her reply: 'for thou hast given me a south land; give me also springs of water.'[1] He had given her Debir as her marriage portion; but it was a south land, dry and barren, and unfit for cultivation; so that she wanted also lands abounding with springs of water, so essential in Palestine, where severe droughts occur, to the fruitfulness of the soil. There was nothing wrong or selfish in this request. She had probably examined the country, and, observing that Debir was not well supplied with springs, she was anxious that an addition should be made to the gift, of a field in the neighbourhood, which would supply the lack. And with all the generosity of a loving father, Caleb granted the request. He gave her 'the upper springs and the nether springs,'[2]—'a particular tract of land so called from the springs within it both on the higher and the lower ground;' for he saw, perhaps, that her wish was but a reasonable one, and not, as Calvin represents it, 'the wicked thirst of gain.'

We blame not Achsah, as, under the circumstances of the case, she acted prudently. Let not the young, however, be dissatisfied with their share in the patrimonial estate. Many are the heartburnings in families occasioned by the grasping ambition of those who would claim more than by right belongs to

---

[1] Josh. xv. 18, 19; Judges i. 14, 15.

[2] The word here used is Gulloth (גֻּלֹּת), a word which only occurs in these two places—Josh. xv. 19, Judges i. 15. The root signifies to tumble or roll over; in allusion, perhaps, to the welling up of the springs in a globular form. See Stanley, Appendix, § 54.

them, and who, even at the expense of their nearest relatives, try to get possession of what they have long coveted. Selfish and mercenary is such a spirit, and the man who displays it does so at the cost of a good conscience and the smile of Heaven.

Far from possessing such a spirit was Caleb himself; for both Hebron and Debir had already, at the time he conquered them, been assigned to the Levites,—the former as a city of refuge:[1] so that he had scarcely got possession of them ere he had to give them up again, retaining only for himself and his posterity 'the fields thereof, and the villages thereof.' That some of his descendants would dwell in these cities there can be little doubt, for the Levites only received in their cities as many houses as their numerical strength required; but those houses became their inalienable possession,[2] and it must have been a sacrifice on the part of Caleb to surrender much of what he had so hardly won. It was, however, for the benefit of the whole nation; and he did not hold back from the conquest of Hebron, even after the lot had determined that it should be partially possessed by others.

Respecting Caleb's posterity, we learn from 1 Chron. ii. the following particulars. His first wife, Azubah, bare him a daughter named Jerioth,[3] and three sons—Jesher, Shobab, and Ardon. His second wife, Ephrath, bare him a son named Hur. Besides these, he had several other sons by his two concubines; so that his family was numerous, and his posterity is mentioned in the times of David.[4] He was a noble character, and God honoured him with a long life and with many descendants; and though nothing is said of his death, yet we cannot doubt that he went down to the grave in peace; a grave, it may be, not far distant from the field of Machpelah, where Abraham, the illus-

---

[1] Josh. xxi. 11, 15; 1 Chron. vi. 55–58. Lev. xxv. 33, 34.

[3] Such at least is the reading of the Vulgate in 1 Chron. ii. 18: 'Azuba de qua gemnit Jerioth.'

[4] 1 Sam. xxv. 3, xxx. 14.

trious ancestor of all the tribes of Israel, was buried by the side
of Sarah his wife.

And what of Othniel, the brother of Caleb? His sons were
Hathath and Meonothai;[1] and he it was who became a judge
in Israel, and who, after they had been subject to Chushan-rishathaim eight years, delivered them from his yoke. The Lord
raised him up for that purpose: 'And the Spirit of the Lord came
upon him, and he judged Israel, and went out to war: and the
Lord delivered Chushan-rishathaim king of Mesopotamia into
his hand; and his hand prevailed against Chushan-rishathaim.
And the land had rest forty years' (Judges iii. 9–11).

[1] 1 Chron. iv. 13, 14.

DEFILE BETWEEN JERUSALEM AND JERICHO.

CHAPTER XII.

THE LOT OF JUDAH AND BENJAMIN.

HE camp of Joshua was still at Gilgal; the land was now at rest from war; and at length the work began of dividing Canaan among the several tribes who had not yet received their inheritance. This was done by lot, which decided, not the size of the inheritance—for that was determined according to the numbers[1]—but the position which each tribe was to occupy. 'The lot causeth contentions to cease, and decideth between the mighty.'[2] For it is not regulated either by the

[1] Num. xxvi. 52, 53.   [2] Prov. xviii. 18.

opinion, the caprice, or the authority of men ; but—where, as in this case, it has His sanction—by the Lord Jehovah Himself.[1] It was, therefore, a wise method to adopt; and probably each tribe would submit to the decision arrived at cheerfully, and would view the inheritance assigned to it as the immediate gift of God.

The mode in which the lots were cast has been variously explained. Some suppose that the names *of the tribes* were written down, and cast into an urn ; and that the tribe whose name was first drawn, selected that portion of the land which it deemed best. Others think that the names *of the provinces* were cast into the urn, and that each tribe drew according to its rank. But neither of these methods would have been impartial; and ' we must therefore assume,' says Keil, ' that there were two urns— one containing the names of the tribes, and the other those of the ten divisions of the land—and that a name was taken at the same time from each of the urns.' By such a plan there would be no room left for any dispute ; and as Joshua and Eleazar are mentioned as distributing the inheritance (xiv. 1), it is not improbable that the former drew the names from one of the urns, and the latter from the other.

But the casting of the lots did not proceed without interruption ; for as soon as the tribes of Judah and of Joseph had received their inheritance, the camp was removed from Gilgal to Shiloh (chap. xviii. 1): the land which had not been appropriated was carefully surveyed, and lots were then cast for the seven tribes which remained. Different explanations of this fact have been attempted by the commentators, some of which are wholly at variance with the instructions originally given to Moses, and therefore must be at once rejected. The true explanation appears to be, that the casting of the lots commenced before any very accurate survey of the land was made, founded on the

[1] Prov. xvi. 33.

general knowledge of it already obtained by the people; but that the exact dimensions of each portion were determined afterwards. Thus, whilst the camp was still at Gilgal, the country was divided into nine different lots, which were named, perhaps, according to their relative positions, but the boundaries of which were not very clearly defined. The lots were cast, and two of these portions fell to the tribes of Judah and of Joseph, who at once took possession of them, under the direction of their princes. Joshua himself belonged to the latter tribe,—that is, to the tribe of Ephraim; and it was natural, therefore, that he should leave Gilgal, and pitch his camp in the midst of his own tribe. This he did; and Shiloh became, from that time, the great centre of all his operations. For another reason also this was done,—namely, that the worship of God, which had so long been interrupted, might now be recommenced; and the probability is, that the spot was selected in accordance with the divine command; for God had said, 'When ye go over Jordan, and dwell in the land which the Lord your God giveth you to inherit, and when He giveth you rest from all your enemies round about, so that ye dwell in safety; then there shall be a place which the Lord your God shall choose to cause His name to dwell there: thither shall ye bring all that I command you' (Deut. xii. 10, 11). Here, then, without further delay, the tabernacle was erected, and here it continued until the days of Saul. But we shall return to this locality again; and meanwhile, following as nearly as we can the topographical order[1] of the tribes, from south to north, we will first survey the territories of Judah and of Benjamin, which were contiguous to each other.

---

[1] This is not the order in which they were assigned;—that order was as follows:—Judah, Ephraim and Manasseh, Benjamin, Simeon, Zebulun, Issachar, Asher, Naphtali, Dan; but it will be more simple and convenient to take the topographical order, by which means we shall be able to proceed through the country step by step, and obtain a general notion of its character, and of the relative positions of the tribes.

' JUDAH, thou art he whom thy brethren shall praise,' said
the aged patriarch Jacob; and to Judah the first lot fell, he
having succeeded, in part, to the privileges of the first-born.
Rich and valuable was his inheritance in many respects : ' the
part of Palestine which best exemplifies its characteristic scenery
—the rounded hills, the broad valleys, the scanty vegetation;
the villages or fortresses—sometimes standing, more frequently
in ruins—on the hill tops ; the wells in every valley, the vestiges
of terraces, whether for corn or wine. Here " the lion of Judah "
entrenched himself to guard the southern frontier of the chosen
land, with Simeon, Dan, and Benjamin nestled around him.'[1]
His boundaries were as follows : on the south it commenced
from the outmost coast of the Dead or Salt Sea eastward; thence
passed on to the south side of the heights of Akrabbim; proceeded thence to Zin, not far from Kadesh, and thence to Hazar-
addar and to Azmon, places now unknown; and from Azmon it
fetched a compass to the river of Egypt—the Wady el-Arish
thus extending far into the desert.[2] Its western extremity here
was the Mediterranean Sea. A list of thirty-six cities, situated
in the south of the territory, is given in Josh. xv. 21–32, the
sites of which, with but few exceptions, are quite unknown.
Beersheba, where the patriarchs sojourned, and which was thirty-
one Roman miles south-west of Hebron, is one of the exceptions
to this general loss; and Kerioth is perhaps identical with the
present Kereitein, ' a site of ruins on the hill-slopes on the west
side of the valley which descends southward from Mâ'in towards
the desert.'[3]

The eastern boundary was the whole length of the Dead
Sea; and the northern boundary passed from that sea, where the
Jordan entered it, up to Beth-hoglah, and thence to Beth-arabah,
and to the stone of Bohan, the son of Reuben. Of the two

[1] ' Sinai and Palestine,' p. 159.   [2] Num. xxxiv. 3–5; Josh. xv. 2–4.
[3] Van de Velde; ' Memoir,' p. 328.

latter places we know nothing; but Beth-hoglah was identified by Dr Robinson with a fine fountain called 'Ain Hajla, two miles west of the Jordan.[1] Beth-hoglah was assigned, not to Judah, but to Benjamin, as also was Beth-arabah (chap. xviii. 21, 22). Through the valley of Achor, the boundary then went up towards Debir, turned northward towards Gilgal,[2] passed to En-shemesh (the fountain of the sun), and thence to En-rogel (the fountain of the spies), the so-called well of Job and Nehemiah, on the south-east of Jerusalem. Passing up by the valley of the son of Hinnom, it went up to the top of the mountain that lies before the valley of Hinnom westward; and from the top of the mountain it was drawn to the waters of Nephtoah, probably the fountain of Lifta, which lies a little more than half an hour west-north-west of Jerusalem.[3] Thence it proceeded to the cities of Mount Ephron (nowhere else mentioned), and on to Baalah or Kirjath-jearim, 'the city of forests,' one of the cities of the Gibeonites, identified by Robinson with 'Kuriet el-Enab.[4] It now described a curve westward to Mount Seir,—not, of course, the Idumean mountain of that name, but a range running in a south-westerly direction, where Robinson discovered a village named Soris or Sores, and near to which is another village called Kesla, supposed to be identical with Chesalon or Mount Jearim. Thence it proceeded to Bethshemesh, 'the house of the sun,' now represented by ruins on the west side of 'Ain Shems, south of Wady Surat; and from this point it passed to the Mediterranean Sea, embracing Timnah, Ekron, Shichron, and Jubniel,—the latter now called Jubna, a town three hours south-west of Ramleh. The sea formed its western boundary; but ultimately, as we shall hereafter find, the coast country was

[1] 'Researches,' vol. ii., p. 544.

[2] A place of that name distinct from the Gilgal of Josh. iv. 19.

[3] Stewart, 'The Tent and the Khan,' p. 349.

[4] 'Researches,' vol. ii., p. 11; vol. iii., p. 156; Van de Velde's 'Memoir,' pp. 347 and 304

assigned to the tribes of Simeon and Dan. In the low ground or valley of the lot of Judah, were fifteen cities, the names of which are given in Josh. xv. 33-36, and the sites of several of which have been discovered. In the actual plain were sixteen cities; in the southern part of the hill country were nine cities; on the Philistine line of coast were Ekron, Ashdod, and Gaza, with their towns and villages; in the south-western hills were eleven cities; north of these, around Hebron, were nine cities; east of these was a group of ten; north of Hebron a group of four; to the westward of Jerusalem, Kirjath-jearim and Rabbah; and in the wilderness or desert, between the mountains and the Dead Sea, there were six cities (Josh. xv. 37-62).

From this enumeration of the cities assigned to Judah, we should infer that the territory must have been somewhat thickly populated by the original inhabitants; but no doubt many of the so-called cities were very small, and, like eastern villages of the present day, were occupied by only a few families. The tribe of Judah numbered, at this time, 76,500 who were twenty years old and upwards; and as they did not require so large a portion of the country, many of the cities, as well as the line of coast, were afterwards given up to the tribes of Simeon and Dan, whilst nine cities were given to the priests (Josh. xxi. 9-19). It is remarkable that Jerusalem, which afterwards became so prominent in the history of the tribe, was not included in this allotment, but was assigned to Benjamin. Attempts were probably made by the children of Judah to wrest it from the Jebusites, who then possessed it; but they were unsuccessful, and it remained in the hands of the Jebusites until the days of David the king.[1]

The physical aspects of the territory of Judah were much diversified. In the south was the undulating pasture-land, sometimes designated 'the wilderness of Judah;'[2] in the east, imme-

---

[1] Josh. xv. 63; 2 Sam. v. 6, 7.   [2] Judges i. 16.

diately adjoining the Dead Sea, was Midbar, or THE WILDERNESS, a wild and desolate country, full of rocks and caves, the haunts of wild beasts and robbers, one of whose six cities—Engedi, ‘the fountain of the kid’—became celebrated in the history of Saul and David.[1]   West of this was the hill country, on the mountain tops of which were ‘the fenced cities of Judah,’ so similar in position and appearance as not to be easily distinguished one from another.   Among these was Bethlehem, ‘the house of bread,’ called originally Ephrath or Ephratah,[2] which, though little among even the thousands of Judah, became the birth-place of David the son of Jesse, and afterwards of Him who was David's Son and Lord.   Its present representative, *Beit-lahm*, stands on a hill of Jura limestone, six Roman miles east of Jeru-salem, and near it may be seen flocks and shepherds as in days of old ; and, in the time of barley harvest, reapers in the fields, with women and children gleaning after them.   The hills of Judah are admirably adapted for the cultivation of the vine ; and here, in the palmy days of the country, it grew luxuriantly on terraces formed on the mountain sides, and carefully guarded by walls and watch-towers.   ‘Binding his foal unto the vine, and his ass's colt unto the choice vine ; he washed his garments in wine, and his clothes in the blood of grapes,’ was the prophecy of Jacob relative to his son Judah, indicating that the vine would be as common as any other tree, and the wine obtained from it as plentiful as water ; and, though the language is that of poetry, the prediction was almost literally fulfilled, for to Judah belonged ‘the valley of Eshcol,’ and other choice localities, where the vine abounded, and the grapes were the richest that the whole land produced.

On the west, between the hill country and the Mediterranean

---

[1] 1 Sam. xxiv. 1–4.

[2] The phrase, Ephratah, does not occur in the Hebrew of Josh. xv. 48–62, but is inserted in the Septuagint version.

Sea, was the SHEPHELAH, or lowland, long the territory of the Philistines, from whom the whole country received the name of Palestine. But, as the tribes of Simeon and Dan were subsequently located here, we shall reserve our remarks respecting this part of the country for the next chapter.

The territory thus assigned to Judah was both prominent and extensive, and singularly remarkable were the fortunes of the tribe. In the days of the Judges, Othniel alone, among the rulers, is named as belonging to it; and, at a later period, the Benjamite Saul was anointed king over the whole land. But in the prophecy of Jacob the sceptre was given to Judah; and when it fell from the feeble hands of Saul, David the Bethlehemite obtained it, and, with occasional interruptions, it remained in the possession of the tribe until Shiloh came. Bright and glorious was Judah's history during the reigns of David and of Solomon; and though, when Rehoboam came to the throne, the ten tribes separated from the kingdom, yet it continued to prosper in spite of all its enemies. Often pillaged of its wealth, that wealth, partly acquired by maritime commerce carried on through the ports on the Red Sea, remained considerable even to the last; and when the ten tribes were led away captive into Assyria, Judah remained in her strongholds and bade defiance to Sennacherib and his hosts.[1] Nor would she have ever fallen but for the practice of idolatry which several of her kings were determined to introduce; and it was to cure her of that practice, that the king of Babylon was permitted to set up his throne in Jerusalem, and to lead captive into Babylon the inhabitants of the land.[2] And the end was answered; for when, at the close of the seventy years' captivity, the Jews were permitted to return to their own country, they did so, not to set up again altars unto Baal, or to re-establish the grove-worship of Astarte, but to rebuild the temple of the Lord God of their fathers, and hence-

---

[1] 2 Kings xix.   [2] 2 Kings xxiv., xxv.

forth to worship only Him.[1]   That worship, it is true, degenerated into mere formality ; but it continued to be observed, to the
exclusion of the worship of the gods of the heathen, up to the
time when Jesus of Nazareth trode the hills of Judea, and walked
within the porches of the temple beautified by Herod.

Close upon the northern boundary of Judah was little
Benjamin with his flocks.   His eastern boundary was the Jordan ;
his northern boundary coincided with the southern boundary of
Ephraim, passing through the mountains towards the west ; and
his western boundary, leaving that of Ephraim, which ran on
to the Mediterranean Sea, came down from the mountains to
Kirjath-jearim.   Here the southern boundary commenced, and
coincided with the northern boundary of Judah.   Two groups
of cities—the one of twelve, the other of fourteen—were found
in the territory of Benjamin.[2]   Of the former, *Jericho* and *Bethel*
were the most distinguished : among the latter were *Gibeon*,
which already has been the subject of remark ; *Mizpeh*, where
Samuel dwelt as judge,[3] and where Saul was elected king ;[4]
Zelah, where Saul and Jonathan were buried ;[5] and *Jebusi*, or
Jerusalem, which became the capital of the whole land of Palestine, and the scene of the grandest and most momentous events
that ever occurred in the history of the world.   Of Benjamin,
Moses said, ' The beloved of the Lord shall dwell safely by
Him ; and THE LORD shall cover him all the day long, and he
shall dwell between His shoulders ;' and when, by ' the rocky
sides of Jerusalem,' the tribe of Benjamin took up its abode, the
prediction was literally fulfilled.   Small was this tribe in number
—45,600—but distinguished was its history, and striking was
its character.   ' In his mountain passes—the ancient haunts of
beasts of prey—Benjamin " ravined as a wolf :" in the morning
descended into the rich plain of Philistia on the one side, and of

[1] Ezra iii., iv.   [2] Josh. xviii. 11–28.   [3] 1 Sam. vii. 16.
[4] 1 Sam. x. 17–24.   [5] 2 Sam. xxi. 12–14.

Jordan on the other, and "returned in the evening to divide the spoil." In the troubled period of the Judges, the tribe of Benjamin maintained a struggle, unaided, and for some time with success, against the whole of the rest of the nation. And to the latest they never could forget that they had given birth to the first king. Even down to the times of the New Testament, the name of Saul was still preserved in their families; and when a far greater of that name appealed to his descent, or to the past history of his nation, a glow of satisfaction is visible in the marked emphasis with which he alludes to the "stock of Israel, the tribe of Benjamin," and to God's gift of Saul the son of Kish, a man of the tribe of Benjamin."[1]

The two distinguishing features of the territory of Benjamin were its passes and its heights. The latter were of considerable elevation, being 2000 feet and upwards above the level of the maritime plain; and the former, caused in part by the torrents which ran down either side of this lofty water-shed, were the only means of access to the land of the Philistines on the east, and to the fords of the Jordan on the west. To some of the events which occurred in these passes—the battle of Ai, in one of those on the east, and the battle of Beth-horon, in one of those on the west—we have referred already; and in later times they were the scenes of other conflicts not less important in the general history of the land. Indeed, all the leading events in the fastnesses of the tribe of Benjamin received a special character from the heights or the passes of the territory assigned to it; and some of those events appear far more striking when viewed in connection with the physical aspects of the localities where they occurred.

Gibeah, or 'the hill,' will furnish us with illustrations of this fact. Its site was discovered by Dr Robinson on a high Tell, called Tuleil el-Fûl, or the 'hill of beans,' one hour and a quarter

---

[1] Stanley, pp. 198–9.

north of Jerusalem, which commanded an extensive view of the
country in all directions, and especially towards the east.   Near
to it, though distinct from it, was Gaba (Josh. xviii. 24), which Dr
Robinson identified with Jeba, a small village on another eminence, and probably the 'Gibeah in the field' of Judges xx. 31 ;
from which, across the deep ravine on the north, could be seen
another village called Mŭkhmâs, the ancient Michmash, lying
directly over against Jeba,[1] in a direction about north-east.
The former Gibeah is not mentioned among the cities of Benjamin in Josh. xviii. ; but we find it in the history of the Judges
as the scene of the sad and shameful story of the Levite and his
concubine, which gave rise to a disastrous war, in which there
fell of the Israelites and of Benjamites sixty-five thousand men.
The Levite having made the conduct of the men of Gibeah known
through all the land of Israel, a council of the tribes was held at
Mizpeh ; and it was resolved *to go up* against Gibeah, and to
demand the men who had committed that great sin.   The Benjamites refused, and came forth against the Israelites to battle,
and twice obtained a victory over them.   But, having asked
counsel of the Lord, the Israelites made a third attack upon the
Benjamites.   They set *liers in wait* about Gibeah ; they then
went up against Gibeah as they had done before, and when the
Benjamites came out to attack them, they fled, and drew them
away from the city.   The liers in wait then hasted and rushed
upon Gibeah, and ere long the Benjamites, who were in pursuit
of the Israelites in the valley, looked round and saw ' the flame
of the city ascending up to heaven.'   They were dismayed ; they
turned their backs and fled towards the way of the wilderness.
But the battle overtook them—they were enclosed on every side ;
and there fell of them eighteen thousand men, who were all men
of valour.   Seven thousand more fell in their flight towards the
rock Rimmon, and on that rock six hundred more abode four

[1] ' Researches,' vol. i., pp. 440 and 577.

months.   This spot Robinson discovered in a village called Rŭm-môn, situated on and around the summit of a conical chalky hill, distant from Gibeah about seven Roman miles.   It is described by Mr Finn as a strong natural fortification on the south and west sides, in the latter of which he found two caverns, and two larger ones on the eastern side, in which we may well suppose the six hundred fugitives took up their abode.[1]

Gibeah was the home, if not the birth-place of Saul; and here, after he had been anointed king, a conflict took place between him and the Philistines.   The latter had fixed their garrison at Michmash, which, as we have seen from Dr Robinson's remarks, was a little north of Gibeah, a deep ravine lying between them called the Wady es-Suweinit.   The Philistines had sent spoilers out of Michmash, who spread themselves in three different directions; when Jonathan, Saul's son, left his father's camp at Gibeah, accompanied by his armour-bearer, and proceeded through the passage towards the garrison of the Philistines.   'In this valley,' says Dr Robinson, 'are two hills of a conical, or rather a spherical form, having steep rocky sides, with small wadys running up behind each, so as almost to isolate them.'[2]   And what says the Scripture narrative?   'There was a sharp rock on the one side and a sharp rock on the other side: and the name of the one was Bozez, and the name of the other Seneh.'[3]   Passing these rocks, Jonathan and his armour-bearer ventured towards Michmash; and when the men of the garrison saw them, they said, 'Come up to us, and we will shew you a thing.'   Jonathan took this as a sign that the Lord had delivered them into the hand of Israel; and, climbing up the steep ascent on his hands and feet, he attacked the Philistines, and his armour-bearer slew after him.   A panic seized the garrison; the

---

[1] See Judges xx.; 'Researches,' vol. i., p. 440; Van de Velde's 'Memoir,' p. 345.

[2] 'Researches,' vol. i., p. 441.   [3] 1 Sam. xiv. 1-23.

shock of an earthquake was just then experienced; the Philistines turned their swords one against another; and the watchmen on the heights of Gibeah observed them melting away, and wondered at the cause. Great was the discomfiture of the Philistines; and the Lord saved Israel that day, and the battle passed over to Beth-aven.

It would lead us too far away to refer to other events which occurred in the territory of Benjamin; and we mention these only as illustrative of the character of the country allotted to that tribe. Its hills and its passes were the scenes of many conflicts and of many victories, extending through the whole history of David and the kings, repeated subsequent to the captivity and during the times of the Maccabees, and occurring again, more terribly than before, after the rejection by the Jews of Jesus the Messiah. Little did the Benjamites know, when they took possession of their inheritance, that those hills would ever witness such events as those which came to pass. Wisely were they hidden from them, even as the future of the history of Palestine is wisely hidden from us. Its future will perhaps be as momentous as its past; but to man it is not given to uplift the curtain which hides that future from our view, and all that we can do is *patiently to* WATCH AND WAIT.

JOPPA.

CHAPTER XIII.

THE LOT OF SIMEON AND DAN.

THE congregation of the children of Israel had assembled at Shiloh, and there the tabernacle had been set up when, after some delay,—arising, as may be supposed, from an unwillingness on the part of the people to prosecute the work of dividing the land on such inaccurate a measurement as that on which it had commenced,—Joshua proposed that three men out of each of the seven tribes should go through the whole country and describe it, and that, on their return, these seven tribes should receive their inheritance by lot. See chap. xviii. 1–6.

The proposal was agreed to, and the men selected entered on their task. Josephus says that Joshua sent with them 'some geometricians, who could not easily fail of knowing the truth on account of their skill in that art;' and, moreover, that he 'gave them a charge to estimate the measure of that part of the land that was most fruitful, and what was not so good;' for some portions of it being much better than others, Joshua thought that it should be estimated, not by its extent, but by the richness of its soil. The same writer says that the survey occupied seven months, at the end of which period the men returned to the camp at Shiloh.[1]

It has been thought that this must have been an accurate and scientific survey, for the men described the land by cities, dividing it into seven parts, in a book or tablet; and there can be little doubt that they were well able to do this, as the Israelites had learnt the art of mensuration in Egypt, where, on account of the annual overflowing of the Nile, it had been practised from the earliest times.[2] 'It is reasonable to suppose,' says Sir J. G. Wilkinson, 'that, as the inundation subsided, litigation often occurred between neighbours respecting the limits of their unenclosed fields; and the fall of a portion of the bank, carried away by the stream during the rise of the Nile, frequently made great alterations in the extent of land near the river side. A mode of determining the quantity which belonged to each individual was, therefore, very necessary, both for settling disputes with a neighbour, and for ascertaining the tax due to government. But it is difficult to fix the period when the science of mensuration commenced. If we have ample proofs of its being known in the time of Joseph, this does not carry us far back into the ancient history of Egypt; and there is evidence of geometry and mathematics having already made nearly the same progress at the earliest period of which any monuments remain, as in the later era of the Great Remeses.'[3]

This valuable art, then, was acquired by the Israelites during

---

[1] Antiq. v. i. 21.   [2] Herod. ii. 109; Diod. i., p. 69.
[3] 'Popular Account,' vol. ii., p. 248.

their residence in Egypt, and now they were able to turn it to account for their own mutual benefit. And yet it is doubtful, after all, whether a *complete* geometrical measurement of the land was taken; for the Canaanites, who were still very numerous, would scarcely have allowed the men to pass quietly through every corner of it and measure it with a line.[1] Rather was it, as we conceive, as accurate a survey as could be obtained under the circumstances, and sufficiently so to enable Joshua to divide the rest of the country among the seven tribes, who had not yet received their inheritance, with a due regard to their respective claims. That it did not embrace the territories already assigned to Judah and Joseph, is expressly stated; it was found, however, that the former had obtained a larger tract of country than they required; and this survey having proved, as we may well suppose, that the unassigned lands were by no means too extensive for the seven tribes, it was resolved that the children of Judah should give up to Simeon a portion of their inheritance.

Accordingly, 'the inheritance of the children of Simeon was within the inheritance of the children of Judah'—chap. xix. 1, 9. 'But whether,' says Keil, 'it was a compact territory or not, cannot be determined with certainty, because only the cities allotted to Simeon are given, and the situation of many of them is unknown.'

In the south of the territory of Judah, thirteen cities were given to Simeon,[2] together with the villages situated near them. Among these were BEERSHEBA, on the borders of Palestine and the Wady es Seba; MOLADAH, which Robinson identified with el Milh, where he found two wells forty feet deep, and the stones of a ruined town, scattered over a space nearly half a mile square, all unhewn; and ZIKLAG, which subsequently was in the possession of Achish, king of Gath, and was presented by him to David when he was persecuted by Saul, but at a little

[1] See Keil on Joshua, p. 414.   [2] Josh. xix. 2, 6, comp. 1 Chron. iv. 28–31.

later period was set on fire by the Amalekites. The sites of the rest are not known, with the exception, perhaps, of Hormah, called also Zephath, which Robinson identifies with the pass Es-Sufâh, on the extreme south of the Land of Promise.

A second group of four cities was ceded to Simeon—Ain, Remmon, Ether, and Ashan—with all the villages that were round about them to Baalath-beer, or Ramah of the south. The situation of Ain is unknown; Remmon was in the southern boundary of the territory of Judah; and Ether and Ashan were in the Shephelah or low country of Judah, where Van de Velde heard of ruins and ancient sites, one of which was called by the people at Beit-Jibrin, Tell 'Athar.[1]

In some maps of Palestine, even of modern date, a distinctly marked territory is assigned to Simeon on the borders of the Mediterranean Sea; but there is no evidence that the tribe ever possessed more than a few cities and villages in that locality. The prophecy of Jacob respecting it—' I will disperse them in Judah, and scatter them in Israel '—was literally fulfilled; and reduced in numbers from 59,300 fighting men to 22,200,[2] they were but little capable of making aggressions on the tribes of Canaan, and could scarcely retain what cities they had received. Judah took Gaza, Askelon, and Ekron, cities of the Philistines, and probably gave them to Simeon; but the Philistines afterwards retook them, and in their hands they were found in the days of Samuel the prophet.[3]

Yet in the days of Hezekiah the tribe of Simeon appears to have possessed a spirit of enterprise of more than ordinary daring. Finding themselves in want of pasture lands for flocks, five hundred men of the tribe, having for their captains Pelatiah, Neariah, Rephaiah, and Uzziel, the sons of Ishi, made a brilliant and successful attack on certain Hamitic tribes dwelling in tents

---

[1] ' Memoir,' p. 311. [2] Comp. Num. i. 22, 23, xxvi. 12–14.
[3] Comp. Judg. i. 18 ; 1 Sam. vi. 17.

beyond the southern boundaries of Palestine. The locality was
'at the entrance of Gedor,' or, as the LXX. read it, Gerar, on
'the east side of the valley,' which, there is little doubt, was
between the southern boundary of Judah and Mount Seir,
whither, it is said, these marauders went.[1] It was a daring act;
and had we the details of the story, they would probably prove
as romantic as many of the stories of Bedouin life. But doubtless
the parties were well repaid; for 'they found fat pasture and
good, and the land was wide, and quiet, and peaceable,'—a description which agrees with the accounts of this territory given
by modern travellers. 'The wadys are full of trees, and shrubs,
and flowers; while the eastern and higher parts are extensively
cultivated, and yield good crops. The general appearance of
the soil is not unlike that around Hebron, though the face of the
country is very different. It is, indeed, the region of which
Isaac said to his son Esau, "Behold, thy dwelling shall be the
fatness of the earth, and of the dew of heaven from above."'[2]

No other facts are related of this tribe in the Sacred Scriptures. It gave to the nation neither judge nor prophet, nor,
indeed, any other illustrious person,—excepting, perhaps, Judith,
who traces her descent from Simeon;[3] but her story is so romantic as to render it doubtful whether she was more than the
heroine of a fiction. We may suppose, therefore, that this tribe
became absorbed in that of Judah; so that by nothing short of a
miracle, or rather a series of miracles, would any Israelite of
the present day, or indeed any Israelite after the captivity in
Babylon, be able to prove that he belonged to the house of
Simeon.

DAN was the next neighbour to Judah, the territory assigned
to that tribe being west of that of Benjamin, and its utmost
coast the Mediterranean Sea. Judah ceded to Dan some of his

---

[1] 1 Chron. iv. 39–42.   [2] Robinson's 'Researches,' vol. ii., p. 154.
[3] Judith ix. 2.

northern cities, and Ephraim some of his cities in the south; and thus another tribe was provided for out of the over-abundance of these two.

The lot of Dan was narrow in its boundaries, but rich and fertile in its general character. It formed part of the great maritime plain, the southern portion of which was occupied by the Philistines, and was so fruitful as to be designated 'a little Egypt.'[1] Some of its cities are of considerable interest.

Of these, ZORAH and ESHTAOL, on the south, were received from the tribe of Judah. Of the latter there is now no trace; but the former, which became the birth-place of Samson, is now represented by a village called Sur'ah, in the Wady es-Surar, a few miles west of Jerusalem. In the same neighbourhood was Ir-shemesh (the city of the sun), equivalent to Beth-shemesh (the house of the sun), the ruins of which were found by Dr Robinson near 'Ain Shems, consisting of many foundations and the remains of ancient walls of hewn stone.[2] This city was assigned to the Levites,[3] but, in the days of Ahaz, was taken by the Philistines,[4] who probably had in it a temple to the sun, long prior to the conquest of Canaan by the Israelites. Shaal-abbin and Jethlah are unknown; and Ajalon, Eltekeh, Gibbethon, and Gath-rimmon were given up to the Levites. Of the other cities mentioned we know little or nothing, with the exception of Timnath, Ekron, and Japho; but these are somewhat celebrated both in earlier and in later times.

TIMNATH, or TIMNAH, was recognised by Dr Robinson in a village called Tibneh, one hour south-west of Zorah; and from the latter place to the former there is a considerable descent, whence it is said of Samson that he *went down* to Timnath, where he saw the woman whom he wished to marry. At that time Timnath had its beautiful vineyards; and such vineyards there

---

[1] See Stanley's 'Sinai and Palestine,' p. 256.
[2] 'Researches,' vol. ii., p. 224. [3] Josh. xxi. 9, 16. [4] 2 Chron. xxviii. 18.

are now in all these hamlets along the base of the hills and upon the mountain sides, which, says Dr Thomson, extend 'far out from the villages, climbing up rough wadies and wild cliffs, in one of which Samson encountered the young lion.'[1] EKRON was the most northerly of the cities of the Philistines, and is at present represented by a village called Akir, in a plain to the north of the Wady Surar. No remains of antiquity exist at 'Akir; but 'this may be accounted for,' says Dr Robinson, ' by the circumstance, that probably the ancient town, like the modern villages of the plain, and like much of the present Gaza, was built only of unburnt bricks.' Josephus says that the god of Ekron was a fly, and of that insect Dr Thomson found plenty at this spot. It was from Ekron that the ark of the covenant was sent back, after it had been captured by the Philistines, upon a new cart drawn by two milch-kine; and these, being left to their own course, took the 'straight way' to Beth-shemesh. 'In coming, therefore, from 'Ain Shems to Akir,' says Dr Robinson, 'we might almost be said to have followed the track of the cart on which the ark was thus sent back.'[2] It was remarkable, however, that the unguided oxen should find their way to Beth-shemesh so readily, for it lies by the side of a long rocky spur which strikes down from the mountains south of Latron. 'It might be said by those ignorant of the country, that, the whole distance being a level plain, there was no great miracle needed to secure the safe transmission of the ark over the comparatively short distance; but let them make a similar experiment, and stake their scepticism on its success, if they have courage to do so; or let them even try to reach Ain es Shems themselves without a guide, and see how they will succeed.'[3] Doubtless, then, these oxen were under the direction of that God, the symbol of whose presence they had, as it were, in charge, and who can as easily

[1] 'The Land and the Book,' p. 566.   [2] 'Researches,' vol ii., p. 228.
[3] 'The Land and the Book,' p. 535

guide the movements of inferior creatures as He can control the wayward passions of mankind.

JAPHO, or JOPPA, was the celebrated harbour of Palestine, now called JAFFA, the history of which is full of interest, and would, if written in detail, fill a large volume. It formed the northern boundary of the territory of Dan, whose border ' went up to,' or ' over against Japho,'[1] and was distant from Jerusalem about 36 miles. A very high antiquity is assigned to it by Mela, who affirms that it existed prior to the Deluge ;[2] and rabbinical writers derive its name from Japhet, one of the sons of Noah, whilst classical writers refer it to Iopa, the daughter of Aeolus and the wife of Cepheus. A few years ago a remarkable Phœnician sarcophagus was found at Sidon, on the lid of which was an inscription of twenty-one long lines, in Phœnician characters. A copy of this inscription was sent by Dr Thomson to the Chevalier Bunsen, by whom it was transmitted to Professor Dietrich, who published a translation of it, accompanied by an elaborate critique. From this translation, which is given at length by Dr Thomson, we learn that the sarcophagus was that of Asheminazer, king of the Sidonians, who says, among other things, that Baal, lord of the kings, bestowed on him 'Dor and Joppa, and ample corn-lands which are at the root of Dan.' Of the date of this inscription nothing very certain can be affirmed, but that it is very ancient there can be no doubt; and Dr Thomson seems inclined to ascribe it to the times of the Judges, when Laish, conquered by the Danites, was a Sidonian city.[3] By the Duc de Lugnes, who deposited this sarcophagus in the Louvre at Paris, and who has published a learned commentary on the inscription, it is assigned to the end of the seventh century before the Christian era.[4]

---

[1] Josh. xix. 46.   [2] Pliny, 'Nat. Hist.' v. 13, 14.
[3] 'The Land and the Book,' p. 138, etc.
[4] See Stanley, 'Sinai and Palestine,' p. 275.

The whole territory of Dan was, as we have already re-
marked, exceedingly rich and fertile, being distinguished, like the
rest of Philistia, for its numerous corn-fields, 'the great source
at once of the power and the value of Philistia; the cause of its
frequent aggressions on Israel, and of the unceasing efforts of
Israel to master the territory.' The history of Samson is bound
up with the physical characteristics of the country which was
the scene of his wondrous exploits. There was 'the standing
corn of the Philistines,' with 'the vineyards and olives,'—the
former nearly ready for the sickle, the latter laden perhaps with
quantities of ripening fruit; and Samson, having caught three
hundred foxes and tied them tail to tail, put burning firebrands
between their tails, and sent them into the midst of the standing
corn and burnt it.[1] The rock Etam, to which he escaped for
refuge from his enemies,[2] was in the territory of Judah, probably
in the neighbourhood of Bethlehem. Gaza, the gates of which,
with the door-posts, he carried away to the top of a hill near
Hebron, was a frontier city of the Philistines; and here the brave
Nazarite, having betrayed to his wife the secret of his strength,
first lost his eyes and then sacrificed his life;[3] but he was buried
in the midst of his own people, between Zorah and Eshtaol,[4]
doubtless with all the respect which his brethren and his father's
house could show him. In his administration of twenty years
was fulfilled the prophetic word of Jacob, 'Dan shall judge the
people;' but the dying patriarch added, 'Dan shall be a serpent
by the way, an adder in the path, that biteth the horse heels, so
that his rider shall fall backward;' for he judged the people 'not
without a certain blame and contempt, compared with the veno-
mous viper or cerastes, which, treacherously lurking in the sand
or the trace of the carriage-wheels, not easily noticed on account
of its grey colour, and suddenly darting forth, attacks with more

[1] Judg. xv. 1–6.   [2] Judg. xv. 7, 8; 2 Chron. xi 6.
[3] Judg. xvi. 1–3, 21.   [4] Judg. xvi. 31.

tal bite horse and rider; a reptile held by the ancients to be so formidable, that they believed, if it was killed by a man on horseback with a spear, that "the poison would run up the weapon, and kill, not only the rider, but the horse as well."'[1]

The last census of the tribes of Israel showed that in the tribe of Dan there had been an increase of 1700 fighting men; the numbers being in the first instance 63,700, and in the second, 64,400. It is not surprising, then, to find that the territory of the Danites proved too narrow for them,[2] especially when it is stated that 'all their inheritance had not fallen unto them among the tribes of Israel.'[3] But they were a bold and enterprising people, and, subsequent to the death of Samson, 'they sought them an inheritance to dwell in.' They first sent five men of their family as spies, from Zorah and from Eshtaol, who went to Mount Ephraim, and lodged in the house of one Micah, who had a Levite as his priest. From the Levite they obtained counsel, and crossing the great plain of Esdraelon, they proceeded northwards beyond the waters of Merom, and came to Laish, a town belonging to the Zidonians, situated 'on the reedy margin of the marsh,' through which the Jordan first flows. It was several miles from Zidon, the parent city; and the spies found the inhabitants 'dwelling carelessly, after the manner of the Zidonians, quiet and secure;' moreover, 'they had nothing to do,' and 'there was no magistrate in the land,' and therefore no government; so that the town was evidently in a defenceless state, and might easily be taken by a small force. What did the five men? They returned to Zorah and to Eshtaol, and said to their brethren, 'Arise, that we may go up against them: for we have seen the land, and, behold, it is very good.' At once six hundred men were armed for the enterprise, who first pitched at Kirjath-jearim, in the territory of Judah, a place identified by Robinson with Kuryet-el-'Enab, near to Beth-shemesh; thence they pro-

---

[1] Kalisch on Genesis, p. 757.   [2] Josh. xix. 47.   [3] Judges xviii. 1.

ceeded to the house of Micah, in Mount Ephraim, whom they robbed of his ephod, his teraphim, and his priest; and at length they arrived at Laish, and finding its inhabitants still quiet and secure, smote them with the edge of the sword, and set the city on fire. These lazy Zidonians well merited their fate; but the Danites were a set of wild and 'angry fellows,' almost equally as lawless as were the victims of their cruelty. Their conduct was unjust and base, and is mentioned by the writer of the book of Judges only as an illustration of the character of the times.

On the site of the city they had destroyed they built another, which they called Dan; and here they set up the graven image of Micah. 'And Jonathan the son of Gershom, the son of Manasseh, he and his sons were priests to the tribe of Dan until the day of the captivity of the land.'[1] As long as the tabernacle of the Lord Jehovah remained at Shiloh, the graven image remained in Dan. And in the days of Jeroboam idol-worship was again established in the city; for there he set up a golden calf, and thither the people went up to worship.[2] In how many instances has a city which was established by iniquity continued for years, and even for centuries, to be a curse to its inhabitants and to the surrounding country! 'Woe to him that buildeth a town with blood, and stablisheth a city by iniquity;' and woe also to the town thus built, and to the city thus stablished; for the character of its founder will be impressed upon it, and upon it, therefore, must rest the frown of God.[3]

'From Dan to Beersheba' became a common expression in Israel; and the meaning of it is explained by the fact, that Dan

---

[1] Judges xviii. 30, 31; comp. Josh. xix. 47.

[2] 1 Kings xii. 29, 30; 2 Kings x. 29.

[3] There is a Dan mentioned in Gen. xiv. 14, which some suppose to be the Dan-Jaan of 2 Sam. xxiv. 6, and to be a different town from the Dan mentioned above. (Kalisch on Genesis.) It is quite as probable, however, that these places were all identical, and that the name Dan was inserted in the MSS. of Gen. xiv. by a later copyist, the word originally having been Laish.

was the most northerly city in the land, and Beersheba the most southerly, so that the two cities were, proverbially at least, the extremities of Canaan. But 'Dan has ceased to be a city for ages. Not one solitary habitation is there. The fountain still pours forth its river of delicious water, but herds of black buffaloes wash and wallow in its crystal pools. You cannot even examine the site with satisfaction, so dense is the jungle of briars, thorns, and thistles which have overspread it.'[1]

It was to this northern colony of the Danites that the prophecy of Moses pointed : 'Dan is a lion's whelp : he shall leap from Bashan.' Of the southern Dan little more remains to be noticed beyond the fact intimated in the song of Deborah, that, when she summoned the Israelites to go forth against Sisera, ' Dan remained in ships ;' whence it would appear that, dwelling as they did on the shores of the Mediterranean, the tribe had already entered, to some extent, on a seafaring life. It is scarcely probable, however, that they became anything more than fishermen ; for none of the Israelites gave themselves to maritime pursuits, but were content to trade by sea through the medium of the Phœnicians. Perhaps, then, the ships in which the Danites remained, were only Phœnician vessels, or but small fishing boats ; and we imagine that, thorough landsmen as they were, all that they did was to venture out a little distance from the land under the care and direction of more expert seamen. That they were on friendly terms with the Phœnicians at a later period, we gather from 2 Chron. ii. 14, where we learn that Huram sent to Solomon a cunning man, whose mother was of the daughters of Dan, and whose father was a man of Tyre. Such intermarriages, though forbidden by the law, were perhaps not infrequent ; but whether they were or not, it is certainly a remarkable coincidence that this one should be met with in the tribe of Dan, whose intercourse with the Phœnicians was, no doubt, main-

[1] 'The Land and the Book,' p. 216

tained by means of the Tyrian mariners who visited the port of
Joppa.

The tribe of Dan is mentioned in 1 Chron. xxvii. 22, but is
omitted in the genealogies of 1 Chron. ii.-xii.   It is also omitted
from the list of the tribes sealed in the Apocalypse (Rev. vii.),
and that because of its idolatry.   ' On this account,' says Hengstenberg, ' did Ezekiel, ch. xlviii., in determining the respective
positions of the tribes, assign the most remote place on the north
to Dan, at the farthest distance from the sanctuary, to which
Judah immediately adjoined.   John only proceeds a step farther,
and excludes Dan altogether.'   As such, then, the *tribe* of Dan
has no place among the sealed ones ; and though we must by no
means infer from this that *individuals* belonging to it are not
found among the redeemed, yet are we admonished by the fact
of the sinfulness of idolatry, and warned against the danger of
setting up false gods in our hearts.   ' Little children, keep yourselves from idols,' is the injunction of the same Apostle who wrote
respecting the sealing of the twelve tribes of Israel, and who
affirms that there shall in no wise enter into the New Jerusalem
' anything that defileth, neither whatsoever worketh abomination,
or maketh a lie; but they only which are written in the Lamb's
book of life.'

THE TOMB OF JOSEPH

CHAPTER XIV.

THE LOT OF EPHRAIM AND MANASSEH.

IN the very centre of the land of promise—the glory of all lands, the land flowing with milk and honey—was the lot of Ephraim and of the half-tribe of Manasseh. Of Joseph, Moses said,—

'Blessed of the Lord be his land,
　For the precious things of heaven,
　For the dew,
　And for the deep that coucheth beneath,
　And for the precious things brought forth by the sun,
　And for the precious things put forth by the moon,
　And for the chief things of the ancient mountains,
　And for the precious things of the lasting hills,
　And for the precious things of the earth, and fulness thereof,
　And for the good-will of Him that dwelt in the bush :

> Let the blessing come upon the head of Joseph,
> And upon the top of the head of him that was separated from
>   his brethren.
> His glory is like the firstling of the bullock,
> And his horns are like the horns of unicorns :
>   With them shall he push the people together to the ends of
>   the earth ;
>   And they are the ten thousands of Ephraim,
>   And they are the thousands of Manasseh.'[1]

In striking agreement is this beautiful language with the blessing pronounced upon Joseph by his aged sire,[2] so that we shall expect to find the inheritance of the tribe one of great value; nor, if we look at it carefully, shall we be at all disappointed. It is described in Joshua, chapters xvi. and xvii., first as a whole; after which, the portion allotted to Ephraim is described more fully. 'It is remarkable, however,' says Keil, 'that of the whole of the inheritance assigned to the children of Joseph only the southern boundary is given, whilst nothing is said respecting that on the north. But this may be explained on the ground that this double tribe had no definite boundary on the north, but merely had a number of cities allotted to them within the line which formed the boundary of the tribes of Asher and Issachar (chap. xvii. 10, 11); and partly from the fact that the Josephites did not expel the Canaanites from the northern part of the territory assigned them, but only gradually brought them into subjection, and dwelt by the side of, or amongst them. Hence the limits of their land in this direction were not always the same; and at one time, when they expressed some discontent at the portion allotted to them, Joshua told them that they might enlarge their possessions if they could drive the Canaanites out.'

Of the southern boundary, then, it is said, that commencing at the Jordan by the brook near Jericho, called ' the waters of

[1] Deut. xxxiii. 13–17.   [2] Gen. xlix. 22–24.

Jericho on the east,' it passed to the north of that city, through
the desert, or the Wady Kelt, to the mountains in the vicinity of
Bethel. Thence it proceeded to the southern side of Bethel or
Luz, and passed along the territory of Archi to Ataroth, and
went down westward to the coast of Japhleti to Beth-horon the
nether, and to Gezer, coming out on the coast of the Mediterranean Sea.[1]

The position of Jericho has been already indicated. That of
Bethel, the ancient Luz (Gen. xxviii. 19), is now represented by
the village of Beitin, twelve Roman miles north of Jerusalem,
the ruins of which occupy 'the whole surface of the hill-point,
sloping towards the south-east, and cover a space of three
or four acres.'[2] From the Arabs, who had pitched their tents
on this spot for the summer, to watch their flocks and fields of
grain, Dr Robinson obtained the finest milk and butter he found
anywhere in Palestine. The land of the Archites is supposed to
be the district now called Beni-Zeid; and Ataroth is identical
with the modern Atara, four miles south of Jijilia, situated on
the summit of a high hill in the midst of a richly cultivated district.[3] Beth-horon the nether, now Beit-Ur et Tahta, is on the
way from Jerusalem to Ludd, at a distance from the former of
twelve Roman miles. Gezer was probably situated between
Beth-horon and Lydda. The boundary-line left the latter city
on the south, and running to the north-west, terminated at Joppa,
the celebrated port.

It is exceedingly difficult, as Keil has observed, to understand
the description of the northern boundary of Ephraim—for such
it appears to be—given in Josh. xvi. 5-8; and hence he supposes
that there is here a corruption of the text. But, referring the
critical reader to his pages, we may observe that none of the
places here mentioned—Michmethah, Taanath-shiloh, Tappuah,

---

[1] Josh. xvi. 1-5; comp. xviii. 11, 14.
[2] Robinson's 'Researches,' vol. i., p. 448.   [3] Ibid. vol. ii., p. 265.

and the river Kanah—have been identified with certainty;[1] so that all we really know, is that the territory of Joseph was divided into two portions, somewhere near the midst, the southern portion being the lot of Ephraim, and the northern portion that of the half-tribe of Manasseh or the descendants of Gilead. The other half-tribe of Manasseh, or the descendants of Machir, had already its inheritance in the fertile districts of Gilead and Bashan, on the east of the Jordan; and now, partly adjoining it on the west of the river, this second half found itself as well provided for. Josh. xvii. 1, 2.

All the male descendants of Manasseh had been satisfied when the daughters of Zelophehad, whose father had died in the wilderness without any male issue, presented themselves before Joshua, and before Eleazar the priest, and requested that they too might have an inheritance; for, after the death of their father, they had received a promise from Moses, who had inquired of the Lord on their behalf, that they should receive a possession among their brethren.[2] The claim was a just one; and Mahlah, Noah, Hoglah, Milcah, and Tirzah, who remembered the promise given them by Moses, and who did well to urge their right to an inheritance, received one without delay. There were six families of the Manassites; and their land was divided into ten portions, five of which were assigned to Abiezer, Helek, Asriel, Shechem, and Shemida, and their descendants, and five to the family of Hepher—that is, to the daughters of Zelophehad—his son. Josh. xvii. 5, 6.

Several important cities were assigned to Manasseh within the territories of Asher and of Issachar; namely, Beth-shean, Ibleam, Dor, Endor, Taanach, and Megiddo; but the Manassites were unable to drive out the Canaanites from these cities. When, however, the children of Israel became strong, they com-

---

[1] See Van de Velde's 'Memoir' on these places.
[2] Josh. xvii. 3, 4; comp. Num. xxvii. 1-9.

pelled the Canaanites to pay tribute, but did not utterly drive them out.[1] The children of Joseph, including both the Manassites and the Ephraimites, displayed some want of courage and independence. Not satisfied with the inheritance they had received, they came to Joshua, and urging that they were a numerous people, asked why but one lot had been assigned to them. But Joshua replied, 'If thou be a great people, then get thee up into the wood-country, and cut down for thyself there in the land of the Perizzites, and of the Rephaim, if Mount Ephraim be too narrow for thee.' The region here referred to was the mountainous tract near Beth-shean, which extended to Endor on the coast, and which was originally in possession of the Perizzites and the Rephaim, and was thickly covered with wood. Go then, said Joshua, and clear this country of the forest. But they complained that they could not, because the inhabitants that dwelt in the neighbouring valley had chariots of iron. It was a cowardly reply; and Joshua only repeated his instructions with a delicate vein of irony. 'The captain gives the same reply as before, but more fully and explicitly. Since, says he, you are a numerous people, and possess great strength, unless you are very timid you will easily obtain possession of the mountain; and, although it is covered with wood, you will clear. And not only will you take the mountain, but all adjacent places; for you are furnished with such resources that you will easily conquer even the Canaanites, with all their chariots of iron.'[2] These mountains, which extended southwards towards the limits of the inheritance of Benjamin, consisted of a range of limestone hills, in the heart of which were wide plains, 'streams of running water, and continuous tracts of vegetation.' And conquered they were, so that even the members of other tribes wandered to their heights for shelter and for power,[3] and 'Mount Ephraim,'

[1] Josh. xvii. 12, 13; comp. Judges i. 27, 28.
[2] Masiuo, quoted by Keil.   [3] See Stanley, p. 229.

the designation of the entire district, became the scene of many
a terrible conflict and of many a decided victory.

Almost in the centre of the lot of Ephraim the tabernacle
was erected by Joshua, and around it gathered the whole congregation of the children of Israel.[1] This event took place, as
we have already observed, immediately after the tribe had received its inheritance; and a highly important event it proved.
The spot was called Shiloh, and the locality was 'on the north
side of Bethel, on the east side of the highway that goeth up
from Bethel to Shechem, and on the south of Lebonah,'[2]—where
Dr Robinson found ruins bearing the name of Seilûn, which
answers perfectly to Shilon, the full form of the Hebrew name.
'The position is in itself a fine one for strength, if it were ever
fortified, though it is commanded by the neighbouring hills.
Among the ruins of modern houses are many large stones, and
some fragments of columns, showing the place to have been an
ancient site. At the southern foot of the Tell is a small ruined
mosk, standing partly beneath a noble oak-tree.'[3]

Here, then, the tabernacle was reared; here the ark of the
covenant of the Lord remained until the days of Eli the priest;
here was an annual feast to the Lord, during which the daughters of Shiloh came out 'to dance in dances,' who, on one of
these occasions, were carried off by the neighbouring tribe of
Benjamin as wives (Judges xxi. 19–23); and here Samuel was
dedicated to the Lord, and spent the days of his childhood in
the service of the sanctuary (1 Sam. i. 24–26). But ultimately
God forsook it; for He 'refused the tabernacle of Joseph,
and chose not the tribe of Ephraim; but chose the tribe of
Judah, the Mount Zion which He loved.'[4] The proud and
haughty spirit displayed by Ephraim in many instances, was
highly offensive in the sight of Heaven; and, though long borne

---

[1] Josh. xviii. 1–3.   [2] Judges xxi. 19.
[3] 'Researches,' vol. ii., p. 269.   [4] Ps. lxxviii. 67, 68; Jer. vii. 12–14.

with, it was at length given up, and its glory and dominion passed away.

Twelve miles north of Shiloh was the vale of Shechem, a locality to which reference was made in a former chapter, in connection with the event that took place on Mount Ebal and Gerizim.[1] We return to it again, inasmuch as its beauty is illustrative not only of the prophecy of Moses, but also of that of the dying Jacob. 'Here,' says Van de Velde, in his description of this vale, 'there is no wilderness; here there are no wild thickets, yet there is always verdure—always shade, not of the oak, the terebinth, and the caroub-tree, but of the olive grove, so soft in colour, so picturesque in form, that for its sake we can willingly dispense with all other wood. Here there are no impetuous mountain torrents, yet there is water—water, too, in more copious supplies than anywhere else in the land; and it is just to its many fountains, rills, and water-courses that this valley owes its exquisite beauty.'[2] Now it will be remembered that to these lovely groves Abraham was attracted when first he entered the land of promise; and that here Jacob settled after he had crossed the brook Jabbok and the northern passes of the river Jordan; for here 'he bought a parcel of a field, where he had spread his tent, at the hand of the children of Hamor, Shechem's father, for a hundred pieces of money.'[3] And this parcel of a field, subsequently wrested from him by the Amorite, but retaken from them by his quiver and his bow, he gave to his son Joseph,[4] blessing him also with 'blessings of the heaven above, and blessings of the deep that lieth under.' Here, in particular, were 'the precious things of heaven, of the dew, and of the deep that coucheth beneath;' here were 'the precious things of the lasting hills,' and 'the precious things of the earth, and the fulness thereof;' for, though 'the valley is far from

---

[1] See Chap. VII.
[2] 'Syria and Palestine,' vol. i., p. 386.
[3] Gen. xxxiii. 19.
[4] Gen. xlviii. 22; John iv. 3.

broad, not exceeding in some places a few hundred feet,' yet the
herbage is everywhere rich and nutritious, and you are charmed
with the music of the murmuring brook, and with the melody of
numerous singing birds; whilst, as you approach Samaria, two
hours distant, you pass through gardens plentifully stocked with
many kinds of fruit-trees, ' among the branches of which clusters
of grapes hang down in wreaths and festoons.'

It is not surprising that a spot so fertile, and moreover hallowed by its connection with the lives of the patriarchs, should
become the first capital of the country after its conquest by the
Israelites. 'Its central position and its peculiar fertility made
it the natural seat of settled habitation in the north, even to a
greater degree than the vale of Mamre and Eshcol ensured, as
we have seen, the same early privilege for Hebron in the south.'[1]
The tabernacle and the ark of the covenant remained at Shiloh,
but the place where the national assemblies met was Shechem.
There Joshua gathered all the tribes together prior to his death;[2]
and there, at a much later period, all Israel came together to
make Rehoboam king.[3]

It was at Shechem that the Israelites buried, probably with
the most solemn funeral rites, the bones of the patriarch Joseph.
The fact is not recorded until after the account of the death of
Joshua;[4] but there can be little doubt that the rites of sepulture
were performed soon after the erection of the tabernacle at
Shiloh. The dying patriarch had said to his brethren, 'God
shall surely visit you, and ye shall carry up my bones from
hence;' and being carefully embalmed, his mummy was preserved in the family of Ephraim through the long period of the
bondage, through the forty years' wanderings in the wilderness
of Sinai, and through the wars of Joshua with the inhabitants of
Canaan; and now, at length, the word of prophecy was fulfilled,

[1] Stanley, p. 236.   [2] Josh. xxiv. 1.
[3] 1 Kings xii. 1.   [4] Josh. xxiv. 32.

and Joseph's remains were deposited in their last earthly resting-place.

The history of the tribes of Ephraim and Manasseh, and its connection with the territory they occupied, can be but very briefly sketched. After the death of Joshua the house of Joseph went up against Bethel, which was still in the hands of the Canaanites ; and being shown the entrance to it by one of its inhabitants, they entered the city and smote it with the edge of the sword, but suffered the man and his family to depart, who went into the land of the Hittites, and there built a city which he called Luz.[1] Under a palm-tree near Bethel[2] sat Deborah the prophetess, who was probably a woman of Ephraim, and who, when the Israelites had long been oppressed by Jabin, king of Canaan, rose up, like the modern Joan of Arc, to rescue her people from the giant's grasp. She and Barak having gathered the people together to Mount Tabor, a battle ensued with Sisera, the captain of Jabin's army, near ' that ancient river, the river Kishon ;' and Sisera's army being discomfited, he himself fled to the tent of Jael, the wife of Heber the Kenite, who, when he was fast asleep and weary, cruelly put him to death. From the magnificent ode of Deborah, sung after the victory, we learn that the Ephraimites and the Manassites both took part in the struggle ; for ' out of Ephraim was there a root of them against Amalek ;' ' out of Machir came down governors.' And it would have been strange indeed if these tribes, so near the field of battle, had stood aloof ; and had they done so, they must have shared in the curse pronounced on Meroz, who ' came not up to the help of the Lord, to the help of the Lord against the mighty.'

At a later period, when the Midianites had entered the land of Canaan, and had pitched their tents in the great plain of Esdraelon, whence they had made incursions as far as to Gaza, destroying the produce of the earth, and compelling the Israelites

---

[1] Judges i. 22–26.   [2] Judges iv. 5.

to take refuge in the dens and caves of the mountains, rose up Gideon, a Manassite; and this mighty man of valour, with his three hundred men, armed only with trumpets, and with lamps concealed in earthen pitchers, discomfited the Midianitish host, though they were in number like grasshoppers for multitude. And that first victory was followed up by a second; for at Beth-shittah, 'the house of the acacia,' and Abel-meholah, 'the meadow of the dance'—places in the Jordan valley under the mountains of Ephraim—the Ephraimites, to whom messages had been sent, took the passages of the river, intercepted the flight of the princes of Midian, Oreb and Zeeb, and slew them there. The proud spirit of the Ephraimites was somewhat roused, how-ever, because Gideon had not called them into the conflict earlier, and they chode with him sharply. But he knew how to deal with them, and said, ' Is not the gleaning of the grapes of Ephraim better than the vintage of Abi-ezer?' What had he done, that is, in comparison with them ? They had slain even the princes of Midian ; had he obtained a victory so signal ? ' Then their anger was abated to him when he said that.' Their vanity was gratified, and they cared for little else. They thought they had done a greater thing than Gideon, and therefore they said no more ![1]

' Faint, yet pursuing them,' Gideon and his three hundred men followed the rest of the fugitives (at the head of whom were Zebah and Zalmunna) over the Jordan eastward, and having overtaken them beyond Succoth and Penuel, the inhabitants of which cities refused him bread, he chastised the men of Succoth and broke down the tower of Penuel, and slew the princes Zebah and Zalmunna, as they, by their own confession, had slain some of the brethren of Gideon at Mount Tabor. After this the people wanted to make Gideon king ; but he declined the honour, if such it was, and said, ' I will not rule over you, neither shall my son rule over you: the Lord shall rule over you.'[2] Sad it was that

---

[1] Judges viii. 1–3.   [2] Judges viii. 4–23.

such a man should relapse into idolatry ; but of the golden ear-rings of the Midianites ' he made an ephod,' implying not only the preparation of a priestly garment, but the construction of a graven image, which he set up in Ophrah, and which became a snare to him and to his house. A natural result followed. After his death his family was divided ; and Abimelech, one of his sons, slew all his brethren, Jotham only excepted, and induced the people to proclaim him king at Shechem. Jotham heard of it, and on the top of Mount Gerizim uttered his remarkable parable respecting the trees which desired a king,—a parable which proved prophetic, for, three years afterwards, the men of She-chem avenged upon Abimelech, their king, the blood of the sons of Gideon which he had shed.[1]

By another sad event is the history of the Ephraimites stained. Jephthah the Gileadite having delivered Israel from the Am-monites, the men of Ephraim, true to their character, went to him and demanded why he had not called them to fight with Ammon, and threatened that they would burn his house with fire. A conflict ensued between the two tribes on the eastern side of the Jordan, and the Ephraimites were smitten by the Gileadites, and fled. But the Gileadites took before them the passages of the river, and intercepted their flight. A difference of dialect had arisen in Israel, and the Ephraimites were unable to pronounce the aspirated sound *sh ;* and when an Ephraimite came to the fords, and, denying that he was an Ephraimite, asked permission to pass over, the Gileadites said to him, Say now Shibboleth, שִׁבֹּלֶת (that is, a stream or flood), but he said Sibboleth, סִבֹּלֶת (that is, burdens), and was then slain without mercy. Thus were the Ephraimites punished for their audacity, for there fell of them at that time forty and two thousand.[2]

By the capture of the ark of the covenant in the days of Eli the priest, and by its subsequent removal to the hill of Zion,

---

[1] Judges ix. 1-27. [2] Judges xii. 1-6.

through the instrumentality of David the king,[1] the pride of
Ephraim was once more humbled. But soon after the revolt of
the ten tribes, the erection of the city of Samaria by Omri gave
renown to the tribe of Ephraim; for that city was situated in the
very heart of their territory, on an oblong hill, six miles from
Shechem, and almost on the edge of the great maritime plain.
' This was the mountain Shomron (corrupted through the Chaldee
"Shemrin" into the Greek "Samaria") which Omri bought of
Shemer for the great sum of two talents of silver, and built
on the mountain, and called the name of the city which he
built Shomron (or Samaria), after the name of Shemer, owner of
the mountain.' ' What Omri in all probability built as a mere
palatial residence, became the capital of the kingdom instead of
Shechem. It was as though Versailles had taken the place of
Paris, or Windsor of London. But in this case the change was
effected by the admirable choice of Omri, in selecting a position
which, as has been truly observed, combined in a union not elsewhere found in Palestine, strength, beauty, and fertility. Its
fertility and beauty are shared to a great extent with Shechem,
in this respect the common characteristics of these later capitals,
all probably alike included in the bitter praise of the prophet,
"Woe to the crown of pride, to the drunkards of Ephraim,
whose glorious beauty is a fading flower, which are on the head
of the fat 'ravines' of them which are overcome with wine."
But having these advantages, which Shechem had, it had others
which Shechem had not. Situated on its steep height, in a plain
itself girt in by hills, it was enabled, not less promptly than
Jerusalem, to resist the successive assaults made upon it by the
Syrian and Assyrian armies. The first were baffled altogether;
the second took it only after a three years' siege, that is, three
times as long as that which reduced Jerusalem.'[2]

---

[1] 2 Sam. vi. 1–12.

[2] Stanley, p. 242; comp. Van de Velde, vol. i., p. 374, etc.

Samaria, or rather Sebaste, its successor, built by Herod, is now represented by considerable remains, which consist principally of colonnades, the grandest of which runs along the south side of the hill, down a broad terrace, which descends rapidly towards the present village. Along this line are nearly one hundred columns, and many others lie scattered about on lower terraces. The glory of Ephraim has passed away, to return not again until the millennial age, when the scattered tribes of Israel shall be restored; when 'Ephraim shall not envy Judah, and Judah shall not vex Ephraim;' when amity and peace shall prevail among all nations, and the noise of battle shall be heard no more.

MOUNT TABOR.

CHAPTER XV.

THE LOT OF ISSACHAR AND ZEBULUN.

NEXT to the mountains of Ephraim, and to the territory assigned to Manasseh, lies the vast plain of Esdraelon, or Jezreel, extending, in length, from Mount Carmel on the west, to the Jordan on the east; and, in breadth, from En-gannim on the south, to Mount Tabor on the north. The eastern part of this plain fell to the lot of Issachar; the western portion was assigned to Zebulun.

Of the sixteen cities which belonged to Issachar, mentioned in Joshua xix. 17–22, nine are altogether unknown; but the sites of the remaining seven have been identified, and by means of these, and the boundary lines of the neighbouring tribes, the limits of Issachar's inheritance can be fixed with tolerable accuracy.

Commencing on the western side of the Jordan, a little south of Bethshan, which belonged to the tribe of Manasseh, the border passed under Mount Gilboa, and swept round the foot of the range called the mountains of Ephraim to En-gannim; thence running north-westward to the foot of the range of Carmel, it crossed the river Kishon, turned to the east and ran to Mount Tabor, and thence to the valley of the Jordan, a little below the Lake of Gennesaret.

En-gannim, which was afterwards assigned to the Levites, was identical with the Ginnea of Josephus, and with the present town of Jenin, which lies on the southern edge of the plain, 'in the midst of gardens of fruit-trees, which are surrounded by hedges of the prickly pear.'[1] Six miles northward of it is Jezreel, now Zerin, on the western extremity of Mount Gilboa. It 'lies comparatively high, and commands a wide and noble view, extending down the broad, low valley on the east to Beisan, and to the mountains beyond the Jordan; while towards the west it includes the whole great plain quite to the long ridge of Carmel. It is a most magnificent site for a city; which, being itself thus a conspicuous object in every part, would naturally give its name to the whole region. There could be little question that, in and around Zerin, we had before us the city, the plain, the valley, and the fountain of the ancient Jezreel.'[2] The name Jezreel, יִזְרְעֶאל, signifies, 'God is sowing,' and indicates the richness of the neighbouring soil. Here was the royal residence of Ahab, and here the vineyard of Naboth, which the haughty monarch demanded that he might turn it into a garden of herbs.

Nearly six miles north of Jezreel is Shunem, now Solam, near to which, in all probability, were Haphraim and Shihon. Chesulloth is supposed to be represented by the village of

---

[1] Robinson's 'Researches,' vol. ii., p. 215; and Wilson's 'Lands of the Bible,' vol. ii., p. 84.

[2] Robinson, vol. ii., p. 320.

Iksal, the Xaloth of Josephus, situated in a rich and fertile plain at the foot of Mount Tabor, on which mount stood the city TABOR, which must have belonged partly to Issachar and partly to Zebulun, as it is mentioned as one of the sixteen cities of the former tribe, but as given to the Levites by the latter.

Of the territory in which these cities stood it seems impossible to speak in terms too high. The mountains which rise up from the plain—Gilboa, Tabor, and the Little Hermon—are the birth-places of innumerable springs and rivulets, which, running east or west, spread beauty and fertility through their tracks; and the soil, being rich and loamy, is productive of the choicest vegeta-tion, so that ' the aspect of the plain in spring time is that of a vast waving corn-field, olive-trees here and there springing from it.' One of its rivers is the Kishon, which takes its rise in Mount Tabor,[1] and, fed also from other sources, winds round to the north-west, and, after running about seven miles, empties itself into the Mediterranean near Mount Carmel. It was here that the battle took place, already referred to, between the Israelites, under the command of Deborah and Barak, and the host of Sisera. ' And the princes of Issachar were with Deborah; even Issachar, and also Barak: he was sent on foot into the valley.'[2] They met together on the broad summit of Mount Tabor, for it is said, ' Barak went down from Tabor, and ten thousand men after him;' whilst Sisera, with his nine hundred chariots of iron, took up his position in the valley of Megiddo; and there the terrible conflict took place, and ' the stars in their courses fought against Sisera.' ' There came down from heaven,' says Josephus, ' a great storm, with a vast quantity of rain and hail; and the wind blew the rain in the face of the Canaanites, and so darkened their eyes, that their arrows and their slings were of no advantage to them, nor would the coldness of the air permit the soldiers to make use of their swords; while this storm did not so much in-

---

[1] See Robinson's ' Researches,' vol. ii., p. 364.   [2] Judges v. 15–21.

commode the Israelites, because it came in their backs.'[1] Meanwhile the torrent of the Kishon was suddenly swollen, as it is wont to be by heavy rains, and pouring down the valley in which the hosts of Sisera lay, it swept them down before it, and 'they had no alternative but to make for the narrow pass which led to Harosheth.' 'The space, however, becomes more and more narrow, until within the pass it is only a few rods wide. There, horses, chariots, and men become mixed in horrible confusion, jostling and treading down one another; and the river, here swifter and deeper than above, runs zigzag from side to side of the vale, until, just before it reaches the castle of Harosheth, it dashes sheer up against the perpendicular base of Carmel. There is no longer any possibility of avoiding it. Rank upon rank of the flying host plunge madly in, those behind crushing those before deeper and deeper in the tenacious mud. They stick fast, are overwhelmed, and swept away by thousands.'[2]

In the same locality Gideon also gained his victory; and here too it was that, at a later period, the prophets of Baal were slain by command of the prophet Elijah, whence it is supposed that the present name of the Kishon, Nahr Mŭkatta, or the river of slaughter, took its rise. But many have been the conflicts witnessed on the plain of Esdraelon, both in ancient and in modern times. It has been, in fact, the great battle-field of Palestine, and it may yet again be the scene of other contests —contests which shall tell upon the future destinies of the land.

Moses said of Zebulun and Issachar, 'Rejoice, Zebulun, in thy going out; and, Issachar, in thy tents. They shall call the people unto the mountain; there shall they offer sacrifices of righteousness: for they shall suck of the abundance of the seas, and of treasures hid in the sand.' 'Issachar,' said Jacob, 'is a strong ass couching down between two burdens: and he saw that rest was good, and the land that it was pleasant; and bowed his

---

[1] Antiq. v. v. 4.　　　　　[2] 'The Land and the Book,' p. 436.

shoulder to bear, and became a servant to tribute.' The latter words especially are strikingly descriptive of the character of the tribe, which, though its numbers were considerable—amounting at the conquest to 64,300—dwelt, and rejoiced to dwell in tents, living a nomadic life, and seldom taking part in the great struggles of the nation. One of the judges, Tola, was of the tribe of Issachar; but we know nothing of him beyond the fact that he dwelt at Shamir, in Mount Ephraim. Between two burdens, or folds, as the word signifies, Issachar couched as a strong-boned ass, such as was used in the work of the fields; and seeing that rest was good, and the land that it was pleasant, he threw aside the military character and betook himself to a pastoral and agrarian life. To such an extent was this the case, that the men of Issachar submitted to pay tribute to surrounding nations, whilst to their neighbours the Manassites they gave up Beth-shean, Ibleam, Taanach, and Megiddo, perhaps because they could not take them from the Canaanites themselves, and thought that the Manassites would be more successful.

But all this was characteristic of human nature. When men CAN live in ease, they *will*. Who that inherits a magnificent estate would not far rather dwell upon it, cultivating its soil, developing its resources, and enjoying its productions, than go into the battle-field and expose himself to the hardships of a soldier's life? A desire for military fame, or a sense of duty to his country, will often induce a man to take the latter course; but few there are who would not prefer the former, and to whom it would not be a trial and a task to exchange a home of quietness for a scene of turmoil and of strife.

At a later period, however, the men of Issachar were of a different spirit, for it is said, that 'among all the families of Issachar were valiant men of might, reckoned in all, by their genealogies, fourscore and seven thousand.'[1] Moreover, of the

---

[1] 1 Chron. vii. 5.

numbers who went up to Hebron, ready armed, to make David the king, were men of Issachar 'that had understanding of the times, to know what Israel ought to do: the heads of them were two hundred; and all their brethren were at their commandment.'[1] According to Josephus, there were of the armed men of Issachar twenty thousand; and it is supposed that those who had understanding of the times were men who were distinguished for their skill in astronomical and physical science, by which they were enabled to predict the course of events. 'The learning of this tribe is no doubt particularly referred to here, because it was matter of great importance that not the military tribes, but the tribe which was celebrated for its scientific attainments, and also for its sound judgment in political questions, declared for David.'[2]

Nor should it be forgotten that Baasha, one of the kings of Israel, belonged to the tribe of Issachar; but he was a fierce and warlike man, and obtained the throne by the murder of his predecessor. It was far more to the honour of the tribe that in the days of Hezekiah many of them came, with a multitude of Ephraim, Manasseh, and Zebulun, to keep the feast of unleavened bread at Jerusalem. Long had they been separated from their brethren of the south, and many years had elapsed since they celebrated the Passover; so that they seem to have forgotten what was required of them, and 'had not cleansed themselves, but ate the Passover otherwise than it was written.' Hezekiah, however, prayed for them, and said, 'The good Lord pardon every one that prepareth his heart to seek God, the LORD God of his fathers, though he be not cleansed according to the purification of the sanctuary.' His prayer was heard, and the Lord healed the people.

Issachar and Zebulun were closely allied by birth; and, as tribes, they were not separated, for the inheritance of the latter adjoined that of the former on the north.

[1] 1 Chron. xii. 32.   [2] Bertheau, Commentary on 1 Chron.

Its boundaries are described in Joshua xix. 10–16. It commenced a little below the southern extremity of the Lake of Gennesaret, and proceeded westward towards the Mediterranean Sea through Sarid, and as far as Maralah,—places, unfortunately, not now known. It is further described as reaching to Dabbasheth—'the camel's hump;' supposed, therefore, to have been upon the heights of Carmel; and to the stream that is before Jokneam,—in all probability, the Kishon. Such is the general boundary line on the south; respecting which it is stated further, that from Sarid it turned eastward toward the sun-rising, unto the border of Chisloth-tabor, and then went to Daberath, and up to Japhia,—places at the foot or in the vicinity of Mount Tabor. In the district were also Gittah-hepher, or Gath-hepher, the birth-place of the prophet Jonah (now represented by the village el Meshad, about five miles north-east of Nazareth); Ittah-kazin, which is not now known; and Remmon-methoar, now Runmanneh, seven miles north of Nazareth. Neah, Hannathon, and the valley of Jiphthah-el are not known, but these places were on the northern boundary. Of the five cities mentioned in verse 15, none have been discovered except Bethlehem, now Beitlahm, half way between Nazareth and Mount Carmel; and three others —Kartah, Dimnah, and Kitron, mentioned as belonging to the tribe of Zebulun in chap. xxi. 34, or in Judges i. 30—are not included in this enumeration.

'Zebulun,' said Jacob, 'shall dwell at the haven of the sea; and he shall be for an haven of ships: and his border shall be unto Zidon.' And of Issachar *and Zebulun* Moses said, 'They suck of the abundance of the seas, and of treasures hid in the sand.' Remarkably were the prophecies fulfilled; for, though the territory of Zebulun did not reach to the coast of the Mediterranean, it extended towards it, and on the east it embraced a considerable portion of the shores of that celebrated lake on which, in after times, so many incidents occurred in connection with the history of our Lord. We can easily understand the expression, 'His borders shall reach unto Zidon,' as signifying that it should extend towards the land of the Phœnicians, of which Zidon, and not Tyre, was at that time the capital. And there is every reason to believe that, as tradition states, the tribe of Zebulun traded on the sea in purple dyes, and perhaps employed themselves in the manufacture and exportation of glass; for is not glass a treasure hid in the sand? It has been supposed, indeed, that glass is a modern discovery; but this is a mistake, as it was made in Egypt as early as the times of Joseph; for the process of glass-blowing is represented on the paintings at Beni-Hassan, belonging to the times of Osirtasen I., and glass bottles have been found in the tombs of the kings, bearing the names of the Pharaohs of that period.[1]

The tribe of Zebulun was also celebrated for its scribes; for 'out of Zebulun,' said Deborah, 'came they that handle the pen of the writer.'[2] Their commercial pursuits would almost compel them to the study of the arts and sciences; and it appears that, as early as the times of the Judges, they had acquired distinction in this line of business. Yet, when necessary, they could lay aside the pen for the sword; for they were 'a people who jeoparded their lives unto the death in the high places of the field.'[3] This is high praise, and leads us to think of the Zebulunites as rushing, during the battle on the Kishon, into the very midst of the enemy, and, utterly fearless of their lives, pursuing them when pursuit was no longer necessary.

The population of this tribe was numerous, amounting, at the conquest, to 60,500; yet they were not able to drive out the Canaanites from their territories; 'but the Canaanites dwelt among them, and became tributaries.'[4] The only judge of this tribe was Elon, who 'judged Israel ten years;' the only prophet

[1] See Wilkinson's 'Popular Account,' ii., pp. 58–60.
[2] Judges v. 14.   [3] Judges v. 18.   [4] Judges i. 30.

was Jonah, who was sent to preach unto the Ninevites. But it is probable that some of our Lord's disciples, the fishermen of the Sea of Galilee, belonged to it; though of this we have no certain proof.

Of the Zebulunites of David's time a noble testimony is given. There went up to him to Hebron, 'of Zebulun, such as went forth to battle, expert in war, with all instruments of war, fifty thousand, which could keep rank: they were not of a double . heart.'[1] The tribe, then, had retained its military character, and possessed qualifications of the highest order. Soldiers who can keep rank, who are expert in the use of warlike instruments, and who do not waver in the hour of battle, will be prized by any general or monarch; and such were the men who, from among the Zebulunites, rallied round the standard of David the king. In the 68th Psalm—a Psalm written, as Hengstenberg thinks, on the occasion of the removal of the ark to Mount Zion—it is intimated by David that the princes of Zebulun were there; and princes in character must the fifty thousand have been; nor can we wonder that their name should be held in honour.

It is scarcely possible to refrain from the mention of one town situated in the territory of Zebulun, belonging though it does to a later period of history. Nazareth was there, the never-to-be-forgotten spot where He, of whom Joshua was a type, spent the days of His childhood and His youth. It derives all its importance from this fact, for it is nowhere mentioned either in the Old Testament or by Josephus; and it was so obscure and insignificant a place, that Nathanael, himself a Galilean, in which province it stood, said, 'Can there any good thing come out of Nazareth?' But it was immortalized by its connection with the early life of the Lord Jesus; and from the beginning of the Christian era it has been deemed as second in interest only

[1] 1 Chron. xii. 33.

to Bethlehem, where Christ was born.   It is situated six miles
W.N.W. of Mount Tabor, hid in a narrow vale, a picture of
quietness and repose.   Near to it are Nain, En-dor, Deburieh,
and Yaffa; the two latter places corresponding with the Da-
beroth and Japhia which we have already mentioned.

Of the general features of this neighbourhood, travellers
speak in the highest terms.   'Fifteen gently rounded hills seem
as if they had met to form an enclosure' for this beautiful basin;
'they rise round it like the edge of a shell, to guard it from intru-
sion.   It is a rich and beautiful field, in the midst of these green
hills, abounding in gay flowers, in fig-trees, small gardens, hedges
of the prickly pear; and the dense rich grass affords an abundant pasture.'[1]   With Mount Tabor itself, and the prospect
from its summit, Dr Robinson was in raptures.   It is, he says,
'a beautiful mountain, wholly of limestone; bearing among the
Arabs, like so many other mountains, only the general name,
Jebel et Tur.   It stands out alone towards the south-east from
the high land around Nazareth; while the north-eastern arm of
the great plain of Esdraelon sweeps round its base, and extends
far to the north, forming a broad tract of table land, bordering
upon the deep Jordan valley and the basin of the Lake of
Tiberias.'[2]   Its height is about one thousand feet above the
plain; its summit is broad, and upon it are ruins belonging to
different ages.   The view, as described by Dr Robinson and
others, is extensive and magnificent; and if the men of Issachar
and Zebulun, when they took possession of their lands, climbed
this mountain, and took a survey of their country and of the
adjoining territories, they would see cause to be well satisfied
with the lot they had obtained.   Indeed, the providence of God
was over each of the tribes; and not by chance did the inherit-

[1] Stanley, p. 361; and Richardson.   See also 'The Land and the Book.'
[2] 'Researches,' vol. ii., p. 351, etc.   See also 'The Tent and the Khan,' by
Dr Stewart, pp. 430–5.

ance of any one of them turn up, but by His special guidance and direction. Nor is it by chance that the lot of any man falls to him; but He who gave Canaan to the Israelites, and placed Judah in the south of it and Zebulun towards the north, gives to each nation its country, and to each family of each nation its estate therein, whether that estate consist of broad acres or of a humble cottage without a foot of land.

SEA OF GALILEE.

CHAPTER XVI.

THE LOT OF NAPHTALI AND ASHER.

'DO NAPHTALI, satisfied with favour, and full with the blessing of the Lord ; possess thou the west and the south.'[1] Such were the brief but significant words of Moses relative to the tribe which sprang from the second of the sons of Bilhah. The lot of this tribe fell to the north of Zebulun, and extended from the tribe of Asher on the west, to the Jordan toward the east. Its exact boundaries cannot now be ascertained, as the places mentioned in Joshua xix. 33, Heleph, Adami, Nekeb, Jabneel, and Lakum, are unknown; but supposing, with Keil, Allon Zaanannim, 'the oak by Zaanannim,' to be the same as that mentioned in Judges iv. 11, with the further explanation, 'which is by Kedesh,' then, as Kadesh, or Kedesh, was situated on the hills north-west of Lake Huleh, the boundary line in Joshua xix. 33 is described as running from the south-west to the north-east up to the sources of the Jordan. Josephus says, that the

---

[1] Deut. xxxiii. 23. By the south in this passage, is probably meant the south of the northern Dan, which had just been mentioned in the previous verse.

territory of Naphtali extended, in that direction, 'as far as the city of Damascus and the Upper Galilee, unto Mount Libanus and the fountains of the Jordan.'[1] From the Jordan the boundary turned westward to Aznoth-tabor, and thence to Hukkok,— supposed by Dr Robinson and others to be identical with a village called Yâkuk, situated on the northern border of the plain of Wady Sellameh, about seven miles west of the Lake of Gennesaret.[2] There can be no doubt, however, that the eastern boundary of Naphtali was identical with the western shore of the above lake until it joined the boundary of Zebulun. From Asher on the west the southern boundary of Naphtali was identical with the northern boundary of Zebulun, extending 'to Judah upon Jordan toward the sun-rising.'[3]

But what can be the meaning of this latter expression? How could the boundary of Naphtali extend towards the territory of Judah? The only satisfactory answer to the question has been furnished by Raumer, referred to by Keil, and is substantially the following :—On the eastern side of the Jordan and of the Lake of Gennesaret were a number of 'villages of tents,' which were taken by one Jair, and named, after himself, 'Havoth-Jair,' or 'Chavvoth-Jair,' i.e., villages or towns of Jair.[4] This Jair was, on his mother's side, descended from Manasseh; but, on his father's side, he was a descendant of Judah.[5] Now, according to the law of Moses, 'every one of the children of Israel kept himself to the inheritance of the tribe of his fathers ;' and hence the possessions of Jair were reckoned as belonging, not to the tribe of Manasseh, but to that of Judah, and thus it is that the territory of Naphtali, which was just opposite to Havoth-Jair, is said to extend 'to Judah towards the sun-rising.'

Of the sixteen fenced cities named in Joshua xix. 35–39, Ziddim, Zer, Adamah, Ramah, Edrei, En-hazor, Iron, Horem,

[1] Antiq. v. 1, 22.   [2] 'Researches,' vol. iii., p. 81.   [3] Josh. xix. 34.

[4] Num. xxxii. 41.   [5] 1 Chron. ii. 21, 22.

Beth-anath, and Beth-shemesh, are altogether unknown ; but of the remainder some few traces have been discovered, which it will be sufficient briefly to mention.

HAMMATH, according to the Talmud, was the same as the warm baths a little south of Tiberias : hence the name, which is said to signify thermæ, or springs. These warm fountains are mentioned both by Pliny and Josephus ; Dr Robinson and Dr Wilson visited them ; and Dr Stewart speaks of ruins a little to the south of them. Rakkath and Chinnereth were not far distant. Speaking of these fountains, Dr Thomson says : ' I am inclined to think that this was the Hammath given to Naphtali ; and if so, then Rakkath, mentioned in connection with it, may have been the ancestor of Karak, at the outgoing of the Jordan. Tiberias itself *may* occupy the site of Chinnereth, from which the lake derived its primitive name, as it now gets that of Tiberias from its successor. We throw out these suppositions without vouching for their truth, or attempting to establish it. I cannot doubt, however, that there was a city near Tiberias far older and more splendid than that built by Herod. The granite columns mingled among the now visible ruins must have an antiquity much higher than the first century of our era.'[1]

HAZOR is identified by Dr Thomson with the capital of Jabin, which, he says, was situated to the north-west of the Lake Huleh,—an opinion with which Keil agrees ; but Van de Velde supposes Hazor to be identical with Tell-Hazur, south-east of Rameh ; whilst Robinson fixes the site on Tell-Khureibeh, south of Kades. Of this latter place, Kades or Kadesh, which became one of the cities of refuge, we shall speak hereafter. The only city left is Migdal-el, probably the Magdala of Matthew xv. 39, now a wretched little Mohammedan village called Mejdal, on the western shore of the Lake of Gennesaret.

Of the territory of Naphtali, Josephus and others speak in

[1] ' The Land and the Book,' pp. 395–6.

the highest terms. 'The country that lieth over against this lake hath the same name as Gennesareth; its nature is wonderful as well as its beauty; its soil is so fruitful, that all sort of trees grow upon it; and the inhabitants, accordingly, plant all sorts of trees there.'[1] 'Naphtali was,' indeed, 'satisfied with favour, and full with the blessings of the Lord;' for in his territory, as Josephus further says, 'there was a happy contention of the seasons, as if every one of them laid claim to the country.' There grew the walnut, which requires a bracing atmosphere; there the palm, which flourishes best in heat; and there the fig, which a temperate air suits best. To dwell upon the beauties of the Lakes of Gennesaret and Huleh would lead us beyond our limits; and we must therefore refer our readers to the pages of Wilson, Robinson, and other travellers. Of the latter lake Dr Thomson says, that it is 'unrivalled in beauty, no matter where and from what point you view it. From the distant heights of Hermon, the hills of Naphtali, the plain of Ijon, or the groves of Banias, in mid-winter or mid-summer, in the evening or the morning—stop just where you are. There lies the Huleh, like a vast carpet, with patterns of every shade, and shape, and size, thrown down in nature's most bewitching negligence, and laced all over with countless streams of liquid light.' And 'thus far north, if not considerably farther, extended the territory of the favoured Naphtali.

The one event in the history of this tribe which is at all prominent, stands connected with the exploit of Deborah. We have already referred to her character, and to the victory gained over Sisera, the captain of the hosts of Jabin; but it must not be forgotten that a considerable share of the honour of that victory is due to Barak, the son of Abinoam. He belonged to the tribe of Naphtali, and, knowing well the prowess of that tribe, to him Deborah sent, inviting him to take part in the glorious struggle.

[1] 'Wars,' iii. x. 8.

At first he hesitated; for there was much timidity in the character of the men of Naphtali, and not a little want of self-reliance. But roused, as it would seem, by the noble woman's appeal, he, who was at first fearful, became bold as a lion and swift as the hind, and, dashing forward at the head of his forces into the high places of the field, he discomfited the adversary, and then joined the wife of Lapidoth in the lofty strains of that inimitable ode : ' Praise ye the Lord for the avenging of Israel, when the people willingly offered themselves.—So let Thine enemies perish, O LORD: but let them that love Thee be as the sun when he goeth forth in his might.'[1]

The boundaries of the inheritance of Asher are given in Josh. xix. 24–31; but here, as in other cases, it is difficult to trace them, as many of the places mentioned are quite unknown. We can only give the general outline.

The border began at Helkath, somewhere inland, on the north-east (ver. 25), and extended thence toward the coast of the Mediterranean to Mount Carmel; and, skirting the foot of it, reached to Shihor-libnath, a river said by some to be the Belus of Pliny and Tacitus, and so called because in its vicinity glass was invented,—Shihor-libnath signifying the glass river. The Belus, however, was north of Carmel; whereas this river was the southern extremity of the tribe of Asher, and must have been beyond Dor, as that place was included in the tribe, though afterwards given to the Manassites (chap. xvii. 10). It was probably the Nahr Belka, or else the Zarka, which is still farther south.[2]

From this river the border turned eastward to Beth-Dagon— the house of Dagon—a place not now known, and reached to the border of Zebulun in the valley of Jiphthah-el (ver. 27). The eastern boundary running to the north is then given; but the

[1] See Judges iv. v.
[2] See Keil; but compare Stanley, and Van de Velde's 'Memoir,' etc.

places mentioned, Beth-emek, Neiel, Cabul, Hebron, Rehob, and
Hammon, are unknown.   It ran to Kanah, a large village not
far from Tyre, and reached to Zidon the great.   It then turned
southward to Ramah, somewhere between Zidon and Tyre, and
reached the fortified city of Tyre; and turning thence to Hosah,
a place not now known, its outgoings were at Achzib, on the
coast, nine Roman miles from Acco, called by the Greeks
Ecdippa, and now known as Zib.   The territory of Asher did
not, then, embrace the whole of the coast line, but only that
from Achzib to Shihor-libnath.   Tyre and Zidon, however,
were assigned to this tribe; though, like several other places,
they were never conquered.[1]   But was Tyre in existence at this
time?   Josephus affirms that it was not erected until within
240 years before the building of the temple of Solomon; and
hence it has been affirmed that the Tyre here mentioned was not
the insular Tyre, but a more ancient fortress, built upon the
mainland at a distance from the coast, and afterwards called
Palætyrus.   But 'Josephus,' says Keil, 'is so thoroughly reckless in his statements and dates, that he never deserves credence
when other witnesses are opposed to him.'   The great antiquity
of Tyre has been established on the clearest evidence, and it is
surprising that Dr Robinson and others should accept the date
of its origin given by the Jewish historian.   Its Hebrew name,
Tsor (whence Syria), signifies 'the rock,' or 'the rock-city,'
which was quite unsuitable to Palætyrus, as that place stood
upon a fruitful plain.   Isaiah styles Tyre the 'daughter of
Zidon,'[2]—an expression which signifies that it was a colony of
that city; but Zidon itself (Sidon) was founded prior to the days
of Jacob,[3] and the probability is that its 'daughter' was born
not many years later.   Mr Kendrick supposes that there was a
city on the mainland, near the coast, in the times of Joshua; and
that, from the first, the island, from the excellence of its natural

---

[1] Judges i. 31·   [2] Isa. xxiii. 12.   [3] Gen. xlix. 13.

harbour, was a naval station to that city, and, as a place of security, the seat of the worship of the national deities.[1]

The cities of Asher are said to have been twenty-two in number; among which are mentioned, Ummah, Aphek, and Rehob, —the last distinct from the Rehob before named (vers. 28, 30). The names given in Joshua do not, however, tally with this number, so that there were probably others which are not mentioned.[2]

The occupation of the land of Canaan by the Israelites did not materially affect the interests of the Phœnicians, for it does not appear that the Israelites ever made war upon them ; and Asher ' is simply said to have dwelt among the Canaanites, probably in friendly relations with his maritime neighbours.' 'Judah and Benjamin, who inhabited the interior of the country of which the Philistines occupied the sea-coast, were the most warlike part of the nation; and the fertile district around the maritime cities which were included in their grant (Josh. xix. 44–47), must have appeared to them a very enviable possession, when contrasted with their own mountains, and the desert region bordering on the Dead Sea. Their hostilities were therefore perpetual. But Issachar and Zebulun, Asher and Naphtali, to whose share the fertile region of Galilee, the sea-coast, and the valley of the Upper Jordan had fallen, were not urged by any similar motives to make aggressions on their neighbours. Their agricultural industry would find its reward in the markets of Tyre and Sidon, whose population far exceeded the means of subsistence which their own territory could supply. The traffic between Assyria, Babylonia, Arabia, and the Phœnician cities must have passed through their territories ; and throughout the East the merchant is usually compelled to pay tribute to every tribe which gives him passage and a safe-conduct.'[3]

---

[1] Kendrick's 'Phœnicia,' p. 345.   [2] Comp. Keil *in loco*.
[3] ' Phœnicia,' pp. 63–4.

Jacob's prophecy respecting Asher was brief, but favourable —'Out of Asher his bread shall be fat, and he shall yield royal dainties ;'[1] and that of Moses is equally expressive—'Let Asher be blessed with children ; let him be acceptable to his brethren, and let him dip his foot in oil. Thy shoes shall be iron and brass ; and as thy days, so shall thy strength be.'[2] The very name Asher signifies 'happy ;' and in this fruitful territory there was everything that could render the tribe such,—the 'fat,' the 'royal dainties,' the 'oil,' and the 'iron and brass ;' and it is not surprising that, in the midst of their plenty, the Asherites took no part in the contest with Jabin. 'Asher continued on the sea-shore, and abode in his creeks.'[3] 'Being merchants,' says Fuller, 'they preferred profit before peril, especially being in a safe place where the iron chariots of Jabin, king of Canaan, could not approach them.'

Moses prayed, 'Let Asher be blessed with children ;' but though the tribe numbered, at the second census, 53,400 adult males, and was thus the fifth in population of all the tribes, yet in the days of David it had become comparatively insignificant, so that its name does not appear in the list of the rulers of the tribes.[4] In the days of Hezekiah, when the tribes were invited to celebrate the Passover, the posts passed from city to city, 'even unto Zebulun: but they laughed them to scorn, and mocked them.' 'Nevertheless,' it is added, 'divers of Asher, and Manasseh, and of Zebulun, humbled themselves, and came to Jerusalem.'[5] There is little doubt that the proximity of Asher and Zebulun to the Phœnicians led them to forget the Lord God of their fathers, and to do homage to the gods of Tyre and Zidon. The religion of the Phœnicians was founded on a deification of the powers of Nature. Baal, the sun, and Ashtoreth, the moon, were its two principal divinities ; and to these, and also

---

[1] Gen. xlix. 20.   [2] Deut. xxxiii. 24, 25.   [3] Judges. v. 17.
[4] 1 Chron. xxvii. 16–22   [5] 2 Chron. xxx. 10–12.

to other gods, temples were erected and rites instituted, some of which latter were most libidinous, and others cruel and inhuman. The worship of Moloch was accompanied by the practice of compelling children to pass through fire, and that of Baal by loud cries and self-torturing of the body. The Israelites found this religion fully established when they entered Canaan; and how soon they became inoculated with the poison, their subsequent history clearly testifies.[1] In the time of the Judges, and in the days of Samuel, they became worshippers of Baal and of Ashtoreth; and hence they were delivered into the hands of their enemies, from whom they were delivered only when they returned to the Lord God of their fathers. The tribe of Asher was probably the first to fall into the snare. For it is surprising how the human mind is fascinated with the rites of heathenism. Heathenism seems to operate on those who come into contact with it like a charm, so that they are often taken in the net before they are aware of it. Its splendid temples, its gorgeous ceremonies, its magnificent processions, its sensual gratifications, make their appeal to the worst passions of our nature; and when once the barrier of principle is broken down, and the fear of the true Jehovah is cast off, the heart becomes an easy conquest, and there false gods revel as they will. No wonder that the northern tribes laughed the messengers of Hezekiah to scorn; for what cared they respecting the Passover at Jerusalem, if, as is more than probable, they joined in the worship of Baal in the cities of Tyre and Zidon?

But the day of vengeance came. First the ten tribes were led into captivity by the Assyrians; and afterwards Nebuchadnezzar, the proud king of Babylon, laid siege to Tyre, and took it; an event *predicted* by the prophet Ezekiel,[2] but not *recorded* in the Jewish scriptures.[3] Nor was this the only judgment upon

---

[1] Judges ii. 11–13. [2] Ezek. xxvi. 2–10.

[3] It is, however, preserved from the Tyrian Annals by Josephus, Ant. x. xi. 1.

Tyre. Having recovered something of its former greatness, it was again besieged by Alexander the Great (B.C. 322); and, after a long and obstinate resistance, taken and destroyed by fire. Eight thousand persons were slain, and thirty thousand were sold as slaves. The population was, in this way, nearly exterminated, and Alexander sent colonists to occupy their place. To its subsequent history we need not allude; but its fall, together with that of Zidon, was intended as a warning to all nations who, in the pride of their hearts, set themselves to oppose the one true God.[1]

The tribe of Asher gave to the Israelites neither judge nor ruler; but there is one name which stands connected with it, which, though it belongs to the Christian era, should not be overlooked. Anna the prophetess, the daughter of Phanuel, a widow of about fourscore and four years, which departed not from the temple, but served God with fastings and prayers night and day, was of the tribe of Aser;[2] and when the child Jesus was brought into the temple, she recognised Him as the Christ, gave thanks unto the Lord, and spake of Him to all them that looked for redemption in Jerusalem. Thus was the honour of this tribe rescued from oblivion by an aged and pious matron; but for whom, its name would scarcely have had a place in the pages of the New Testament Scriptures.

[1] See Ezek. xxvii. xxviii.　　　　　[2] Luke ii. 36.

HEBRON.

CHAPTER XVII.

THE LEVITICAL CITIES AND THE CITIES OF REFUGE.

ALL the tribes, save one, had now been provided for; the Israelites had given to Joshua himself Timnath-serah, in Mount Ephraim, for an inheritance; and, as the several allotments were assigned to them, the people had probably repaired to those allotments, and had entered on the possession of their lands. But for the tribe of Levi no provision was yet made, and now therefore the heads of that tribe came to Joshua and Eleazar at Shiloh, and reminded them that the Lord had commanded Moses to give them cities to dwell in, with the suburbs for their cattle.[1] The number of cities they were to receive was in all forty-eight, including six cities of refuge; and

[1] Josh. xxi. 1, 2, comp. Num. xxxv. 2–8.

these cities were to be chosen out of all the tribes of Israel, that the Levites might be scattered among the people for the general good.

The Levites were the descendants of Levi, one of the sons of Jacob by Leah; and to this tribe belonged Moses, the lawgiver of Israel, and Aaron, their high priest. It was specially set apart, instead of the first-born of all the tribes, for sacerdotal purposes; and in the wilderness the office of the Levites was to carry the tabernacle and its furniture from place to place.[1] Highly honourable was the task, and it was, no doubt, performed with considerable pleasure; but now that the people had entered Canaan, and that the tabernacle had been set up in Shiloh, the work ceased, and another task would therefore devolve upon the tribe. What that task was, we shall hereafter indicate.

The sons of Levi were Gershon, Kohath, and Merari; and the tribe consisted accordingly of three branches. Of these the Kohathites took the lead, and were subdivided into the families of Amram (whose lineal descendants were Moses and Aaron), Izhar, Hebron, and Uzziel.[2] On the family of Aaron the priesthood was conferred;[3] but the posterity of Moses were also reckoned as Levites, and were placed on an equality with the rest of the entire tribe.[4] The Levitical cities were chosen by lot; and the first lot was drawn by the Kohathites, the second by the Gershonites, and the third by the Merarites. The following tables represent the several allotments, the names of the cities of refuge being printed in capitals, and the modern names of those cities which have been identified being given in opposite columns.

I. (a)—THE KOHATHITES IN THE LINE OF AARON.

1. *Cities in the territories of Judah and Simeon.*

| 1. HEBRON (Arba), | . | . | el Khulil, | . | . | 20 m. S. |
| 2. Libnah, | . | . | Arab el Menshiyeh, | | | 26½ m. S.W. |

---

[1] Num. iii 12, etc.
[3] Num. xviii. 1-7.
[2] Exod. vi. 18.
[4] Num. iii.; 1 Chron. vi. 19, 20.

3. Jattir,	Attir,	33 m. S.
4. Eshtemoa,	Senaar,	24½ m. S.
5. Holon,	...	...
6. Debir,	Kirjath-Sephr,	23 m. S.S.W.
7. Ain,	...	...
8. Juttah,	Yutta,	23 m. S.
9. Beth-shemesh,	Ain Shems,	15 m. W.S.W.

2. *Cities in the territory of Benjamin.*

10. Gibeon,	el Jib,	5½ m. W.N.W.
11. Geba,	Jeba or Jiba,	6½ m. N.N.E.
12. Anathoth,	Anata,	2¾ m. N.N.E.
13. Almon,	'Almit,	4 m. N.N.E.

Such were the cities assigned to the priests; and they were all, as the figures in the third column indicate, within a comparatively short distance of Jerusalem, where ultimately the tabernacle was set up, and the temple was erected, that being the spot which God chose, in preference to Shiloh, to place His name there. Could this be by chance? No; the hand of Providence was in the matter. God Himself so ordered it, and so disposed the lots, that just that portion of the tribe of Levi who would be required to conduct the services of the temple should live in its vicinity. And there, accordingly, we find them in the days of David and Solomon, when, their number having considerably increased, they were divided into twenty-four courses, each course officiating in its turn during two weeks of the year.

I. (*b*)—THE REST OF THE KOHATHITES.

1. *Cities in the territory of Ephraim.*

1. SHECHEM,	Nabûlûs,	32 m. N.
2. Gezer,	el Kubab (?),	15 m. W.N.W. (?)
3. Kibzaim,	...	...
4. Beth-horon,	Beit-Ur,	15 m. N.W.

2. *Cities in the territory of Dan.*

5. Eltekeh,	...	...
6. Gibbethon,	...	...

| 7. Aijalon, | . | . | . | Yalo, | . | . | . | 11 m. N.W. |
| 8. Gath-rimmon, | . | . | . | ... | . | . | . | ... |

3. *Cities in the territory of Manasseh, W.*

| 9. Taanach, | . | . | . | Ta'anuk, | . | . | 43 m. N. |
| 10. Bileam (1 Chron. vi. 70), | ... | . | . | . | . | ... |

II.—THE GERSHONITES.

1. *Cities in the territory of Manasseh, E.*

| 1. GOLAN, | . | . | . | ... | . | . | . | ... |
| 2. Beeshterah, | . | . | . | Mezarib (?), | . | . | ? |

2. *Cities in the territory of Issachar.*

3. Kishon,	.	.	.	...	.	.	...
4. Dabareh,	.	.	.	Debûrieh,	.	.	63 m. N.
5. Jarmuth,	.	.	.	Rameh,	.	.	80 m. N.
6. En-gannim,	.	.	.	Jenin,	.	.	46½ m. N.

3. *Cities in the territory of Asher.*

7. Mishal,	.	.	.	Misalli,	.	.	73 m. N.W.
8. Abdon,	.	.	.	Abdeh,	.	.	86 m. N.W.
9. Helkath,	.	.	.	Ukkrith,	.	.	89 m. N.
10. Rehob,	.	.	.	...	.	.	.	...

4. *Cities in the territory of Naphtali.*

11. KEDESH,	.	.	.	Kades,	.	.	95 m. N.
12. Hammoth-dor,	.	.	...	.	.	.	...
13. Kartan,	.	.	.	...	.	.	.	...

III.—THE MERARITES.

1. *Cities in the territory of Zebulun.*

1. Jokneam,	.	.	.	el-Kaimûn,	.	.	68 m. N.E.
2. Kartah,	.	.	.	el-Harti,	.	.	73 m. N.E.
3. Dimnah,	.	.	.	...	.	.	.	...
4. Nahalal,	.	.	.	Malul,	.	.	.	...

2. *Cities in the territory of Reuben.*

5. BEZER,	.	.	.	Bozor (?),	.	.	80 m. E.N.E. (?)
6. Jahazah,	.	.	.	...	.	.	.	...
7. Kedemoth,	.	.	.	...	.	.	.	...
8. Mephaath,	.	.	.	...	.	.	.	...

3. *Cities in the territory of Gad.*

9. Ramoth,	.	.	. es-Salt, .	. .	39 m. N.E.
10. Mahanaim,	.	.	. ...	. .	...
11. Heshbon,	.	.	. Heshban,	. .	37 m. E.
12. Jazer, .	.	.	. Seir,	. .	37 m. E.N.E.[1]

It will be seen from these tables that nearly the same number of cities were assigned to the Levites from each of the other tribes; another proof, surely, that the hand of Providence directed the drawing of the lots. Thus, according to the prophecy of Jacob, were the Levites literally *scattered* in Israel; whilst the prayer of Moses for them was also answered: 'Bless, LORD, their substance, and accept the work of their hands.' God honours those who honour Him. When the Israelites made the golden calf and worshipped it, 'Moses stood in the gate of the camp, and said, Who is on the Lord's side? let him come unto me. And all the sons of Levi gathered themselves together unto him.'[2] They were commanded by the Lord God of Israel to take their swords, and to slay every man his brother, and every man his companion, and every man his neighbour; and terrible as the injunction was, they obeyed, and thus consecrated themselves that day to the Lord. To this event the song of Moses has reference. 'By his untimely and ungodly zeal for the honour of his own house, the forefather of the tribe of Levi brought a curse upon himself, which still rested on his tribe (Gen. xlix. 5–7, xxxiv. 25 *sqq.*); by their well-timed and holy zeal for the honour of the house of God, his descendants had now extinguished the curse, and changed it into a blessing. If their ancestor had violated truth, fidelity, and justice, by the vengeance which he took upon the Shechemites from a mistaken regard to blood-relationship, his descendants had now rescued truth, justice, and the covenant, by executing the vengeance of Jehovah upon their own blood-relations. Hence Moses referred to this tribe in the

---

[1] Comp. 1 Chron. vi. 54–81.   [2] Exod. xxxii. 26–29.

following words (Deut. xxxiii. 9): "Who says of his father and mother, I saw them not; who is ignorant of his brother, and knows nothing of his own sons." The disposition manifested by Levi on this occasion, and his obedience in such difficult circumstances,—viz., his readiness to esteem father and mother, friend and brother, lightly in comparison with Jehovah,—was that which qualified the tribe of Levi, above every other, to serve in the house of Jehovah, and rendered it worthy to be chosen as the lot and inheritance of Jehovah (cf. Deut. xxxiii. 9, 10). The command of Moses to the Levites, who were assembled round him, to avenge the honour of Jehovah on those who perished in their rebellion, was a temptation intended to prove whether they were fit for their future vocation, namely, to devote them entirely to the service of Jehovah.'[1]

Around each of the cities of the Levites a thousand square cubits of land were granted to them for pasturage and cultivation,—equal to 305 English acres. But this was by no means an equivalent for a twelfth portion of the whole land of Canaan; nor was it sufficient to meet the necessities of the tribe. Hence the law of tithes was established; and each of the tribes was required to give a tenth of the produce of their flocks and of their harvest to the Levites year by year, out of which, however, the Levites gave one-tenth to the priests.[2]

But essential service was rendered to the nation by the Levites for all that they received. They became, to a great extent, the instructors of the people. Not only did the *priests'* lips keep knowledge, but the Levites, as a tribe, exerted great influence in the land; for, in the days of Jehoshaphat, for example, 'they taught in Judah, and had the book of the law of the Lord with them, and went about through all the cities of Judah, and taught the people.' In connection with the temple

[1] Kurtz, 'History of the Old Covenant,' vol. iii., p. 169.
[2] Num. xviii.

service, their office was 'to wait upon the sons of Aaron, in the courts, and in the chambers, and in the purifying of all holy things.' Of the priests there were twenty-four courses; but of the Levites there were four times twenty-four, who officiated as singers, porters, and servitors.[1] And though, as a general rule, the Levites, not of the sons of Aaron, were not at liberty to exercise sacerdotal functions, yet Samuel, who, though a Levite, was not of the line of Aaron, did offer sacrifices,—as, indeed, did David, David's sons, and several others, who did not belong to the tribe of Levi at all. This fact is somewhat difficult to account for; but the obvious inference is, that 'during a long period after the conquest of Canaan, the Israelites extensively preserved the patriarchal organization of their households; that the head of the family, at regular intervals, performed the sacerdotal functions in the name of the other members; that, in general, the priestly power remained combined with secular authority. So that among the Hebrews, as was the case among all ancient nations, kings, military leaders, or other public dignitaries, offered sacrifices for the people, and discharged other religious offices; that these rites were performed at any place where an occasion arose, and not exclusively at the tabernacle; that the Levites, weakened and humbled in consequence of political misfortunes and reckless warfare, were far from possessing any special claim to the priesthood, could still less obtain or exercise great hierarchical power, and appear almost everywhere in a condition of dependence, and sometimes of helplessness.'[2]

Amid the varied fortunes of the Israelites, the tribe of Levi exerted a powerful influence on the nation. But the Levitical institute, being permanent and hereditary, was liable to abuse; and had it not been for the checks it received from the prophets and their order, it would probably have degenerated much further than it did. Wisely and mercifully did God raise up from

---

[1] 1 Chron. xxiii. xxiv.   [2] Dr Kalisch on Gen. xlix. 1–28.

amongst the people, and that irrespective of tribe, family, or station, a number of men, from time to time, who, putting the trumpet to their mouth, cried aloud and spared not, but denounced the sins of the priests and Levites as well as of the nation generally ; and thus they who in their official pride called themselves 'the temple of the Lord,' and were disposed to think themselves much holier than others, were taught that they too were amenable to a higher power, and that God had respect, not to ceremonial observances and to ritual institutions merely, but to purity of heart and to holiness of life.

It would, however, lead us beyond our limits to dwell on the history and character of the Levites ; nor are there many of their cities, save the cities of refuge, which possess any considerable amount of interest. As the foregoing tables show, the sites of several of them are unknown ; but those of several others have been discovered by recent travellers, where, as at Jazer in Gilead, Nahalal, Mishal, and elsewhere, ruins have been observed, manifestly of great antiquity.[1]

But, passing by these cities, we proceed to speak of the cities of refuge, and of the design of their appointment. They were evidently selected before the Levitical cities were chosen,—three of them, indeed, by Moses prior to his death, and the remaining three by Joshua, just after the division of the land. The purpose for which these cities were set apart, was to afford an asylum from the blood-avenger for the person who had involuntarily committed homicide. Both in patriarchal times and under the law of Moses, human life was held in the highest degree sacred. The wilful murderer was to be put to death ; and even the man who had accidentally killed another might be pursued by the Goel, גֹאֵל, or blood-avenger,—the person next of kin to the man slain, —who might take vengeance on him for the loss of his relative.[2]

---

[1] See Robinson's 'Researches,' and Van de Velde's 'Memoirs.'
[2] Num. xxxv. 10, 11; Joshua xx. 3–6.

Here was justice; but with it mercy was tempered: for the involuntary manslayer might flee to one of the cities of refuge, the roads to which were always open; and on arriving within a circle of 2000 cubits, was safe from the avenger of blood, until at least the case was investigated by the constituted authorities.

Ere we proceed further to explain the law, we will advert to the cities selected for this purpose. They were, as we have seen, all Levitical cities, or, rather, they were all given to the Levites after being selected. Three of them were situated on the eastern side of the Jordan, and three on the western side; and it is said that the former three were, respectively, nearly opposite the latter three. On the eastern side of the Jordan were ' Bezer in the wilderness, in the plain country of the Reubenites ; and Ramoth in Gilead of the Gadites ; and Golan in Bashan of the Manassites.'[1] BEZER (Βοσορ) is supposed to have been nearly opposite Jericho, and was probably one of the strong and great cities mentioned in 1 Macc. v. 26 ; but its exact site has not been ascertained. RAMOTH, or RAMOTH MIZPEH, has been identified with the present es-Salt, a place in the mountains of Gilead, visited by Burckhardt in the year 1810–11. Here probably Jephthah dwelt ; here one of Solomon's chief governors resided (1 Kings iv. 13); and here occurred the unfortunate siege of Ahab, when, the city being in the hands of the Syrians, he was persuaded to go up and attack it, was wounded in his chariot, and lost his life. 1 Kings xxii. 3, etc. GOLAN was, no doubt, situated somewhere on the eastern side of the Sea of Galilee, and probably gave its name to the tract of country called Gaulonitis ; but the site of it has not been ascertained.[2]

The cities on the west of the Jordan are well-known sites. Of HEBRON we have already spoken. Connected as it was with such hallowed associations, it is not surprising that it should be chosen as a city of refuge; and ' lying in deep repose in the vale

[1] Deut. iv. 43; Joshua xx. 8.   [2] Comp. Keil in loco.

of Mamre,' it looked like such a city—calm, peaceful, and secure.
It is now called el-Kulil, or 'the friend;' it is situated among
the mountains of Judah, twenty miles south of Jerusalem, and
contains at present a population of about five thousand. Every
traveller in Palestine pays it a visit; and the descriptions given
of the beauty and fertility of the surrounding country lead us to
conclude that, in gaining such a possession, the Levites were
highly favoured. The surrounding lands were, however, retained
by Caleb.   In the mountains of Ephraim, between Ebal and
Gerizim, was the second of the three, SHECHEM, a little to the
west of the present Nablous, or Neapolis.[1] This city also was
known to the patriarchs; and its situation, in 'a valley, green
with grass, grey with olives,' with 'gardens sloping down on
each side,' and 'fresh springs rushing down in all directions,'
rendered it not less desirable as a residence than Hebron.   And
what shall we say of KEDESH, in Naphtali? It still exists,
bearing the name of Kades, in a high tract of country on the
west of the Hûleh, where there are remains which show that it
was once a place of considerable importance.[2]

Such, then, were the cities of refuge. And now let us return
to the consideration of their purpose. Here is a man who has
unawares killed another. He has suddenly thrust him, or, not
seeing him, has let a stone fall upon him, and thus, though he
bore him no enmity, has caused his death. The nearest kinsman
of the person slain is made acquainted with the fact; and it is
his duty at once to pursue the homicide, and to avenge upon him
the blood of his relative. But the homicide flees, and, finding
one of the roads leading to the nearest city of refuge, pursues it
with the utmost speed, the Goel following close upon his heels.
If the latter is a revengeful man, and overtakes him ere he
reaches the borders of the city, he takes away his life; if he is a

---

[1] See Stanley's 'Sinai and Palestine,' p 231.
[2] See Robinson, vol. ii., p. 439; and 'The Land and the Book,' p. 266.

generous man, he gives him the advantage, and allows him to
reach the spot in safety. There he is received by the elders of
the city; and there, at the entering in of the gate of the city,
where was the forum, or place of judgment, the case between
the parties is investigated. If the elders find that, though he
has fled thither, the homicide is guilty of wilful murder, they at
once deliver him up to the Goel; but if they find that he is
really guiltless—that the act was indeed unintentional and unpremeditated,—they are bound to deliver him from the avenger of
blood, and he must remain within the precincts of the city until
the death of the then living high priest.[1]

Heathen nations had their *asyla*—groves, temples, altars, and
even cities—to which offenders might flee for protection. But
in process of time they were much abused, and many of the
vilest characters were permitted to claim in them exemption
from punishment. The city of Ephesus, for example, was re-
sorted to as an asylum by wilful murderers; and hence the
Emperor Tiberius deemed it necessary to interfere, and to limit
both the number and the privileges of such cities. The superiority of the Jewish law, then, is evident. Even the altar itself
was to afford no asylum to the guilty; for the Mosaic ritual
said, 'If any man come presumptuously on his neighbour to slay
nim with guile, thou shalt take him from Mine altar.' Exod. xxi.
14. In no instance did the Jewish law connive at sin. It was
strict, even to severity; yet, in the appointment of the cities of
refuge, there was mercy mingled with justice. Doubtless it was
a great trial for a man who had unfortunately killed another, to be
separated from his home and family for weeks, months, or even
years; for he was strictly confined to the borders of the city,
inasmuch as if he went beyond them, and the Goel found him,
he might kill him. Num. xxxv. 26, 27. But in this way the
Israelites were taught to be specially careful of human life. Nor

---

[1] Num. xxxv. 2, 25; Deut. xix. 1-7, Josh. xx. 2-6.

was the punishment, after all, severer than that which our own laws frequently inflict for manslaughter; for in the city of refuge the poor refugee was well provided for, and, though he might not return to his home until the death of the high priest, his friends and relatives might visit him and converse with him, and he would look forward to the day of his release with hope and joy.

But why must the homicide remain in the city until the death of the high priest? Not because, as some have represented, the high priest was the representative of the whole people, and that his death, therefore, was so important that every other death was forgotten, and could no longer be avenged; but because, being anointed with the holy oil, he was the mediator of the people in the presence of God, and because he only could enter the holiest place of all on the great day of atonement, to present the annual expiation for the whole congregation of the children of Israel. Thus ' his death might be regarded as a death for the sins of the people, by which the unintentional manslayer received the benefits of the propitiation, and, being cleansed from that sin, might return to his native city without further exposure to the revenge of the avenger of blood.'[1] To the unfortunate homicide, then, the death of the high priest would be a most desirable event; and hence the Rabbins say, that to induce such fugitives not to pray that it might be hastened, the relatives, and especially the mothers of the high priests, provided them with food and clothing, thus making their asylum as agreeable as they could. The Rabbins say further, that if the fugitive died before the high priest, he was buried in the city of refuge; but that, after the high priest's death, his bones were delivered to his relatives to be reinterred.

A difficulty presents itself here, arising fom the fact, that the punishment might, in some cases, extend over a considerable period, and in others be exceedingly brief; for the high priest

[1] See Keil *in loco.*

might live many years after an homicide had fled to one of these cities, or he might die almost immediately after. To meet this objection, Philo, after his usual method, has recourse to an inner and allegorical interpretation, in which he represents the high priest as signifying, not a man, but the Word of God. But so mystical is his notion, that it is impossible to understand it; and it is doubtful, indeed, whether he understood it himself.[1] There is no need, however, to depart from the literal interpretation of the words of the law. Whether the high priest died soon after the fugitive had entered the city of refuge, or not until several years after, there he must remain; for the law said, 'Ye shall take no satisfaction for him that is fled to the city of his refuge, that he should come again to dwell in the land, until the death of the priest.' Num. xxxv. 32. As to any injustice to the fugitive, we may safely leave it to that Providence which watched over the interests of every Israelite. He who ordained these laws, would take care that they should not press with undue severity on the persons whose welfare they had in view; and, under any circumstances, the city of refuge was a provision of mercy, which few would fail gratefully to acknowledge.

It is a remarkable fact, that a law of blood-revenge exists amongst the Bedouin Arabs to this day; and it is highly probable that the Mosaic legislation on this subject was founded, in part, on usages at that time existing in the East. But, among the Arabs, affairs of blood are usually made up by a heavy fine; and it is said in the Koran, that whoso killeth a believer by mistake, the penalty shall be the freeing of a believer from slavery, and a fine to be paid to the family of the deceased, unless they remit it as alms.[2] Very different from this was the law of Moses; and far more sacred, therefore, is human life in

---

[1] See his treatise on 'Fugitives,' which is full of the strangest imaginable notions concerning the cities of refuge.

[2] See Sale's Koran, chap. iv.; and Layard's 'Nineveh and Babylon,' p. 305.

the estimation of the Jewish code than in that of the Mohammedan or of any other system. The Jewish code declares that man was made in the image of God; that whoso sheds man's blood, by man shall his blood be shed;[1] and that even the homicide, though not guilty of wilful murder, shall not be liberated by the payment of a fine, but only by the atoning death of the high priest; and thus it proclaims the life of a man to be of greater worth than thousands of gold and silver.

And here a somewhat interesting inquiry arises, to which we must devote, at least, a few pages. Were the cities of refuge typical of Christ? Did they, in any way, shadow forth to the Israelites the better refuge provided for every transgressor of the law? That they are not spoken of as types, must be at once admitted; and if nothing was typical under the Old Testament economy but what is expressly represented as such, then we must unhesitatingly reply to this question in the negative. But we are by no means disposed to admit this principle. It has the sanction of Bishop Marsh and many other writers, but its advocacy was simply a reaction from the opposite extreme of the Cocceian and Hutchinsonian schools of interpreters; and calmer views of the subject are leading us back into the middle path, in which, here as well as almost everywhere else, it is best to tread. If we look at the persons, such as Melchizedek, Moses, David, and Jonah; or at the events, such as the deliverance of the Israelites out of Egypt; or at the things, such as the ark of Noah, and the brazen serpent, which *are* referred to by the sacred writers as types; we can scarcely suppose that they intended these only to be regarded as such, but rather that they mention them as specimens; and certainly, if, as St Peter

---

[1] Gen. ix. 6. In all heathendom human life is deemed of little value; and hence wholesale massacres of their subjects take place by the command of kings and princes, sometimes to gratify their revenge, and often, as in Dahomey and elsewhere, in accordance with ancient customs. How much wo owe to Judaism and to Christianity!

tells us, the ark of Noah was a figure of Christ, the cities of refuge may be considered as such.

For what is the position of a sinner? It is that of one who is guilty of innumerable sins, and whom the law, just and inexorable, follows with its threats of vengeance, demanding nothing less than blood for blood. What can he do? He cannot turn round and face the law, and plead that his offences were undesigned; for many of them were not, but were premeditated and deliberate. And even for sins of ignorance the law asks for satisfaction, and will not listen to the plea that its requirements were not known. In this condition he hears the angel of mercy crying to him, 'Escape for thy life, look not behind thee, neither stay thou in all the plain; escape to the mountain, lest thou be consumed;' and he is pointed to Christ Jesus, the great High Priest of the New Testament economy, whose death atoned not only for unpremeditated violations of the law, but for sins of the most deliberate nature; and in Him he is assured he will find a hiding-place. Claiming Christ as his substitute, who for him has satisfied the law's demands, and for him has entered into the holiest place, and for him presents the all-prevalent intercession, he is safe—safe from the accusations of a guilty conscience, safe from the threatening of the avenging sword.

That the Israelites, as a people, viewed the cities of refuge in this light, and saw in them types of a better refuge than one which was merely temporary, we do not affirm;. but, as the whole of the Mosaic institute was of a typical character, we cannot doubt that the more pious portion of them did discern through the veil a deeper meaning, and, conscious of their need of a place of rest and safety for the soul, reposed by faith on the promised Saviour—the Prophet like unto Moses, the Priest like unto Melchizedek—who was afterwards to appear. Moses, in his final address to Israel, said, 'The eternal God is thy refuge, and underneath are the everlasting arms: and He shall thrust out the enemy from before thee, and shall say, Destroy them.'[1] And how often David spoke of God as his refuge, the language of several of his Psalms testifies. 'The Lord also will be a refuge for the oppressed, a refuge in times of trouble. And they that know Thy name will put their trust in Thee: for Thou, Lord, hast not forsaken them that seek Thee.'[2] Had he these cities of refuge in view when he thus spake? Did he think, in particular, of Hebron, the royal city, and of the fugitives who frequently repaired thither from the pursuit of the blood-avenger? It is possible, and not improbable; and if so, to David and to others like-minded, both before him and after him, these cities would be looked upon with special interest; and when they visited them they would say, Here has many a poor refugee found shelter and repose; but in God, and in the Christ to be revealed, thousands have found that rest from sin, and that spiritual repose, without which the soul must ultimately sink and die.

But, in whatever light *the Israelites* viewed the cities of refuge, *to us* they present lessons of the deepest interest, which we shall do well to ponder. They tell us of the breadth and majesty of the law of God, which requires satisfaction even for sins of ignorance, or for sins committed unintentionally; so that for such sins an atonement must be offered, as well as for sins of a more flagrant character. They tell us, therefore, of the sinner's need of a hiding-place from the angel of wrath, who is abroad, as of old, executing vengeance on transgressors—a hiding-place in which he can hear of one who has borne the penalty of his sin, and to which he can appeal, and say, 'Here is my Substitute; spare me for His sake.' To every guilty one they cry, Flee! flee! tarry not, but flee, lest the avenger overtake thee, and thou art slain; and they intimate that such a hiding-place as the sinner needs has been provided, and to that hiding-place they urge him to repair.

Then comes in the teaching of the New Testament; and here

---

[1] Deut. xxxiii. 27.   [2] Ps. ix. 9, 10; comp. Ps. lvii. 1, lxii. 7, etc.

the true city of refuge stands before the sinner more conspicuously than did Hebron, or Shechem, or Kadesh to the homicide, inviting him to enter and find rest and peace. It is not the church, it is not the altar; it is Christ Himself who is the one and only sacrifice for sin, and therefore the one and only hiding-place to which the sinner can repair. A man under the condemnation of the law may fly to a sacred building, or may rush to the altar as the holiest place in it (and time was when human laws would not touch him whilst he was there); but the law of God pays no respect to sacred edifices or to consecrated shrines, and were a man to die at the very foot of the altar ere he had found his way to Christ, his sins would rest upon his head, and for those sins he would have to give account. In no place, person, or thing —in no buildings, sacrifices, or rites, is there any refuge for the guilty, save the atonement of the cross; but there such a refuge is provided as will meet the case of sinners of every class, not excepting the wilful murderer himself.

And once in *this* city of refuge, the refugee must never leave it, but must make it his abiding home. For our High Priest never dies. He died unto sin once; but He now lives unto God for ever. All, then, who repair to Him must dwell in Him continually; and, indeed, if they are right-minded, they will have no desire to forsake Him for a moment. More and more closely will they cleave to Him. Nearer and yet nearer will they strive to walk with Him. The world, home, friend, will have no attractions for them, compared with those of their best and truest Friend; and with holy hope and joy will they anticipate their removal from this world of toil, because they will then be *for ever with their Lord.*

> ' Then, onward yet a step, thou hard-worn soul,
> Though in the Church thou know thy place,
> The mountain farther lies—there seek thy goal,
> There breathe at large, o'erpast thy dangerous race.

JOSHUA'S LAST CHARGE

CHAPTER XVIII.

THE LATER YEARS AND DEATH OF JOSHUA

IT is ever pleasant to contemplate the close of a good and great man's life. For though in many instances it is spent in comparative retirement, yet there is generally something connected with it which speaks both of the past and of the future, which tells us of the blessedness of such a life, and which assures us of the fidelity of Him who has said, 'I will never leave thee nor forsake thee.' The last days of Jacob were calm and beautiful as the summer's setting sun; the death of Moses, though unseen by man, was like the entrance of a conqueror into a royal city; and the close of Joshua's career was worthy of his former life—the going home of a victor crowned.

How eventful had the life of Joshua been! He had shared

the bondage of his people in the land of Mizraim; he had witnessed their deliverance from the oppressor's hand; he had passed with them through the waters of the Red Sea on dry ground; he had heard the law given on Mount Sinai, and had seen the manifestation of the glory of the Lord; he had journeyed through the wilderness with the ransomed host; he had seen Miriam, Aaron, and Moses taken from their midst; he had left behind him, in the desert, the bones of a whole generation of his people; he had crossed the Jordan, he had conquered Canaan, he had driven out thousands of its godless tribes; he had divided the land by lot among the Israelites, and had witnessed, in part, their settlement on the soil; and now what more remained for him to see or do? He had accomplished, if ever man did, the great mission of his life; now therefore he might retire with satisfaction from the busy scenes of life, and wait until his Lord should call him to his rest.

But ere we come to his very last days, there are some other events which demand attention, the record of which occupies the whole of the twenty-second chapter. It will be remembered that the Reubenites, the Gadites, and the half-tribe of Manasseh had accompanied their brethren over Jordan to aid them in the conquest of the land, but with the express understanding, that afterwards they should return to the possessions granted them on the east.[1] And now, having fulfilled their engagements, they were dismissed by Joshua with this address of commendation: 'Ye have kept all that Moses, the servant of the Lord, commanded you, and have obeyed my voice in all that I commanded you: Ye have not left your brethren these many days unto this day, but have kept the charge of the commandment of the LORD your God. And now the LORD your God hath given rest unto your brethren, as He promised them: therefore now return ye, and get you unto your tents, and unto the land of your possession, which

[1] Num. xxxii. 1–42; Josh. iv. 12.

Moses, the servant of the LORD, gave you on the other side Jordan.' This was high praise, but these auxiliary troops, as they have been called, fully merited it; and to them it must have been gratifying beyond measure to receive from their illustrious commander such approving words. History furnishes some striking parallels. It has been the duty and the privilege of many an eminent military general, at the close of an arduous campaign, to dismiss a portion of his forces, and to send them back to their country and their friends with the highest commendations of their bravery and their heroism; and, to a soldier, this is an honour of which he is justly proud; and though he returns, perhaps, laden with scars, or with a mutilated body, yet the thought of having done his duty to his country, and of receiving the approbation of his commander and his sovereign, compensates him, to some extent, for all he has endured.

But Joshua was careful to add a word of instruction to these auxiliaries: ' Take diligent heed,' said he, ' to do the commandment, and the law, which Moses, the servant of the Lord, charged you, to love the Lord your God, and to walk in all His ways, and to keep His commandments, and to cleave unto Him, and to serve Him with all your heart, and with all your soul.' Such advice was, no doubt, necessary; for, isolated as they would be from their brethren, these two tribes and a half would be specially exposed to the danger of forgetting the Lord God of their fathers, and of assuming an independent attitude even in matters of a religious nature. Even the flowing of a river, and that not a very large one, between one territory and another, has tended, not a little, to distinguish the inhabitants, and to foster among them differences of opinion both in politics and religion. This word of exhortation, then, was valuable, and with it, and his blessing, Joshua sent them away; ' and they went unto their tents.'

The word tents is here used for houses; for they had left their families in walled cities, and therefore not in tents.[1] It has been supposed by some, that the 22d chapter is an interpolation ; and by others, that the event is not related in chronological order. But without this chapter the history would evidently be incomplete ; and whether the return of these tribes took place now or at an earlier period, is a matter of no moment ; and, as one observes, ' even if they did return at an earlier period, the account of their return would be in its right place here, because it was proper for the historian to relate everything which belonged to the subjugation and occupation of the land, before he allowed the thread of his narrative to be broken by descriptions of other events.'[2] At the same time, we see no reason for the opinion that the event is not narrated in chronological order. It is more probable that these troops would remain in the land until after its division among the several tribes, than that they would be dismissed previously, as their presence might be necessary to prevent the rising up again of the yet unconquered inhabitants of the country.

Their return must have been a somewhat imposing sight, and must have been witnessed by their brethren with no little interest. Their number was about fifty thousand ; and as rank after rank and file after file crossed the Jordan, now no doubt at its lowest ebb, and wended their way on the opposite banks towards the mountains of Bashan, many who remained on the western banks would watch them until they were lost to sight, and they themselves would bid adieu to their friends, not perhaps without regret, and yet full of joy and hope at the prospect of a reunion with their wives and children. And what scenes would be witnessed when they reached their homes ! Weather-beaten and sun-burnt, they would present to their friends a singular appearance ; and not without difficulty, perhaps, would the parties be able to recognise one another. We remember witnessing the landing on

[1] Num. xxxii. 17.
[2] Lightfoot, quoted by Keil, ' Commentary on Joshua,' p. 460, *note.*

our shores of a regiment of soldiers who had survived the perils
of the Crimean war; and we remember seeing them drawn up
soon after in the barrack-yard, the gates thrown open, and many
of their wives and children rushing in to welcome them.   But
so altered were they in their appearance,—their faces being un-
shaven, and their aspect jaded and forlorn,—that in several instances some time elapsed ere they were recognised even by
those who before had known them best.   But a joyous meeting
it was at length; and the big tear started that day from many
a brave soldier's eye as he clasped his loved ones to his embrace
again.   The sacred writer tells us of nothing of this kind, nor
does he even refer to the meeting of these soldiers with their
friends.   But imagination may be allowed to picture to itself
the scene; and we cannot doubt that to many and many a
heart it would be a joyous one indeed.

Not without a share in the spoil did the Reubenites return
to their possessions, but 'with much riches, with very much
cattle, with silver, with gold, with brass, with iron, and with
very much raiment.'   They had taken part in the conquest of
the country, and it was but right that they should have part of
the property of the Canaanites; but Joshua requested that they
would share this booty with their brethren who had remained at
home,—thus following the example of Moses, who, after the
defeat of the Midianites, ordered the people to divide the spoil
into two equal parts, one of which was to be given to those who
took part in the war, and the other to those who quietly remained within the camp.[1]   This was equitable in both cases;
for those who tarried at home did so to take care of the women
and the children, and therefore they also had a right to a portion
of the booty.   So said David at a later period :—' As his part is
that goeth down to the battle, so shall his part be that tarrieth
by the stuff, they shall part alike.   And it was so from that

---

[1] Num. xxxi. 25, etc.

day forward, that he made it a statute and an ordinance for Israel unto this day.' The statute of David, however, was evidently founded upon the earlier commands of Moses and of Joshua.

But now an act of the Reubenites, in itself perfectly justifiable, though apparently far otherwise, caused no little anxiety to Joshua and the people. On their way to their own territories, they erected, on the banks of the Jordan, a large and imposing altar—'a great altar to see to;' hearing of which, the children of Israel gathered themselves together at Shiloh, and proposed to make war against their brethren. But were they not in haste, and ought they not first to have inquired into the motives of their brethren? Some acts may be right or may be wrong, according to the principle which leads to their performance; and the erection of the altar, as afterwards appeared, was dictated by the purest motives. But the law which forbade the erection of more than one altar for sacrifices was express;[1] and it was to punish the Reubenites for a supposed violation of this law that the Israelites proposed to make war upon them. 'For they truly and wisely judged,' says Calvin, 'that the lawful sanctuary of God was polluted, and His worship profaned; that sacred things were violated, pious concord destroyed, and a door opened for the license of superstitious practices, if in two places victims were offered to God, who had, for these reasons, so solemnly bound the people to a single altar. Not rashly, therefore, do the ten tribes, on hearing of a profane altar, detest its sacrilegious audacity.'

With whom, and in what, then, lay the error? Doubtless with the builders of the altar, who ought to have consulted the high priest, and to have considered not only what was lawful, but what was also expedient. Well-nigh had their want of forethought brought them into great distress. The sword was

[1] Lev. xvii. 8, etc.; Deut. xii. 4 and 13, etc.

already drawn; and but for the wise precaution and the brotherly regard of the ten tribes, thousands of the Reubenites would have been put to death. But Phinehas, the son of Eleazar the high priest, together with ten princes, one of each tribe, were sent to inquire into the conduct of their brethren, and to remonstrate with them on account of their supposed rebellion. Observe them! They cross the Jordan, following in the track of the two tribes and a half; they arrive in the land of Gilead; and, probably, to the great surprise of many, present themselves before the chiefs and elders of the people. And how severe is their address! 'What trespass,' say they, 'is this that ye have committed against the God of Israel, to turn away this day from following the Lord, in that ye have builded you an altar, that ye might rebel this day against the Lord?' And referring to the guilt and punishment which the people brought upon themselves in the wilderness when they went after Baal-Peor, and again to the consequences of Achan's sin when he took of the accursed thing, they ask whether these acts of transgression and their results were not enough, but that they must again rebel against the Lord, and provoke Him to be angry with His people.

So serious a charge might have been resented by the Reubenites with indignation, and they might have refused to give an explanation of their conduct. They doubtless saw, however, that this would be unwise and dangerous; and hence they answered mildly, that their motive was not to erect an altar of sacrifice, and thus to contravene the Mosaic statute, but merely to raise an altar of witness, that in time to come the descendants of the ten tribes might not be able to ask their descendants what they had to do with the Lord their God, seeing that they were separated by the river Jordan. That altar—a pattern of the altar reared at Shiloh—was to be a witness between the ten tribes on the western side of the river, and the two tribes and a half on the eastern side, that the latter had an equal right with the former to claim Jehovah as their God, and that they were not a separate and distinct people, but belonged to Israel, though the river was between them. 'This anxiety was not altogether uncalled for. In all the promises, only Canaan, the land on this side of the Jordan, had been mentioned as the land which Jehovah would give to His people for an inheritance; and, therefore, at some future period it would be easy for the false inference to be drawn, that only the Israelites who dwelt in Canaan proper belonged to the people of Jehovah, and none but they had part in Jehovah.'[1] We cannot, then, blame the Reubenites for erecting this altar. They had no desire to rebel against the Lord, by building an altar for burnt-offerings or for sacrifices in addition to the altar that was before the tabernacle; but the thought of being hereafter cut off from Israel and from Israel's God they could not bear, and they had, therefore, reared this altar to be a perpetual sign of their relationship to their brethren.

This explanation was highly satisfactory to Phinehas and the princes, and not less so to the children of Israel, to whom the matter was reported on the return of Phinehas and his companions. All thought of war was relinquished, and the people blessed God; for they were thankful to find that they had misunderstood the motives of the Reubenites, and that there was no real cause of difference between them.

The altar was called by the Reubenites and Gadites 'a witness between us that Jehovah is God.'[2] But where did it stand?' On the east of the Jordan, or on the west? Many would reply, without hesitation, On the east; but if it was to be a witness that the tribes on the eastern side had a part with those on the western side, why should it be erected

[1] Keil *in loco*.

[2] The word, Ed, עד (introduced into our version in verse 44), is not found either in the Septuagint or the Vulgate, and is probably an interpolation.

there? Obviously the end would be accomplished better by
the altar being erected on the same side of the Jordan as
that on which the ten tribes remained; for then, those on the
opposite side could say, 'See, here is the altar we erected
whilst yet we were on your side of the river.' And, accordingly,
it is said in ver. 10, that the Reubenites built the altar when, on
their way to their possessions, 'they came unto the borders of
Jordan.' Nor does ver. 11 contradict this view, which says,
that 'the altar was over against the land of Canaan;' for 'these
words,' as Keil observes, 'are spoken from the stand-point of
those who built the altar, viz., the tribes who lived on the other
side of the Jordan.

To the mind of Joshua himself the settlement of this dispute
must have given great relief. He was now 'old and stricken
in age;' his work was nearly done; and he was looking forward
to the day when he should lay down his important charge, and
be gathered to his fathers in the spirit-land. True, he lived
some years after this event; for it is said that 'a long time
after that the Lord had given rest unto Israel from their enemies
round about,' he called for the elders and gave them his fare-
well address. But at whatever period of his life the occurrence
took place at which we have now glanced, it would give him
great satisfaction to know that the tribes on both sides the
Jordan were one in sentiment and heart; and he would look
forward to the hour of his departure with the hope that *one*
they would remain.

Passing over the years of interval, respecting which we have
no record, we now come to contemplate another of those touching
scenes which the sacred narrative depicts. Affecting was the
last interview of Jacob with his sons, of Joseph with his brethren, of Aaron with Moses and Eleazar, and of Moses with the
people whom he had brought up out of Egypt. Scarcely less so
was this of Joshua with the elders of Israel, at which we must

now look. What a picture for the artist's pencil! There is the
venerable form of the heroic soldier to whom, under God, the
people owe the conquest of the land,—the last link, Caleb only
excepted, of the generation who had come out of the land of
Egypt; and around him are gathered the heads of the tribes,
to listen once more to his sage counsel and advice. Eleazar
the high priest is there, and Phinehas his son; and doubtless
Caleb is there, in his green old age, and perhaps Othniel, with
many others. And Joshua addresses them; and, reminding them
of what God has done for them, exhorts them to courage and
to constancy, and warns them of the consequences of departing
from the Lord, and especially of intermarrying with the remnant
of the nations round about them. Chap. xxiii. 1–13. 'Behold,'
he says, 'this day I am going the way of all the earth: and ye
know in all your hearts, and in all your souls, that not one thing
hath failed of all the good things which the Lord your God
spake concerning you; all are come to pass unto you, and not
one thing hath failed thereof.' 'To-day,' as if he had said, 'I
am looking forward to my decease. But be consoled and com-
forted by the recollection that all God's promises to you have
been fulfilled, and that, though I am taken from you, He will still
be your protector and your God if you obey Him. But as He
has proved Himself true to His promises, so also, if you depart
from Him, will He certainly fulfil His threatenings.' Memorable
and never-to-be-forgotten words! They were indicative of the
paternal solicitude of Joshua for his people. Like the father of
a family who is anxious for his children's welfare after his departure, Joshua was desirous that when he was numbered with the
dead, the Israelites should still possess the approving smile of
Heaven. Could he but indulge this hope, he would die in greater
peace.

But this was not the last interview of Joshua with the elders.
At a little later period he summoned them to Shechem, to a

s

solemn renewal of the covenant before the Lord.   Shechem, and
not Shiloh, was chosen for this event, because it stood between
the mountains Ebal and Gerizim, where the covenant was first
renewed, soon after they had entered Canaan.   The same spot
was to be the witness of the last renewal of the covenant before
Joshua's death, which had witnessed the first renewal of it after
he had become the successor of Moses.

There was, probably, a larger assembly on this occasion than
on the former one ; and from the expression, ' They presented
themselves before the Lord '—chap. xxiv. 1—many have supposed
that the ark of the covenant was brought from Shiloh to Shechem,
that the transaction might be performed in the most solemn
manner, and in the immediate presence of the Lord Jehovah
Himself.[1]   And what said Joshua to the elders on this occasion?
He reviewed God's mercies to His people from the call of Abraham, who, together with his family, was originally an idolater,
dwelling in Ur of the Chaldees, on the other side of the river
Euphrates.   This was the first of a long series of acts by which
God had displayed a special regard for the Israelites.   Abraham
He had conducted through the land of Canaan, promising that
his seed should afterwards inherit it.   To him He had given
Isaac, and to Isaac, Jacob and Esau.   To Esau Mount Seir was
assigned for a possession ; but Jacob and his family went down
to Egypt.   In Egypt Moses and Aaron were raised up, and the
plagues having devastated the land, the descendants of the patriarchs were set free from Pharaoh's yoke.   The Egyptians pursued them, but were drowned in the Red Sea.   The wilderness
became the home of the ransomed people for a period of forty
years ; there the Amorites were conquered ; there the stratagems
of Balak and of Balaam were defeated ; and there innumerable
proofs were witnessed both of the goodness and the power of
God.   Moreover, they had crossed the Jordan ; they had ob-

[1] See, however, Keil, Hengstenberg, and also Calvin.

tained possession of the land of Canaan; the hornet had driven out their enemies before them; and God had given them a land for which they did not labour, and cities which they built not, and vineyards and oliveyards which they planted not; and now they were in possession of this fair inheritance, and could boast of a land which literally flowed with milk and honey. 'Now therefore,' said Joshua, 'fear the LORD, and serve Him in sincerity and in truth: and put away the gods which your fathers served on the other side of the flood, and in Egypt; and serve ye the LORD. And if it seem evil unto you to serve the LORD, choose you this day whom ye will serve; whether the gods which your fathers served, that were on the other side of the flood, or the gods of the Amorites, in whose land ye dwell: but as for me and my house, we will serve the LORD.'

Professedly, the Israelites *were* worshippers of the Lord Jehovah, and of Him only; but *in heart* they still clung to the gods of Chaldea and of Egypt, and hence Joshua here exhorts them to serve the LORD in *sincerity and truth*. Outward idolatry did not exist among them at this time, as some have supposed; for, if it had, they would at once have brought their idols in responding to Joshua's appeal, and have destroyed them. The family of Abraham were not gross idolaters, but mingled with the worship of the true God a regard to their Teraphim or household gods (Penates); and even in Egypt the one Supreme Being was acknowledged, though in connection with many idolatrous elements. What Joshua demanded, then, was the putting away of all false gods *from their hearts*, and the service of the One True God in all sincerity. But it was to be with them a matter of free choice; and if it seemed evil to them to serve the Lord, they were that day to decide whom they would serve— the gods of their fathers beyond the Euphrates, or the gods of the Amorites, in whose land they now dwelt. 'The real object of Joshua was to renew and confirm the covenant which had already been made with God. Not without cause, therefore, does he give them freedom of choice, that they may not afterwards pretend to have been under compulsion, when they bound themselves by their own consent. Meanwhile, to impress them with a feeling of shame, he declares that he and his house will persevere in the worship of God.'[1]

The people answered this appeal, and acknowledging their obligations to the Lord Jehovah, solemnly promised that they would serve Him. But merely human resolutions are very feeble, and Joshua, reminding them of the holiness of God, says, ' Ye cannot,' in your own strength, in your present state of mind and heart, and without the help of divine grace, ' serve God : for He is an holy God ; He is a jealous God ; He will not forgive your transgressions nor your sins. If ye forsake the LORD, and serve strange gods, then He will turn and do you hurt, and consume you, after that He hath done you good.'

To take a religious vow, to enter into covenant with God, to promise deliberately allegiance to His throne, is a most solemn and momentous act ; for God is a jealous God, and requires of all His people unbroken fidelity to their engagements ; nor will He fail to visit with severity every breach of promise. But, so full of gratitude were the people at this moment, that with these views of the divine character before them, and fully conscious as they must have been of the vast importance of the transaction, they again declared that they would serve the Lord, and that they were ready to renew the covenant which Ebal and Gerizim had witnessed long before.

It was enough. Joshua was satisfied of their sincerity, and that day the covenant was renewed accordingly. ' Ye are witnesses,' said Joshua—witnesses, that is, against yourselves— ' that ye have chosen you the Lord, to serve Him.' And they replied, ' We are witnesses.' And now the idols of their heart

---

[1] Calvin *in loco ;* comp. Keil.

being put away, at Joshua's request, so that no vestige of idolatry might remain amongst them, ' a statute and an ordinance' was set in Shechem,—a statute binding the Israelites to observe the law, and an ordinance giving them a title to expect that, on this condition, the Lord Jehovah would be faithful to His promises. And in the book of the law all the transactions connected with this ratification of the covenant were written; and then a large stone was set up as a visible memorial of the event. This stone was set up ' under an oak that was by the sanctuary of the Lord;' which some interpret, ' at the threshold of the sanctuary, which Joshua had caused to be brought with the ark to Shechem.' But the sanctuary here referred to was none other than the spot which Abraham had consecrated to the worship of the Lord Jehovah, under a venerable oak, when he passed through the land journeying towards the south,[1] and on which Jacob also erected an altar, and afterwards buried all the strange gods of his household.[2] Memorable, then, was that spot in the history of the chosen race, and most fitting to be the scene of this very solemn and momentous engagement. And Joshua said unto all the people, ' Behold, this stone shall be a witness unto us; for it hath heard all the words of the LORD which He spake unto us: it shall therefore be a witness unto you, lest ye deny your God.' In the language of poetry things inanimate are often said to see, and hear, and speak; and thus was this stone said to have heard the words of God; and as the people looked upon it, they were to remember that, if they denied their Lord, it would be a witness against them of the heinousness of their sin.

Thus Joshua, following in the footsteps of the illustrious law-giver, had done everything in his power to bind the Israelites as a people to their God. And now all that he could do more was to dismiss them with his blessing. It was his last public act, and he retired from that scene to gather up his feet and die.

---

[1] Gen. xii. 6–8.　　　　[2] Gen. xxxiii. 19, 20, xxxv. 2–4.

Of the death-scene we have no account. We know not where it occurred, whether at Shiloh or at Shechem, nor who were present to witness his departure and to close his eyes. The historian merely tells us that Joshua the son of Nun, the servant of the Lord, died, being a hundred and ten years old; and that they buried him in the border of his inheritance in Timnath-serah, which is in Mount Ephraim, on the north side of the hill Gaash. To the inheritance of Joshua reference has been already made; but the sites of Timnath-serah and the hill Gaash have not been identified with certainty. Dr Eli Smith, however, found a hill called Tibneh, covered with considerable ruins, and to the south of it, another hill with remarkable sepulchral caverns, eight miles south-east of Shiloh, which he supposed to be identical with these two spots;[1] and it is not improbable that the last resting-place of the illustrious commander of the Israelites is here.

The influence of Joshua's example and instructions was such, that Israel served the Lord all his days, and all the days of the elders that overlived him, who had known the works of the Lord. Like every good man who occupies a prominent position in society, he left behind him a bright track of light, in which many walked long after his departure. Of his character we cannot speak too highly. It is transparent as the light itself. He was indeed 'strong and very courageous.' He feared no danger; he shrunk from no hardships; he was deterred by no difficulties. Arduous was the enterprise he was called to undertake, and, to human appearance, the barriers to its accomplishment were all but insurmountable. But Joshua had faith in God. Seldom, if ever, did his confidence in the divine promises give way; and if it did, under special trials, for a moment waver, it rose again and took hold on the arm of Omnipotence afresh. Two traits in his character are peculiarly prominent—his disinterestedness, and his fidelity to the trust reposed in him.

[1] See Van de Velde's 'Memoir' and Map.

Joshua lived, not for himself, but for his people. Unlike Alexander and other conquerors of the East, he sought no glory, was ambitious of no greatness, and aimed at no sinister purposes or ends. There is not a circumstance in his history which indicates that he had any personal designs to gratify ; for, indeed, he was too great a man for this. True greatness consists not in aspiring to place and power, not in the carrying out of ambitious projects, not in *trying to be great*, and wishing that the world *may think us great;* but in lowliness and humbleness of mind, and in self-forgetfulness for the common good. Hence few of the conquerors of the world—the Alexanders, the Cæsars, the Attilas, and the Napoleons, of human fame—were truly great, but miserably little. But Joshua was great—great as a patriot, great as a commander ; for his aim was one, that of promoting to the utmost of his power the highest interests of the people of his charge. Let our rulers, our statesmen, our military commanders, imbibe the spirit of the noble-minded Joshua ; and, instead of that hunting after place which is now so common for the sake of personal or family aggrandisement, there would be a prevalent desire to lose sight of personal advantage for the sake of the public good. Nor would society be in any way a loser, for the most disinterested servant of the state is always its best and most efficient one.

Closely connected with this trait in the character of Joshua was his fidelity to the trust reposed in him. He was not the mere patriot. He was the servant of the people because he was the servant of their God. He felt his responsibility to the Lord Jehovah, who had appointed him to the charge of the hosts of Israel; and whether he pleased the Israelites or not, please the Lord Jehovah he must. Some men, through cowardice or through fear, are no sooner placed in an eminent position in society by the providence of God, than, to keep it, they have recourse to all kinds of mean and dishonourable plans. Instead of doing their duty, whatever it may cost them, they conform to custom and court the favour and the smiles of men. There was nothing of this kind in the conduct of Joshua. To be the idol of the people at any price, was never his desire. His eye was single, his aim was one. He thought of nothing but of fulfilling the task assigned to him, and would sooner have laid down his charge, and retired into private life, than have proved faithless to his trust as the servant of the Lord his God. Hence there was no vacillation in his policy. He was the same man from the time he took the command of the hosts of Israel to the time that he laid it down, and he pursued one line of conduct through the whole of his administration of affairs. If ever he erred, it was in judgment only; and his errors were so few, that they are all but lost amid the cluster of the excellences which adorn his character. He was a man in whom the Spirit of God was, and that Spirit he retained to the close of his long and most eventful life.

It would be easy, were we to look back on the history we have sketched, to illustrate more fully these traits of the character of this truly great man; but we have nearly reached the limits of this volume, and the reader can supply such illustrations for himself. There is but one other thought on which it is necessary to dwell:—Joshua was, in one respect at least, an eminent type of the Lord Jesus Christ. As he conducted the chosen Israel into the rest of the earthly Canaan, so is Jesus, the true Joshua, leading the Christian Israel into the rest of Christian holiness and of heaven. Centuries after the death of Joshua, the Psalmist David said, ‘To-day, if ye will hear His voice, harden not your hearts.’ And the author of the Epistle to the Hebrews, adverting to these words, says, ‘If Jesus’—that is, Joshua—‘had given them rest, then would he not afterwards have spoken of another day.’ That is, if Joshua had led God’s people into the true rest provided for them, then would not

David, under the inspiration of the Spirit, have spoken of another day or period in which rest may be obtained. 'There remaineth therefore,' is the conclusion of the writer, 'a sabbath-rest for the people of God.'[1] Under the brighter economy of the Gospel, there is a rest more true, more spiritual, and more permanent than that of Canaan,—the rest of peace and purity on earth, the rest of glory and of God in heaven. Yes, believers shall enter even into the rest of God. As He, when He had finished the work of creation, rested from His works and entered on a sabbath which shall never end; so, when they shall have accomplished the task assigned them, shall they begin their sabbath-rest, and that sabbath-rest shall be a rest in God and with God which shall know no change or end.

But who is their conductor to that rest? Who guides them to its entrance? Who arms them for the victory over the enemies that assail them? Who sustains them in the valley of the shadow of death, causes the waters to divide, and leads them into the promised land? Jesus is their Joshua; and He it is to whom they look, and on whom alone they can depend. He is not only their Prophet like unto Moses, and their Priest like unto Melchisedec, but their Captain like unto Joshua; and, enlisted under His banner, He leads them on, 'conquering and to conquer,' until at length they triumph in His name over the last enemy, and are admitted into the sabbath-rest of the incorruptible and undefiled inheritance. That inheritance Moses entered, though he saw the earthly Canaan only at a distance. That inheritance Joshua himself obtained when he bade adieu to his inheritance in Timnath-heres, and laid him down to die. And that inheritance thousands now possess, out of every nation under heaven; whilst thousands more are on their journey thither, with the bright prospect of immortality in their view. This is the sphere of toil and conflict; but for every true follower of Christ

---

[1] Heb. iv. 9.—Ἄρα ἀπολείπεται σαββατισμὸς τῷ λαῷ τοῦ Θιοῦ.

there is an abode of perfect rest.　But each one who gains that rest, gains it not by his own unaided skill, but by the grace of God in Christ; and hence the song of the redeemed is one 'To Him that loved us, and washed us from our sins in His own blood, and hath made us kings and priest unto God and His Father; to Him be glory and dominion for ever and ever. Amen.'

INDEX.

THE END.

www.ingramcontent.com/pod-product-compliance
Lightning Source LLC
Chambersburg PA
CBHW060557030726
47498CB00005B/1434